NEW GEOGR

MW00576516

GROUNDING METABOLISM
edited by **DANIEL IBAÑEZ & NIKOS KATSIKIS**

New Geographies 06
Grounding Metabolism

Editors
Daniel Ibañez & Nikos Katsikis

Editorial Board
Daniel Daou
Ali Fard
Taraneh Meshkani
Pablo Pérez Ramos

Founding Editors
Gareth Doherty
Rania Ghosn
El Hadi Jazairy
Antonio Petrov
Stephen Ramos
Neyran Turan

Advisory Board
Eve Blau
Neil Brenner
Sonja Duempelmann
Mohsen Mostafavi
Antoine Picon
Hashim Sarkis
Charles Waldheim
James Wescoat

Editorial Advisor
Melissa Vaughn

Design Labs Administrator
Edna Van Saun

Graphic Design
Rob Daurio & Chelsea Spencer

New Geographies is the journal of Design, Agency, Territory founded, edited, and produced by doctoral candidates in the New Geographies Lab at the Harvard University Graduate School of Design. New Geographies presents the geographic as a design paradigm that links physical, representational, and political attributes of space and articulates a synthetic scalar practice. Through critical essays and projects, the journal seeks to position design's agency amid concerns about infrastructure, technology, ecology, and globalization.

New Geographies 06—Grounding Metabolism has been made possible by grants from the Graham Foundation for Advanced Studies in the Fine Arts and the Aga Khan Program at the Harvard University Graduate School of Design.

All attempts have been made to trace and acknowledge the sources of images. Regarding any omissions or errors, please contact:

New Geographies Lab
Harvard University Graduate School of Design
48 Quincy Street, Cambridge, Massachusetts, 02138

Printed in Cambridge by Universal Wilde
Logo Design by Jean Wilcox

Distributed by Harvard University Press
ISBN 978-1-934510-37-7
www.gsd.harvard.edu/newgeographies

002	**Daniel Ibañez & Nikos Katsikis** Editorial
010	**Jason W. Moore** Toward a Singular Metabolism: Epistemic Rifts and Environment- Making in the Capitalist World-Ecology
020	**Erle C. Ellis** Ecologies of the Anthropocene: Global Upscaling of Social- Ecological Infrastructures
028	**Peter Baccini** Understanding and Designing the Metabolism of Urban Systems
038	**Timothy W. Luke** Urbanism as Cyborganicity: Tracking the Materialities of the Anthropocene
052	**Roi Salgueiro Barrio, Aanya Chugh & Maynard León** Petrified Metabolism as Urban Artifact: Tells and Artificial Topographies in the Khabur Basin, Syria
062	**Sabine Barles** Urban Metabolism: Persistent Questions and Current Developments
070	**Matthew Gandy in Conversation with Daniel Ibañez & Nikos Katsikis** On Circulations and Metabolisms: Challenges and Prospects
078	**Volker M. Welter** The Valley Region—From Figure of Thought to Figure on the Ground
088	**Hadas A. Steiner** After Habitat, Environment
098	**Ken Tadashi Oshima in Conversation with Daniel Ibañez & Nikos Katsikis** On Metabolism and the Metabolists
108	**Douglas Spencer** Nature Is the Dummy: Circulations of the Metabolic
114	**Felipe Correa & Tomás Folch** Resource Extraction Urbanism and the Post-Oil Landscape of Venezuela
122	**Rahul Mehrotra & Felipe Vera** Ephemeral Urbanism: Learning from Pop-up Cities
132	**Paola Viganò** Territorialism I
140	**Rania Ghosn & El Hadi Jazairy** Hassi Messaoud Oil Urbanism
150	**Reinier de Graaf / OMA** Moscow after Moscow
160	**Vicente Guallart** Barcelona 5.0: The Self-Sufficient City
166	**Philippe Rahm** Toward a Thermodynamic Urban Design
174	**Kiel Moe** The Nonmodern Struggle for Maximum Entropy
184	**Pierre Bélanger** Ecology 5.0
188	**Daniel Daou & Pablo Pérez Ramos** "Projective Views on Urban Metabolism": Conference Postscript

Grounding Metabolism

Editorial
by Daniel Ibañez
and Nikos Katsikis

Daniel Ibañez is a registered practicing architect and urbanist. He is a Doctor of Design candidate at the Harvard University, research associate of New Geographies Lab, research manager at the Urban Theory Lab GSD, and co-director of the design firm Margen-Lab. He holds a Master in Architecture (ETSAM, 2007), Master in Advanced Architecture (IAAC, 2007), and a Master in Design Studies in Urbanism, Landscape and Ecology with distinction (Harvard GSD, 2012). His dissertation research, "Metabolic Urbanism," seeks to frame the design disciplines in relation to broader socio-ecological interdependencies through cross disciplinary research on urban metabolism. He is co-editor of a forthcoming book Third Coast Atlas (Actar, 2014) and Thermodynamics Applied to High-Rise and Mix-Use Prototypes (2013) and is on the editorial board of New Geographies. Some of his academic grants and awards include the Fundación La Caixa Fulbright Fellowship, the Real Colegio Harvard Complutense Scholarship and the Harvard GSD Dimitris Pikionis Award.

Nikos Katsikis is an architect and urbanist, and a Doctor of Design candidate at the Harvard Graduate School of Design (GSD), currently completing his dissertation, "From Hinterland to Hinterworld." At the GSD he is research associate in the New Geographies Lab and in the Urban Theory Lab and he will serve as Lecturer in Urban Planning and Design in Spring 2015. He has organized conferences on "Urban Metabolism" (2014), "Regionalism and the Mediterranean" (2013) and "The Limits of the Urban" (2012) and is on the editorial board of New Geographies. He holds a professional degree (2006) and a Master in Architecture (2009) with highest distinction from the National Technical University of Athens. His recent work includes contributions to MONU (2014), Implosions/Explosions: Towards a Study of Planetary Urbanization edited by Neil Brenner (Berlin: JOVIS, 2013), and the forthcoming pamphlet with Brenner, Is the World Urban?: Towards a Critique of Geospatial Ideology (Moscow: Strelka Press, 2014). He is a Fulbright and Onassis scholar.

NG06–Grounding Metabolism interprets urban metabolism as an inherently geographic condition, investigating the possibility for a redefinition of the context for design in a manner that can grasp both the fluidity of metabolic processes and their geographical engraving on the earth.[01]

Although design has been always tempted by the need to position itself in relation to a larger context, the engagement with (and even the definition of) this context has proved increasingly challenging. This situation results not only from the increasing complexity of urban environments–the traditional locus of design inter-ventions–but also from the need to grasp their expanding social and environmental interdependencies across the earth. In what could be characterized as a condition of generalized urbanization, increasingly diffuse agglomeration patterns blend with a dense mesh of infrastructural networks and are strongly interwoven with expanding zones of production, supply, and disposal that cover the whole planet.[02] Where does the synthetic geography of inhabitation end? Is it just decaying with the density of population and built-up space, the transport corridors and the com-muting belts? Or does it have to include the operationalization of a series of often distant but socially and ecologically interdependent territories? The vast zones of food production, resource extraction, energy production? The systems of res-ervoirs and hydroelectric dams? The logistical spaces of trade and circulation?

Within this condition of planetary socio-environmental transformation, the concept of urban metabolism has gained influence among scholars and designers, suggesting an analytical basis for gauging the continuous flows of energy, material, and population exchange within and between cities and their extensive operational landscapes. Metabolic approaches to urbanization promise to interweave these diverse locational contexts, allowing the investigation of the interactions among social and ecological processes in the production of urban environments, and potentially enabling designers to address a broad array of processes operating at multiple spatial scales. Most contemporary discussions on urban metabolism, however, have failed to integrate formal, spatial, and mate-rial attributes. Technoscientific approaches have been limited to a performative interpretation of flows, while more theoretical attempts to interrogate the socio-political embeddedness of metabolic processes have largely ignored their spatial registration. NG06–Grounding Metabolism suggests the need for a more explicit and systematical exploration of the geographical imprint of metabolic processes.

But the geographic structure of the metabolic organization of urbanization has been increasingly elusive over at least the last century. Historically this relation-ship was confined to a contiguous regional scale, with towns or cities co-evolving in a state of social and ecological interdependence with their surrounding hinterlands. Successive waves of capitalist development, the proliferation of world trade, and the development of transport infrastructures have resulted in a gradual socio-metabolic upscaling. Under contemporary globalized urbanization, cities appear more connected to the planetary system of production and exchange than to their surrounding territories. Dissolved in the operations of logistical networks and global supply chains that reshuffle them across distant territories, metabolic processes thus often appear largely ungrounded, detached from any geographic association.

This underlying tension between the fluidity of flows and their materialization in geographical patterns of human occupation of the earth has long characterized the engagement of designers and urbanists with questions of urban metabolism. Since the beginning of the twentieth century, designers have sought to conceptualize and respond to the metabolic reorganization associated with the diffusion of metropolitanism. For influential urbanists such as Patrick Geddes and Lewis Mumford, metropolitanism suggested an exploitative operationalization of the earth that was leading to a socially and ecologically unsustainable specialization of regions, reducing them to mere utilitarian links in a world system of exchange.[03] From Geddes' valley section to Mumford's ecological regionalism, models with evident spatiality, where social and ecological processes were interpreted geographically, promoted the return to putatively more balanced, spatially confined, and self-sufficient regional forms of metabolic organization. This tension between the increasingly globalized metabolic flows and the specificities of their geographic embeddedness is further revealed in the projective attempts of Benton MacKaye and Ludwig Hilberseimer.[04] Through his "new exploration," MacKaye suggested charting the global system of resource circulation—dominated by the forces of industrial capitalism—uncovering its inefficiencies and thus allowing a reshaping of metabolic patterns according to the logics of natural geography. Conversely, Hilberseimer's "new regional pattern" proposed to counterbalance the predominant tendency of regional specialization through a less interdependent redistribution of functions with respect to the geographic terrain. This effort to (re)establish a more geographically informed territorial paradigm that would regulate or confine metabolic flows continued to be a major concern in several important strands of postwar design thinking. Examples of such engagements include the models of human association across geographic scales developed by Team 10, or the subsequent work of Ian McHarg and his ecological interpretation of the valley as a geographic unit.[05]

This geographic appreciation of metabolism gradually dissolved, however, under an increasingly technoscientific paradigm that dominated most post-World War II approaches. The fascination with a systematic interpretation of flows and the exploration of technological solutions fueled some of the most striking architectural utopias of the second part of the 20th century. The projects of the Metabolist group explored the translation of an organicist interpretation of circulation and adaptation into megastructural formations that organized and colonized territories. At the same time critical interrogations of the fascination with technology, networks and flows started questioning the detachment of architecture from the ground, as in the projects of Archigram. A series of ambitious efforts and methodologies started focusing more on the global management of flows rather than on the organization of territories. The work of Buckminster Fuller explored the agency of design as a tool for the "scientific" representation and eventually management of the global flows of resources and commodities. Fuller even advocated a complete redefinition of design practices, shifting their focus from the physical design of geographic space to the organization of the space of flows.[06] Around the same time, the large-scale simulations of the Club of Rome reports, which built upon Jay Forrester's work on systems dynamics, reconstructed the world as a dynamic system interrelating population, resources, and development.[07] These ambitious efforts reflect the uncritical optimism associated with a general technoscientific paradigm that largely transformed urban metabolism from a question of territorial organization to one of ecological analysis and coordination of stocks and flows. The influential work of Eugene and Howard T. Odum simplified the complexities of cities and regions to a set of topologically interrelated functional elements that were measured exclusively as a transformation of energy.[08] In 1965, Abel Wolman's seminal text on "The Metabolism of Cities" called for planning to focus on the analytical investigation of flows of energy and material associated with the function of urban environments.[09]

Along these lines, under the recent paradigm of sustainable development, a tremendous amount of quantitative research has been generated in the environmental sciences to model urban metabolism. The standardization of models and indicators, such as material flow analysis or the urban footprint, has contributed to an unprecedented statistical profiling of the metabolism of cities and regions exposing the scales, dimensions, and dynamics of contemporary systems of inhabitation.[10] These approaches have remained largely descriptive, however, and blind to the underlying socioeconomic tensions associated with their geographical embeddedness. Metabolic interdependencies are rarely investigated as sociospatial constructs, but are simply presented as naturalized elements of organic ecosystems.

Over the last two decades, a set of influential critical approaches has addressed exactly this *problematique*. Stemming mainly from neo-Marxian urban geography and political economy, the concept of metabolism has been reappropriated in a dialectical manner that attempts to analyze the spatial complexities of metabolic processes in ways that also capture their social, natural, political, and technological hybridities.[11] These approaches have contributed to an understanding of metabolic processes as historically contested elements of a socially and ecologically unequal exchange within successive waves of capitalist development. Although they have been instrumental in reintroducing geography and overcoming the society-nature divide, they have been rather reluctant to supersede inherited territorial categories such as that of the "city." Consequently, such approaches have contributed only weakly to a novel understanding of extended patterns of urbanization.[12] Although both technoscientific and critical approaches to urban metabolism have been influential in design discourse, they have yet to be meaningfully connected to an appreciation of the formal organization of the expanding urban fabric, and concomitantly, to the construction of more socially, politically, and ecologically viable models of urbanism.

Within this context, contemporary design disciplines have been rather myopic in addressing the geographic dimensions of metabolic processes. A series of preoccupations, operating in parallel or in combination, seem to characterize the engagement of design with processes of urban metabolism. A fascination with the fluidity of metabolic processes has led to the privileging of design concepts focusing on adaptability, indeterminacy, and flexibility rather than the often sclerotic nature of urban fabrics, infrastructures, and territories. At the same time, within the broader sustainability paradigm, the increasingly widespread concern with quantitative questions of performance and efficiency tends to prioritize energy, material, and climatic optimization and thereby to marginalize the agency

Daniel Ibañez and Nikos Katsikis

of design. Finally, there has been a tendency for a morphological fetishization of metabolism. This attitude has foregrounded a metaphoric interpretation of fluidity and organic forms, undermining the possibility of grasping the complexities of a metabolic interpretation of context. Meanwhile, an important series of more analytical engagements has emerged in contemporary design research. On the one hand, a thematic approach has been invested in investigating specific metabolic processes, charting for example the flows of food, waste, water, and energy. On the other hand, a more territorial approach has engaged with specific functional sites of metabolic activity, such as landfills, mines, agricultural fields, and ports. Although their often-groundbreaking cartographic and diagrammatic investigations have been successful in surfacing the complexities of metabolic processes, they have yet to adequately address the full potential of their projective dimension.

Grounding Metabolism interprets design as a geographic agent that, although reflexive to the spatially transcendent systems of flows and processes, is still focused on the physical configuration of human occupation "on the ground." As a result, any valuable interpretation of context needs to be connected to this specific operation. No matter how expanded it can be, as urbanization continuously reshapes the planetary terrain, design has eventually to be connected to a site-specific formal appreciation of geography. For this reason, Grounding Metabolism foregrounds the geographical imprints of metabolic processes. Instead of a seamless, ethereal, and malleable space of flows, we aim to reveal a different, thick, heavy, and lengthy process of metabolic reorganization of the earth's surface operating at various paces and scales.

We argue that the more seamless and continuous the global metabolic system of exchange becomes, the more it is engraved in a geographically discontinuous organization of the earth's surface. As urbanized regions expand and thicken, extending their metabolic reach, they become increasingly interdependent with the development of specialized regions of service and supply (agricultural regions, resource extraction zones) and a densifying mesh of connectivity infrastructures that enables the increasing volumes of exchange. As this process unfolds, it results in the production of a series of distinctive and rather sclerotic fabrics of urbanization. The articulation of these fabrics, however, is becoming increasingly splintered as the differences inherent in the specificities of natural geography are coupled with the uneven patterns of capitalist development.[13] At the same time, almost all elements of this fabric are revealed as parts of a multiplicity of metabolic cycles operating at a series of both spatial and temporal scales, from the building to the planetary, from the daily to the geologic. On an hourly and daily basis, settlements and infrastructure systems, buildings and cities, ports and highways, dams and pipelines, mines and oil rigs, agricultural lands and irrigation networks, landfills and waste treatment plants are all are parts of a dynamic metabolism of people, energy, water, nutrients, etc. At longer time frames, they are themselves artifacts of a process of not only capital investment but also the reorganization of materials and resources that have often been relocated from distant lands, and as such of a longer-term geo-metabolic alteration of the earth.

Grounding Metabolism offers a promising yet challenging proposition. It does not suggest adopting any sort of "metabolic determinism" in which conditions on the ground are seen as the mere reflection of metabolic processes. Nor does it aim to reintroduce any sort of geographical determinism in which the organization of metabolic processes is derived from the specificities of natural geography. Rather, it aspires to uncover the complexities behind the historically path-dependent, socially

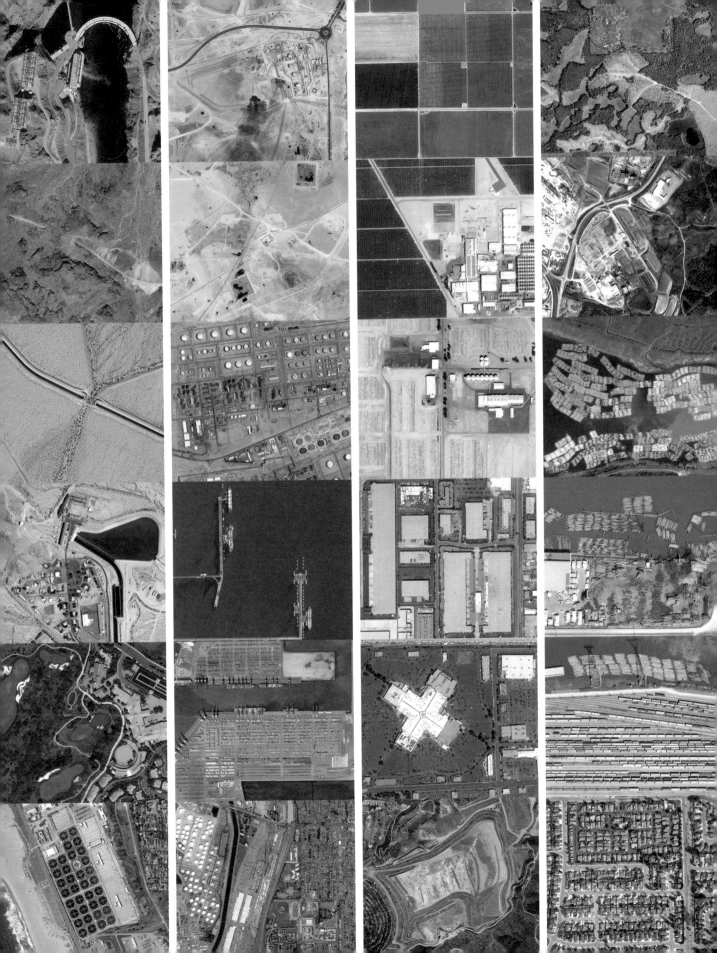

and politically contested negotiations through which metabolic processes and their geographical imprints are co-produced. It aims to reveal metabolism not as a "natural," "organic" process configured automatically as urbanization unfolds, but as a laborious and highly asymmetric effort to coordinate social and environmental systems, always mediated through the forces of capital and power. But such an approach in turn points up a series of potentials and challenges for design, including the following:

- Although the locus of design has been historically limited to urban environments, Grounding Metabolism highlights how almost every metabolic process transcends the "urban" to reach even the most remote territories of the globe, interweaving a multiplicity of sites. Rather than claiming "new" territories for design, it aims to investigate its agency in shaping their socio-ecological circulatory connections and interdependencies.

- Grounding Metabolism helps to overcome a series of historically inherited conceptual and territorial binaries—society-nature, town-country, city-hinterland—that are inadequate to describe the contemporary condition of urbanization. The circulatory dynamics of these socio-ecological processes offer an opportunity to reshuffle old binaries into new categories of analysis and intervention for design.

- Despite the contemporary fascination with the apparently weightless metabolic circulation of energy and material, it becomes evident that contemporary architectures and urbanisms are still deeply interwoven with heavy material transformations and spatially confined processes, tightly connected to the specificities of natural geography. A more informed reading of the metabolic properties of this condition could open up alternative routes to globalized design interventions.

- The geographic interpretation of metabolic processes enables the simultaneous conception of the "construction" of a site vis-à-vis "deconstruction" of others. This composite of sites and territories and their associated social and ecological transformations could offer a nuanced redefinition of the context of design, beyond traditional notions of proximity. The potentials of connecting labor, operations, and power relations with the material specificities of one site to the other is still uncharted territory for design.

- Grounding Metabolism blends the fixity and motion of material circulation. The apparent rigidities of urbanization become gradually liquefied when conceptualized as part of circulatory processes operating at variegated time frames. Long-term material rearrangements can be conceived as part of a process of creative destruction, historically mediated through capital and power relations. This framework opens up opportunities for understanding buildings, infrastructures, or land-use intensities as systematically temporal and in perpetual motion. Life cycles, differential obsolescence, or functional sequences suggest nuanced drivers for the material organization involved in (any) design.

Grounding Metabolism brings together a diverse set of contributions, offering an overview of state-of-the-art approaches to urban metabolism to highlight elements for its geographic interpretation. The first part attempts to place into creative dialogue a series of seminal approaches that are seldom presented side by side. Analytical contributions highlighting the potential for systematic and quantitative modeling and classification of aspects of urban metabolism [**Ellis / Baccini / Barles**] are interwoven with a series of critical approaches [**Moore / Luke / Gandy**], aiming to shed light on the social and political dimensions of metabolic processes that are often obscured behind the abstraction of technical models. Under the lens of urban political ecology, these contributions highlight conceptual, theoretical, and etymological challenges in the construction of a hybrid socio-natural, geographically embedded interpretation of metabolism. These approaches also offer varied perspectives on the dimensions and challenges of the contemporary condition of global metabolic upscaling. In parallel, design questions are introduced early on with a set of historical examples attempting both a design investigation of the formalization of metabolic processes [**Salgueiro, Chugh, and Léon**] and more scholarly explorations of seminal design approaches and concepts that dominated the past century [**Welter / Steiner / Tadashi Oshima**]. The last part of the volume brings together a diverse set of critical texts [**Spencer / Bélanger**] and design investigations highlighting various attempts to engage with the territorial dimensions of metabolism. These include projects highlighting the emergence of neglected territories of design in the vast networks of global hinterlands [**Correa and Folch / Ghosn and Jazairy**] as well as studies of the challenges of reorganizing post-metropolitan forms of urbanization [**Viganó / de Graaf**]. Moreover, they foreground certain urbanistic attitudes to questions of self-sufficiency, ephemerality, material sourcing, and performativity [**Mehrotra and Vera / Guallart / Rahm / Moe**].

In this way, Grounding Metabolism offers a compilation of preliminary notes, positions, and projects to open up relevant questions for designers. It builds toward an understanding of a contemporary design context that is not merely being upscaled but is in constant circulation through the weaving together of a multiplicity of variegated geographies.

Notes

01. The investigation of the potentials of a geographic approach to design has been central not only among the New Geographies editors but also in research undertaken in the New Geographies Lab at the Harvard University Graduate School of Design under director Hashim Sarkis (www.research.gsd.harvard.edu/nglab). See also: Hashim Sarkis. "Geo-Architecture: A Prehistory for an Emerging Aesthetic," Harvard Design Magazine 37 (2014).

02. Neil Brenner and Christian Schmid have recently embarked on an investigation of planetary urbanization, stressing the need to connect analytically concentrated agglomerations and their extended operational landscapes, an agenda already generating considerable research in the Urban Theory Lab, Harvard GSD (www.urbantheorylab.net). See also: Neil Brenner and Christian Schmid, "Planetary urbanization," Urban Constellations (2012): 10–13; Neil Brenner, ed., Implosions/Explosions: Towards a Study of Planetary Urbanization (Berlin: JOVIS, 2013).

03. Patrick Geddes, Cities in Evolution: An Introduction to the Town Planning Movement and to the Study of Civics (London: Benn, 1968); Lewis Mumford, "Regionalism and Irregionalism," Sociological Review 19, no. 4 (1927): 277–288.

04. Benton MacKaye, The New Exploration: A Philosophy of Regional Planning (Urbana, IL: University of Illinois Press, 1990); Ludwig Hilberseimer, The New Regional Pattern (Chicago: Paul Theobald, 1949).

05. Alison Smithson, ed., Team 10 Primer (Cambridge, MA: MIT Press, 1968); Ian L. McHarg, Design with Nature (New York: American Museum of Natural History, 1969).

06. Buckminster Fuller, "U.S. Industrialization," Fortune 21, (2 February 1940): 50–57; Buckminster Fuller and John McHale, World Design Science Decade, Document 4 (Carbondale, IL: World Resources Inventory, 1965).

07. Donella H. Meadows and Dennis Meadows, The Limits to Growth: A Report for the Club of Rome's Project on the Predicament of Mankind (New York: Universe, 1972); Jay W. Forrester, World Dynamics (Cambridge, MA: Wright-Allen Press, 1971).

08. Eugene Odum, Ecology and Our Endangered Life-Support Systems (Sunderland, MA: Sinauer Associated Inc., 1989).

09. Abel Wolman, "The Metabolism of Cities," Scientific American 213, no. 3 (1965): 179–190.

10. See, for example: Peter Baccini and Paul H. Brunner, Metabolism of the Anthroposphere: Analysis, Evaluation, Design (Cambridge, MA: MIT Press, 2012); William Rees and Mathis Wackernagel, "Urban Ecological Footprints: Why Cities Cannot Be Sustainable—and Why They Are Key to Sustainability," Environmental Impact Assessment Review 16 (1996): 223–248.

11. See, for example: Nik Heynen, Maria Kaika, and Erik Swyngedouw, eds., In the Nature of Cities: Urban Political Ecology and the Politics of Urban Metabolism (London: Routledge, 2006); Matthew Gandy, "Rethinking Urban Metabolism: Water, Space, and the Modern City," City 8, no. 3 (2004): 363–379.

12. Hillary Angelo and David Wachsmuth, "Urbanizing Urban Political Ecology: A Critique of Methodological Cityism," International Journal of Urban and Regional Research (2014).

13. Steve Graham and Simon Marvin, Splintering Urbanism: Networked Infrastructures, Technological Mobilities, and the Urban Condition (London: Routledge, 2001).

Daniel Ibañez and Nikos Katsikis

Jason W. Moore

Toward a Singular Metabolism

Epistemic Rifts and Environment-Making in the Capitalist World-Ecology

Critical exploration of the capacity of the concept of metabolism to transcend Nature/Society dualism within a world-ecological framework.

Jason W. Moore teaches world history and world-ecology in the Department of Sociology at Binghamton University. He has published widely on the history of capitalism, environmental history, and the capitalist world-ecology. He is presently completing <u>Ecology and the Accumulation of Capital</u> (Verso) and <u>Ecology and the Rise of Capitalism</u> (University of California Press), and serves on the editorial boards of <u>Review</u>, the <u>Journal of Agrarian Change</u>, and the <u>Journal of World-Systems Research</u>. Professor Moore coordinates the World-Ecology Research Network and blogs regularly at www.jasonwmoore.wordpress.com. Many of his essays are available on his website, www.jasonwmoore.com.

Metabolism is a seductive metaphor. As critical environmental studies across the humanities and social sciences boomed over the past decade, metabolism and its cognates—above all, the "metabolic rift"[01]—has enjoyed a special place in environmentalist and Marxist thought. We can say two things about this special place. One the one hand, Marx's conception of social metabolism has been reinterpreted as the "metabolism of nature *and* society."[02] On the other hand, there has been virtually no critical interrogation of social metabolism as the metabolic exchange between two entities: "nature" and "society."[03] The "separation" of nature and society has been taken for granted.

Why Should This Be a Problem?

In a nutshell, the problem is that the reality is much more messy, and the relations of humans and the rest of nature more intimate, than the dualistic model suggests. Both mainstream and radical metabolism approaches have highlighted the importance of a historical perspective on the linkage of global capitalism (or industrial society) and global environmental change.[04] This is an important contribution. In the second decade of the twenty-first century, however, the metabolism of nature/society no longer serves to advance our understanding of modernity's unfolding contradictions: of financialization, war, climate change, and much more. It has become increasingly clear, for instance, that financialization not only causes socio-ecological problems, but that financial markets are, in themselves, "ways of organizing nature."[05]

Metabolism-centered studies, like much of critical environmental studies, face an unresolved contradiction: between a philosophical-discursive embrace of a relational ontology (humanity-*in*-nature) and a practical-analytical acceptance of the Nature/Society dualism (humanity *and* nature). This dualism—which I shorthand as the Cartesian binary—is

of course manifold.[06] One of Cartesian dualism's essential features is the tendency to circumscribe truth-claims by drawing hard-and-fast lines between what is human and what is "natural." We might call this an *epistemic rift*.[07] At the core of this epistemic rift is a series of violent abstractions implicated in the creation and reproduction of two separate epistemic domains: "Nature" and "Society." The abstractions are "violent" because they remove essential relations from each node in the interests of narrative or theoretical coherence.[08] Not for nothing was this symbolic divorce of Nature and Society consolidated in early capitalism. The epistemic rift was an expression—and also, through new forms of symbolic praxis, an agent—of the world-shaking material divorce of the direct producers from the means of production.[09]

This epistemic rift is premised on the creation of two idealized and independent objects of investigation: Nature/Society. The binary is so resilient because its underlying ontology is mechanical: environmental "factors" can easily be tacked onto the analysis of social processes. Although some version of the phrase "nature-society dialectic" is now commonplace, for the most part such deployments affirm dualism rather than dialectics. How do we see this? Above all, the life and times of metabolism as a "conceptual star" of Marxist thought has resisted the tendency of dialectical praxis to dissolve its analytical objects (nature/society), and to create new categories suitable to comprehending the irreducible messiness and interpenetration of humans with the rest of nature.[10]

Just how one goes about moving from the dualism of humanity *and* nature to the dialectics of humanity-*in*-nature has been a vexing problem for environmentalist thought since the 1970s. My hope, in what follows, is to suggest a different view of this conceptual star. If metabolism is not an exchange between quasi-independent objects—nature/society—but rather a process of life-making within the biosphere, new possibilities emerge. A singular metabolism of humanity-in-nature might allow us to chart a course beyond dualism.

To say humanity-in-nature is to highlight the specific configurations of human and extra-human natures. In this, capitalism may be comprehended as both producer and product of the web of life, as a "rich totality of many determinations" that transcends the Nature/Society divide.[11] This is a view of capitalism as world-ecology, joining the accumulation of capital, the pursuit of power, and the co-production of nature as an organic whole.[12] In contrast to dualist approaches, a world-ecological reading of metabolism could offer a conceptual way forward, one that might unify humans and the rest of nature through "the unbroken coincidence of our being, our doing, and our knowing."[13]

To recast our narrative frames on the basis of this "unbroken coincidence" implies a movement from "the" environment as object to environment-making as action. All life makes environments; all environments make life. Geographical change is inscribed in the ontology of life itself.[14] For humanity in the era of historical capitalism, environment-making has reached a stage of development capable of facilitating a new geological era. This is usually called the Anthropocene; but it is more accurately called the Capitalocene.[15] It is certain that the twenty-first century is a moment of dramatic global change.

But the task of interpreting these dramatic, and accelerating, global changes is daunting, and it is complicated by more than the facts on the ground. For the epistemic rift between the "economic" and the "environmental" limits our capacity to understand the character of the present conjuncture; it constrains our understanding of how the capitalist world-ecology has created and resolved crises over the *longue durée*. Is this a developmental crisis, one amenable to resolution through renewed redistribution and commodification? Or have we entered a period of protracted transition from one mode of production to another, an epochal crisis? In my view, any effective reply to these questions must ground capitalism in the earth itself, and show how modernity does not act upon nature, so much as develop through the web of life. Capitalism produces, but is also produced by, the web of life.

Capitalism as a Way of Organizing Nature: From Environmentalist Arithmetic to Dialectical Reason

The analytical challenge of explaining how capitalism develops through, rather than upon, nature is posed by the turbulence of the twenty-first-century world-system. Financialization, global warming, the rise of China—and much beyond—are neither social nor environmental processes, as conventionally understood. They are, rather, bundles of human and extra-human nature in which the really decisive connections turn on the configuration of power and re/production in the web of life. Not the separation from, but the terms of humanity's place within, nature is crucial to understanding the conditions of capitalist renewal (if any) and crisis. For I think many of us understand well enough intuitively—even if our analytical frames still lag behind—that capitalism is far more than an "economic system," and indeed far more than a social system. Capitalism is a way of organizing nature.[16]

Such a perspective immediately draws our attention toward two great organizing moments. First, capitalism internalizes—however partially—the relations of the biosphere. In the process, the agencies of capital and empire (but not only these) seek to turn the work of the biosphere into capital (abstract social labor). Second, capital's internalization of biospheric process—something that all human organizations do—simultaneously shape the biosphere's internalization of capitalism's process. These are asymmetrical relations, of course, whose valences and vectors change over time. In this, the philosophical point shapes the historical observation: capitalism, like all civilizations, is constituted through a double internalization: capitalism-in-nature/nature-in-capitalism. To say human activity of any sort "organizes" nature is to say that human activity is ontologically coincident with, and constituted through, specifically bundled relations with the rest of nature. The production of nature is therefore always the co-production of nature—not of two ontologically independent units (humanity plus nature) but of an evolving mosaic of interdependent flows, forces, conditions, and relations. This means that the accumulation of capital and the pursuit of power in the modern world-system do not have an ecological dimension, but rather are ways of human organization moving, representing, channeling, and reworking a singular metabolism: the web of life. And in the very act of moving, representing, channeling, and reworking—always unevenly, and in the modern world, systemically combined—human organization acquires new properties, undergoes cumulative and sometimes fundamental change, and brings new contradictions to the fore.

In this, all human activity is environment-making, which extends far beyond the earth-moving of urbanization, agricultural expansion, mining, and so forth. I underscore the point because the global environmental change literature leaves little room for ideas and culture as "material forces."[17] Environment-making is therefore not limited to earth-moving; it encompasses those epoch-making revolutions in cartography, agronomy, economic botany, quantification, and much beyond—the relations of what I have called *abstract social nature*.[18] In this perspective, capitalism names those long-run and large-scale patterns of environment-making that encompass "planetary urbanization"; earth-moving always works through the extra-economic procedures of mapping and quantifying reality.[19]

In contrast, environmentalists have long espoused an exogenous breakdown model, in which overpopulation, resource scarcity, earth-system breakdown, and increasingly today, global warming will cause either planetary disaster or the end of civilization as we know it. The metabolic rift perspective at once converges and diverges from this breakdown model. Its central diagnostic metaphor is "planetary catastrophe."[20] Humanity's ongoing and impending transgression of "planetary thresholds" signals an immediate threat to the planet's capacity to sustain life.[21] In this, metabolic rift arguments find common cause with the Anthropocene argument.[22] Meanwhile, rift analysts represent capitalism as essentially independent of planetary catastrophe: "[T]he system will recognize that money cannot be eaten only when the last tree has been cut—and not before."[23] Here the rift perspective diverges from other environmentalist currents—"peak oil" and its predecessors[24]—that view resource scarcity as the prime mover of civilizational crisis. For the peak-everything approach, industrial civilization winds down long before the last barrel of oil is extracted. Notwithstanding this divergence from environmentalist thought, metabolic rift arguments share with the latter an ontological consensus: the relations of Nature (environments without humans) and Society (humans without nature) are quasi-independent. The two systems interact, but are not mutually constituting. Marx's "interdependent process of social metabolism" has been reduced to the "metabolism of nature *and* society."[25]

This has led to a curious state of affairs in relation both to thinking capitalism's historical limits and to considering Marx's "ecological" thought in the study of historical change. For much of the environmentalist left, the question of limits has been pursued through an arithmetic rather than dialectical procedure: "Marxist ecology = society + nature." There are social limits, and there are natural limits. The problem is that the boundaries between the metabolism of the two units—nature and society—are nowhere specified; and the ways in which social limits make natural limits, and vice-versa, are unspecified. By and large, the metabolic rift approach tends to paint a picture of capitalism rushing headlong into the abyss—perhaps true enough in a broad sense—but there is little sense of how history is co-produced by humans and the rest of nature. This gives rise to a static and ahistorical theory of Natural Limits, in which humans (not-Nature) ultimately push nature (not-Humans) too far, whereupon nature exacts its "revenge."[26] Too often, however, the revenge of nature appears as impending cataclysm, and too rarely as a "normal" cyclical phenomenon of capitalism.

This one-size-fits-all model of ecological crisis is a problem if we acknowledge nature, even in a dualist sense, as a constitutive field and force in modern world history. This history is replete with instances of capitalism overcoming seemingly insuperable "natural limits."[27] Any account of capitalist development unable to come to grips with capitalism's cyclical socio-ecological crises—developmental crises—will be unable to frame a theory of capitalism's cumulative limits today. Ignoring the "normal" operation of capitalism's world-ecological reorganizations, such a dual systems approach to metabolism gives us only one flavor of crisis: the apocalypse. In the absence of a rigorous historical approach to the bundling of human and extra-human natures in the accumulation process, arguments for an epochal crisis today will tend to fall back on arithmetic rather than dialectical reason.[28]

This fetishization of natural limits is problematic analytically, because it blinds us to the ways that capitalism unfolds historically through the web of life. Positing two metabolisms, one social and one natural, the Marxist metabolism school forgets to answer the really revolutionary question: How are distinctive metabolisms of capital, power, and production unified, however unevenly, across the long arc of capitalist history? The problem with the rift perspective's argument is not its identification of distinctive metabolisms

Jason W. Moore

but its hardening of these into the modernist containers of Nature/Society. This would not be such a problem were it not for the considerable influence of Foster's reading of Marx and ecology. Marx's ecological insights have been taken up by a significant layer of critical scholarship in a manner largely defined by Foster's dualistic interpretation of "social metabolism" as "nature *and* society" rather than society-*in*-nature. This hardening into a dualist position has discouraged (until now) a debate over the possibilities for a unified theory of capitalism as the accumulation of capital, the pursuit of power, and the co-production of nature.

The formulation of social metabolism as the "metabolism of nature and society" has won such great popularity among social scientists because it leaves untouched the sacred category of Society. This dualism is the metabolic rift perspective's greatest strength and greatest weakness. For in channeling research into the metabolism of nature and society, metabolism has been reduced to a question of flows and stocks between pre-formed units. This has, in turn, encouraged a divorce between Marx's historical materialism and Marx's theory of value. It is often difficult to discern the analytical difference between the use-/exchange-value binary of metabolic rift analysts and the utility/exchange binary of neoclassical reasoning. The politics between the two are clearly different; but it is difficult to see Marx's central theoretical contribution—on the shaping of capitalist civilization through socially necessary labor-time—at work in Marxist ecology today.

And why should this matter? One of the key sources of understanding how capitalism creates and transcends limits—Marx's theory of value and the analysis of capitalism's crises—is rarely encountered in Marxist analysis, and even less rarely is Marx's political economy revised and renewed as if the relations of capital unfold through nature. In brief, through the law of value, Marx identified the ways in which the worlds of humanity-in-nature became valued *and* not-valued over the past five centuries, converting the globe into a vast storehouse of unpaid work—delivered by "women, nature, and colonies."[29] This cheap nature strategy was the basis for advancing labor productivity within the commodity system.[30] Marx's conception of value-relations, in other words, provides a way of seeing the exploitation of labor-power and the appropriation of unpaid work performed by human and extra-human natures as a singular metabolism of many determinations.

From Dualism to Dialectics: Metabolic Rift to Metabolic Shift

The problem of Nature/Society dualism has been confronted on philosophical terrain since the 1970s.[31] It is on this philosophical terrain that relational critiques of dualism have advanced furthest.[32] And yet, the philosophical victory of humanity-in-nature has rarely penetrated the theory and history of capitalist development. Critical political economy unfolds from the premise that the relations of capital are ontologically prior to the environmental consequences they effect. This ontological premise explains the popularity of a "converging" or "triple" crisis discourse since 2008.[33] Happily, environmental crisis tendencies are now invoked alongside economic contradictions. But this carries us only so far. However welcome the inclusion of environmental factors, the converging crisis discourse rests on an environmentalist arithmetic that is fundamentally dualist.

The problem is that adding "the environment" to a laundry list is precisely that: additive, and not synthetic. This kind of "soft" dualism tends to justify social-reductionist analyses of neoliberalism's crisis tendencies, which cannot be abstracted from capitalism's quest for cheap natures.[34] Nature, in this dominant critical approach, does not call for any fundamental rethinking of capital, value, and the patterns of recurrence, evolution, and crisis in historical capitalism. For world-historical scholars too, environmental factors are now widely recognized, but again in additive fashion: "the" environment can now be added to a long list of consequential factors in modern world history. It is this arithmetic of "nature plus society" that insulates critical political economy and world-historical studies from a view of modernity as producer and product of the web of life. And it is this arithmetic that leads Foster to the conclusion—shaping a decade of metabolic rift analysis—that there is no "feedback mechanism that... turns environmental destruction into increasing costs for capital itself."[35]

But if nature matters as more than consequence, and as more than additive factor, how do we go about reshaping our methodological premises, conceptual vocabulary, and analytical frames to show capitalism-*in*-nature rather than capitalism *and* nature? Any effective response must pursue a translation of the philosophical claim (humanity-in-nature) into workable analytics for the history of capitalism—including, of course, the history of the present.

For the world-ecology synthesis, the historical task is not one of explaining the separation of humanity and nature, but rather of specifying the historical forms of humanity-in-nature, and therefore nature-in-humanity. Humanity's species-being is located at once in and inside our bodies, and at the same time outside of us.[36] The "system of nature" is immediately internalized through our life-activity, which through embodied thought simultaneously externalizes our experiences *and mental* constructs in a never-ending yet asymmetrical and contingent circle of life.[37]

A world-ecological method unfolds from the premise of a fundamental unity between human activity with the rest of nature. The historical specificity of "mode[s] of humanity" derives from their co-produced relation within nature as a whole.[38] There is no ontological divide between the web of life and civilizations, only distinctive variations and configurations within nature as a whole. Even when environments are in some abstract sense pre-formed (the distribution of the continents, for example), historical change works through the encounters of humans with those environments, a relation that is fundamentally co-productive. A mountain range or an ocean is therefore an environmental, not historical, fact; historical change begins when we move from such environmental facts to environment-making, through which humans make environments and vice-versa.[39] Here we recognize that humanity's environment-making proceeds through the nexus of production and reproduction, a process in which humanity "can only proceed as nature does herself," by "chang[ing] the form of the materials."[40] Such a mode of analysis gives analytical—not just moral—teeth to the now-ritualized denunciations of capitalism's destruction, degradation, and disruption of nature.[41] For the focus now shifts to the "reordering of matter" through the *oikeios*— the creative, generative, and manifold relation of species and environments—in its successive historical-geographical forms.[42] The notion that humans relate to nature, in our "physical *and mental* life," as an internal actor "simply means that nature is linked to itself."[43] From this perspective, the problem is not metabolic rift, but metabolic shift.

Toward a Singular Metabolism: Geography, Nature, and the Limits to Capital

Any pursuit of such a holistic and relational perspective not only implies but necessitates a transition from dualism to dialectics. The virtue of the metabolic rift as a heuristic intervention was to highlight the irreducibly geographical character of human activity, no moment of which is independent of the web of life. Marx and Engels's point about the urbanization of the countryside—a process that unfolded in successive historical determinations—was to underscore how the relations of production, class, and accumulation enter into specific historical-geographical forms in the rise of capitalism, from its sixteenth-century origins to the era of large-scale industry.[44] These specific historical-geographical crystallizations do not produce a social metabolism that subsequently confronts a natural metabolism; they are co-produced through a singular metabolism in which humans participate. Metabolisms are always geographical. Capitalist relations move through, not upon, space, which is to say through, and not upon, nature as a whole.

Foster's contribution was to suggest how we might read Marx to understand capital, class, and metabolism as an organic whole. From this perspective, all social relations are spatial relations are relations within the web of life. Metabolism, in this perspective, is about shifts (provisional and specific unifications), not rifts (cumulative separation).

Put in these terms, the apparent solidity of town and country, bourgeois and proletarian, and above all Society and Nature, begins to melt. Metabolism, liberated from dualisms, acts as a solvent. For if metabolism is comprehended as a totality of totalities in which life and matter enter into specific historical-geographical arrangements, we are called to construct a much more supple and historically sensitive family of concepts, unified by a dialectical method that transcends all manner of dualisms—not least, but not only, Nature/Society.

What does this mean for the question of limits? Too much of the discussion around limits has been framed narrowly, focusing too much on resource constraints and too little on how capitalism's drive for limitless expansion presumes an endless frontier of cheap nature. Foster's insight was to see capitalism as an open-system metabolism, one that requires more and

Jason W. Moore

more cheap nature just to stay in place: not just nature as input (e.g., cheap fertilizer) but also nature as waste frontier (e.g., greenhouse gas emissions). Many of the most powerful implications of metabolic rift thinking, however, remain fettered by the very dualisms that Foster initially challenged, not least an unduly narrow view of the "economy" and of accumulation as an economic process (it is surely much more than this) and an undue emphasis on the rarely specified "destruction" of nature.[45] Entropy is all fine and good to embrace, but the web of life is also a place full of life-creating and environment-making activities. A one-way theory seldom gets you where you want to go.

If we take seriously the post-Cartesian implications of an open-flow conception of capitalism's metabolisms in historical perspective, the first thing that comes into focus in the centrality of the "Great Frontier." The Great Frontier was a term coined by the historian Walter Prescott Webb to describe the great shift in the labor-land ratio that inaugurated the rise of capitalism in the sixteenth century.[46] The Great Frontier was, in Webb's apt turn of phrase, the source of unprecedented "windfall profits" (not least American silver). Its opening marked the rise of a civilization that had begun to pivot on the cash nexus. Webb thought the modern world was the product of a great "boom" of economic prosperity that lasted for four centuries; on closer inspection, thanks to the great vertical frontiers of coal and then oil, this Great Boom appears to have last until the dawn of the twenty-first century, with signs of exhaustion apparent by the 1970s. Although the specifics of Webb's analysis have often been superseded in the half-century since he wrote, the basic argument is as sound as ever: modernity's epoch-making reorganizations of human and extra-human natures (labor and land) were in fact a colossally "abnormal" process premised on ruthless conquest and the appropriation of wealth on the frontier. The frontier of what? Of commodification and global value relations. For central to the great arc of modern world history, from the sixteenth century to the present, has been the voracious consumption of, and relentless quest for, cheap natures—"cheap" in relation to the accumulation of capital and its curious privileging of wage-work as the only thing worth valuing. A civilizational conceit of this sort could only emerge on the basis of devaluing both human work outside the commodity system—much of it so-called women's work—and the "work" of extra-human natures.[47]

What this line of thought suggests is that the investigation of capitalism and the "end of cheap nature" has been hobbled by its Cartesian sorting out of the problem; "nature" remains the stuff of metals and oil and corn, to the exclusion of human natures. So I would recommend that our analyses of capitalism's metabolism and its limits begin by unifying the processes of "surplus humanity" and the end of cheap energy, food, and raw materials.[48] We must dispense with the notion that something like climate change as a whole can be analyzed in its quasi-independent social and natural dimensions. And we must embrace the understanding that, with climate change, financialization, or warfare, we are dealing with bundles of human and extra-human natures, that these are varied and bundled "determinations of one essence."[49] Such an embrace would take "limits talk" as a methodological proposition rather than empirical claim, setting aside the millenarian language of catastrophe and privileging a more hopeful and historical view of limits and crises. Crises are full of danger, to be sure, but, as the Chinese would remind us, they are also full of opportunity.

Far from denying geological and biospheric realities, the limits suggested by a monist and relational view of metabolism—the pulse of capitalism as world-ecology—bring into focus the historical agency of extra-human natures as internal to the unfolding crisis of capitalist civilization. I have highlighted capitalism as a world-ecology because this perspective frames the long-run patterns of capital, power, and production in the web of life. Such a perspective defies the convenient and Cartesian notion that capital, power, and production can be placed into their bloodless and disembodied boxes, next to another, bigger but still quite tidy box called Nature. And if we still recognize that the capitalist project creates something called nature in discrete forms (resources, genes, etc.), a world-ecological view of metabolism reveals this view of compartmentalized natures as a "God-trick"[50]: please do pay attention to the Man behind the curtain.

The promise of a singular metabolism perspective is this. It recognizes that the realities signified by capital, power, and nature cannot be encaged within dualist categories. Capital and power (and more than this, of course) unfold within the web of life, a totality that is shaped by manifold civilizational projects. But these projects are not infinitely contingent. Foster and his colleagues are right about the "what" of capitalism's coherence. And yet, their dualism—an ontological and epistemic rift—keeps them from understanding that value-relations, themselves co-produced, make that coherence. These global value-relations create a set of quasi-lawlike rules of reproduction that necessarily admit contingency, for the very sound reason that capitalism's greatest strength has been its flexibility in mobilizing and recombining parts of nature in the interests of endless accumulation. And because value was premised on valuing some nature (e.g., wage-labor) and not-valuing most nature ("women, nature, colonies"), it necessitated a powerfully alienating conception of nature as external.

At the core of the capitalist project, therefore, from its sixteenth-century origins, was the scientific and symbolic creation of nature in its modern form, as something that could be mapped, abstracted, quantified, and otherwise subjected to linear control.[51] This was external nature; it is what we have come to call Nature, even if many of us no longer believe in a Nature that is independent of the Anthropos. It is easy to talk about the "limits to growth" as if they were imposed by this (external) Nature, but the reality is thornier, more complex, and, I would say, more hopeful. For the limits of capitalist civilization include biophysical realities, but are not reducible to them. Politics still matters.[52] And if the limits of capitalism today are limits of a particular way of organizing nature—this is hardly to deny the acceleration of biospheric change through global warming, the Sixth Great Extinction, and more—then we are confronted with the possibility of changing humanity's relation to nature, which is to say also humanity's relation to itself. Is the "collapse" of a civilization that plunges nearly half its population into malnutrition really something to be feared? The Fall of Rome after the fifth century and the collapse of feudal power in Western Europe ushered in golden ages in living standards for the vast majority.[53] We should be wary of making too much of such parallels. But we make too little of them at our peril.

I have long thought that the most pessimistic view is one that holds for the survival of modernity in something like its present form. But this is impossible, for the good reason that capitalism's metabolism is inherently an open-flow system that continually exhausts its sources of nourishment. There are limits to how much new work capitalism can squeeze out of new working classes, forests, aquifers, oilfields, coal seams, and everything else. Nature is finite. Capital

is premised on the infinite. Thus the centrality of the Great Frontier in the history of capitalism, and the centrality of the end of the last frontiers—cheap oil in the Middle East, cheap labor-power in China, cheap food everywhere—in the present conjuncture.[54] It was this Great Frontier that inaugurated a civilizational metabolism in which most nature, including most humans, was sacrificed in service to the productivity of wage-labor. These frontiers of appropriation were the decisive way of making others outside the circuit of capital, but within reach of capitalist power, foot the bill for the endless accumulation of capital. The great secret and the great accomplishment of the capitalist mode of production has been to not pay its bills, which is what frontiers made possible. The end of the frontier today is the end of Cheap Nature, and with it, the end of capitalism's free ride.

Acknowledgments

Special thanks to Richard Walker, Sharae Deckard, Mike Niblett, Dale Tomich, Phil McMichael, Christian Parenti, Mindi Schneider, John Bellamy Foster, Henry Bernstein, Phil Campanile, and Anna Zalik for conversations on metabolism and dialectics. I am especially grateful to Diana C. Gildea and my students at Binghamton University (and elsewhere) for ongoing conversations about the "singular metabolism" of the capitalist world-ecology: Alvin Camba, Joshua Eichen, Benjamin Marley, Roberto José Ortiz, Andy Pragacz, Shehryar Qazi, Kyle Gibson, and Christopher Cox.

Notes

01. John Bellamy Foster, "Marx's Theory of Metabolic Rift," American Journal of Sociology 105, no. 2 (1999): 366–405.
02. Karl Marx, Capital, vol. 3 (New York: Penguin, 1991), 949; John Bellamy Foster, "The Metabolism of Nature and Society," chap. 5 in Marx's Ecology (New York: Monthly Review Press, 2000).
03. But see Jason W. Moore, "Transcending the Metabolic Rift," Journal of Peasant Studies 38, no. 1 (2011): 1–46
04. Respectively, the global metabolism school of Fischer-Kowalski and her colleagues and the metabolic rift perspective of Foster, Richard York, and their students. See Marina Fischer-Kowalski, Fridolin Krausmann, and Irene Pallua, "A Sociometabolic Reading of the Anthropocene," Anthropocene Review, (forthcoming, 2014): 1–26; and John Bellamy Foster, Brett Clark, and Richard York, The Ecological Rift (New York: Monthly Review Press, 2010).
05. Jason W. Moore, "Wall Street Is a Way of Organizing Nature," Upping the Anti 12 (2011): 47–61; Larry Lohmann, "Financialization, Commodification, and Carbon," in Socialist Register 2012: The Crisis and the Left, ed. Leo Panitch, Gregory Albo, and Vivek Chibber (London: Merlin, 2012), 85–107.
06. Val Plumwood, Feminism and the Mastery of Nature (New York: Routledge, 1993).
07. The term is indebted to Jeremy Vetter, "Expertise, 'Epistemic Rift,' and Environmental Knowledge in Mining and Agriculture in the U.S. Great Plains and Rocky Mountains" (paper presented to the annual meeting of the American Society for Environmental History, 29 Mar 2012); and Mindi Schneider

Jason W. Moore

and Philip McMichael, "Deepening, and Repairing, the Metabolic Rift," Journal of Peasant Studies 37, no. 3 (2010): 461–484. Their independent formulations are, however, distinct from epistemic rift as epistemological dualism.

08. Derek Sayer, The Violence of Abstraction (Oxford: Blackwell, 1987).

09. Jason W. Moore, "The Capitalocene, Part II: Abstract Social Nature and the Limits to Capital (unpublished paper, Fernand Braudel Center, Binghamton University), http://www.jasonwmoore.com.

10. Marina Fischer-Kowalski, "Society's Metabolism," in The International Handbook of Environmental Sociology, ed. Michael R. Redclift and Graham Woodgate (Cheltenham, UK: Edward Elgar, 1997), 119–137.

11. Karl Marx, Grundrisse (New York: Vintage, 1973), 100.

12. In addition to Moore, the world-ecology synthesis is pursued by Gennaro Avallone, "Tra finanziarizzazione e processi ecologici: la salute urbana come bene comune," Sociologia Urbana E Rurale 101 (2013): 85–99; Sharae Deckard, "Mapping the World-Ecology," (unpublished paper, School of English, Drama, and Film, University College Dublin, 2012); Benjamin Marley and Samantha Fox, "Exhausting Socio-Ecological Relations," Journal of World-Systems Research (forthcoming); Michael Niblett, "The 'Impossible Quest for Wholeness'," Journal of Postcolonial Writing 49, no. 2 (2013): 148–160; Roberto José Ortiz, "Latin American Agro-Industrialization, Petrodollar Recycling, and the Transformation of World Capitalism in the Long 1970s," Critical Sociology (forthcoming); Christian Parenti, "The Inherently Environmental State: Nature, Territory, and Value," (unpublished paper, School for International Training, 2014); Tony Weis, The Ecological Hoofprint (London: Zed, 2013).

13. Humberto Maturana and Francisco Varela, The Tree of Knowledge (Berkeley: Shambhala, 1987), 25.

14. Richard Lewontin and Richard Levins, "Organism and Environment," Capitalism Nature Socialism 8, no. 2 (1997): 95–98.

15. Jason W. Moore, "The Capitalocene, Part I: On the Nature and Limits of Our Ecological Crisis" (unpublished paper, Fernand Braudel Center, Binghamton University, 2014), http://http://www.jasonwmoore.com; Moore, "The Capitalocene, Part II."

16. This argument is elaborated in Jason W. Moore, "Transcending the Metabolic Rift," Journal of Peasant Studies 38, no. 1 (2011): 1–46; "Ecology, Capital, and the Nature of Our Times," Journal of World-Systems Analysis 17, no. 1, (2011): 108–147; "Wall Street Is a Way of Organizing Nature"; "From Object to Oikeios" (unpublished paper, Department of Sociology, Binghamton University, 2013), http://www.jasonwmoore.com.

17. Marx reminds us that "theory itself becomes a material force when it has seized the masses." Does this not apply also to the bourgeoisie? Karl Marx, "Contribution to the Critique of Hegel's Philosophy of Right," in The Marx-Engels Reader, ed. R.W. Tucker (New York: Norton, 1978), 60.

18. See Moore, "The Capitalocene, Part II."

19. Neil Brenner, ed., Implosions/Explosions (Berlin: Jovis, 2013).

20. John Bellamy Foster, "The Epochal Crisis," Monthly Review 65, no. 5 (2013), 1.

21. Johan Rockström et al., "Planetary Boundaries," Ecology and Society 14, no. 2 (2009), http://www.ecologyandsociety.org/vol14/iss2/art32/main.html.

22. Will Steffen, Paul J. Crutzen and John R. McNeill, "The Anthropocene: Are Humans Now Overwhelming the Great Forces of Nature?" Ambio 36, no. 8 (2007): 614–621.

23. John Bellamy Foster, The Ecological Revolution (New York: Monthly Review Press, 2009), 206.

24. Richard Heinberg, The Party's Over (Gabriola Island, BC: New Society, 2003); Donnella H. Meadows et al., The Limits to Growth (New York: Signet, 1972).

25. Marx, Capital, vol. 3, 949; Foster, Marx's Ecology, chapter 6.

26. Frederick Engels, "The Part Played by Labor in the Transition from Ape to Man," in The Origin of the Family, Private Property, and the State (New York: International Publishers, 1970), 260.

27. See especially Jason W. Moore, "The End of the Road? Agricultural Revolutions in the Capitalist World-Ecology, 1450–2010," Journal of Agrarian Change 10, no. 3 (2010): 389–413.

28. A good example is Foster's Cartesian reformulation of my framing of world-ecological crises, in which long-run cyclical moments of crisis and restructuring shape, and are shaped by, a long-cumulative moment (see Moore, "Transcending the Metabolic Rift"; and "Ecology, Capital, and the Nature of Our Times"). Crucially, Foster characterizes epochal crises as the "convergence of economic and ecological contradictions." Such a formulation makes sense only if we presume the ontological and historical independence of "economy" and "ecology." See Foster, "The Epochal Crisis," 1.

29. Maria Mies, "National Liberation and Women's Liberation," chap. 6 in Patriarchy and Accumulation on a World-Scale (London: Zed, 1986). On value relations as a way of organizing nature, see Moore, "Transcending the Metabolic Rift"; "The Capitalocene, Part I" and "The Capitalocene, Part II.")

30. Jason W. Moore, "The End of Cheap Nature, or, How I Learned to Stop Worrying about 'the' Environment and Love the Crisis of Capitalism," in Structures of the World Political Economy and the Future of Global Conflict and Cooperation, ed. Christian Suter and Christopher Chase-Dunn (Berlin: LIT, 2014), 1–31.

31. Charles Birch and John B. Cobb, The Liberation of Life (Cambridge: Cambridge University Press, 1981); David Harvey, "Population, Resources, and the Ideology of Science," Economic Geography 50, no. 3 (1974): 256–277; Neil Smith, Uneven Development (Oxford: Basil Blackwell, 1984); Raymond Williams, "Ideas of Nature," in Ecology: The Shaping Inquiry, ed. Jonathán Benthall (London: Longman, 1972), 146–164; Alfred Schmidt, The Concept of Nature in Marx (London: New Left Books, 1973).

32. Bruce Braun and Noel Castree, eds., Remaking Reality (New York: Routledge, 1998); David Harvey, Justice, Nature, and the Geography of Difference (Oxford: Basil Blackwell, 1996); Bruno Latour, We Have Never Been Modern (Cambridge, MA: Harvard University Press, 1993); Plumwood, Feminism and the Mastery of Nature.

33. Susan George, "Converging Crises," Globalizations 7, no. 1–2 (2010): 17–22; Foster, "Epochal Crisis"; Philip McMichael, "The Land Grab and Corporate Food Regime Restructuring," Journal of Peasant Studies 39, no. 3–4 (2012): 681–701.

34. Jason W. Moore, "Cheap Food & Bad Money: Food, Frontiers, and Financialization in the Rise and Demise of Neoliberalism," Review 33, no. 2–3 (2012): 125–161; "The End of Cheap Nature."

35. Foster, The Ecological Revolution, 206 (2002 original).
36. A being which does not have its nature outside itself is not a natural being, and plays no part in the system of nature." Karl Marx, The Economic and Philosophic Manuscripts of 1844 (Mineola: Dover Publications, 2007), 157.
37. Ibid.; also Karl Marx, Capital, vol. I (New York: Vintage, 1977), 283.
38. Quotation from Gerda Roelvink, "Rethinking Species-Being in the Anthropocene," Rethinking Marxism 25, no. 1, (2013), 52–69; this argument is developed in Moore, "The Capitalocene, Part I."
39. Richard Levins and Richard Lewontin, The Dialectical Biologist (Cambridge, MA: Harvard University Press, 1985); Moore, "From Object to Oikeios."
40. Marx, Capital, vol. I, 133, emphasis added.
41. Foster, Clark, and York, The Ecological Rift.
42. Quotation from Petro Verri, quoted in Marx, Capital, vol. 1; on the oikeios, see Moore, "Transcending the Metabolic Rift," and "From Object to Oikeios."
43. Marx, Economic and Philosophic Manuscripts, 74, emphasis added.
44. Karl Marx and Frederick Engels, The German Ideology (New York: International Publishers, 1970); Marx, Capital, vol. 1, part 8.
45. Foster et al., Ecological Rift; Foster, Ecological Revolution.
46. Walter Prescott Webb, The Great Frontier (Austin: University of Texas Press, 1964).
47. Moore, "The End of Cheap Nature."
48. Quotation from Mike Davis, Planet of Slums (London: Verso, 2006); see Moore, "The End of Cheap Nature"; "Cheap Food and Bad Money."
49. Karl Marx, Critique of Hegel's Philosophy of Right (1843), https://www.marxists.org/archive/marx/works/1843/critique-hpr/ch05.htm.
50. Quotation from Donna J. Haraway, "Situated Knowledges," Feminist Studies 14, no. 3 (1988): 575–599.
51. Moore, "The Capitalocene, Part II."
52. Christian Parenti, "Shadow Socialism," New Politics 14, no. 4, (2014): http://newpol.org/content/rethinking-state-0.
53. Chris Wickham, Framing the Middle Ages (Oxford: Oxford University Press, 2005); Immanuel Wallerstein, "The New European Division of Labor: c. 1450–1640," in The Modern World-System I (New York: Academic Press, 1974).
54. Moore, "The End of Cheap Nature."

Jason W. Moore

Erle C. Ellis

Ecologies of the Anthropocene

Global Upscaling of
Social-Ecological
Infrastructures

*An attempt at a systematic
classification of the hybrid
socio-ecological fabric
associated with the long
and continuous human
use of the earth's surface.*

Erle Ellis is Associate Professor of Geography and
Environmental Systems and Director of the Laboratory
for Anthropogenic Landscape Ecology at the University
of Maryland, Baltimore County, and Visiting Associate
Professor at the Harvard Graduate School of Design.
His research investigates the ecology of human
landscapes at local to global scales with the aim of
informing sustainable stewardship of the biosphere in
the Anthropocene. Recent projects include the global
mapping of human ecology and its changes over the
long-term (anthromes), online tools for global synthesis
of local knowledge (GLOBE), and inexpensive user-
deployed tools for mapping landscapes in 3D (Ecosynth).

Human populations quadrupled over the past century and will likely reach 10 billion before leveling off midcentury. Per capita rates of food, energy, and other resource consumption have grown even faster than population, accelerating already massive human demands for resources.[01] These dramatic trends have led some to forecast imminent environmental and societal collapse as human demands transgress Earth's natural limits.[02] Yet global and regional indicators show human well-being increasing steadily over the same period.[03]

To understand the extraordinary long-term growth and development of human societies is to recognize the adaptive processes of social-ecological upscaling that have enabled a single species to reshape an entire planet. It is not by using up and destroying environments that human societies have been able to grow and develop over the long-term but rather, by ever-greater scales of social and material exchange and ever-more intensive alteration of ecosystems to better support human populations — often to the detriment of other species and by exploiting non-renewable energy and material resources.[04] Nevertheless, as will become clear, the upscaling of human societies from bands of hunter-gathers to farming communities to global urban industrial networks has made the Earth more capable of sustaining human populations, not less.

Yet what are the prospects for humanity and ecology on a planet ever-more rapidly and completely reshaped by human societies? The challenges are unprecedented and there is no going back. Remarkably, the continued global upscaling of the social-ecological infrastructures that sustain humanity might still offer the greatest planetary opportunities — the global social-ecological design spaces — in which the future prospects for both humanity and nonhuman nature might be dramatically improved.[05]

Emergence of the Anthropocene

Human use of land for agriculture and settlements — the key social-ecological infrastructures that sustain humanity — has already transformed more than three-quarters of the terrestrial biosphere into anthropogenic biomes, or anthromes, yielding a host of novel ecologies characterized by their sustained direct interactions with human populations and infrastructures in the forms of crops, pastures, built structures, and other used lands [**Figure 01**].[06] This profound and permanent transformation of Earth's ecology together with anthropogenic global changes in climate, hydrology, element cycling, biodiversity, and other environmental processes has recently led scientists to recognize the emergence of human systems as a global force transforming the Earth system and the beginning of a new epoch of geologic time, the Anthropocene.[07]

The Anthropocene is commonly portrayed as a recent crisis brought on by the overwhelming demands of industrial societies on Earth's "life support systems."[08] And contemporary rates and scales of industrial environmental change are certainly unprecedented.[09] Left unchecked, these might derail all prospects for a desirable future, especially climate change caused by fossil fuel combustion. Yet the single greatest global change wrought by humanity to date is likely the transformation of the terrestrial biosphere by human use of land [**Figure 02**].[10] While far slower than industrial changes, the evidence from archeology, paleoecology, and environmental history demonstrate clearly that human societies have been reshaping the terrestrial biosphere, and perhaps even global climate, for millennia.[11]

Long before the rise of industry, even before the rise of agriculture, human societies began transforming ecosystems to support their populations and sustained these processes for thousands of years in some regions.[12] Even our predecessors in the genus *Homo*, now extinct, used tools of stone and fire to extract more sustenance from landscapes than would ever be possible without these

021

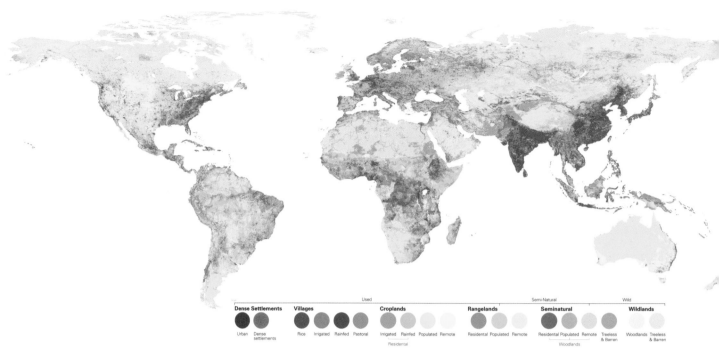

Dense Settlements | Villages | Croplands | Rangelands | Seminatural | Wildlands

Urban Dense settlements | Rice Irrigated Rainfed Pastoral | Irrigated Rainfed Populated Remote | Residential Populated Remote | Residential Populated Remote Treeless & Barren | Woodlands Treeless & Barren

technologies.[13] Rather than simply adapting to environments as they are, our species, like some others, alters environments to sustain its populations, a process known to ecologists and archeologists as niche construction.[14]

Social Construction of the Human Niche

Niche construction confers powerful evolutionary advantages because the social-ecological infrastructures developed by ancestors, such as cleared woodlands or tools for exploiting diverse species, are inherited by their progeny, enhancing the adaptive capacity of future generations. More powerful still is the unrivaled ability of our species to transmit strategic knowledge for producing these infrastructures across societies in generational time, enabling this social-ecological capital to accumulate over generations across the world.[15] As a result, the human niche has been expanded far beyond anything that unaltered nature could provide by processes of cultural evolution far more rapid than biological evolution. These unprecedented capabilities for social-ecological upscaling are what have enabled a single species to transform an entire planet.

Tens of thousands of years ago, hunter-gatherer societies had already spread across the Earth and depended on sophisticated social-ecological strategies to sustain growing populations in landscapes transformed by their ancestors.[16] Over thousands of generations, these societies accumulated advanced technologies enabling more sustenance to be squeezed out of ecosystems, including the ability to utilize a broad spectrum of species once preferred megafauna such as the wooly mammoth

became rare or extinct, to extract more nutrients from them by cooking and grinding, to burn woodlands to enhance hunting and foraging success, and to propagate and later to domesticate the most useful species.[17] Hunter-gatherers transformed their environments and depended on the social-ecological legacies of their ancestors to sustain themselves. Ecosystems began changing across the Earth, setting the stage for even greater rates of social-ecological change driven by the rise of agriculture.

Land-Use Intensification and Social-Ecological Upscaling

Populations sustained by agriculture grew more rapidly than those of hunter-gatherers, ultimately replacing them across Earth's most productive lands. These larger and more demanding populations were driven to adopt more intensive and productive land-use systems to gain their sustenance from the same land using technological innovations such as tillage, irrigation, and manuring, typically adopting them only when existing technologies could no longer produce enough—usually long after technologies first became available—but ultimately yielding long-term increases in land productivity and the social-ecological upscaling of human societies.[18] Long fallow shifting cultivation gave way to shortened fallows, the plow, continuous cropping, irrigation, manuring, and other increasingly productive land-use technologies. Still, relationships between a given population and its land system productivity remained dynamic and complex, driven not only by populations but also by social and economic processes regulating resource demand, land availability

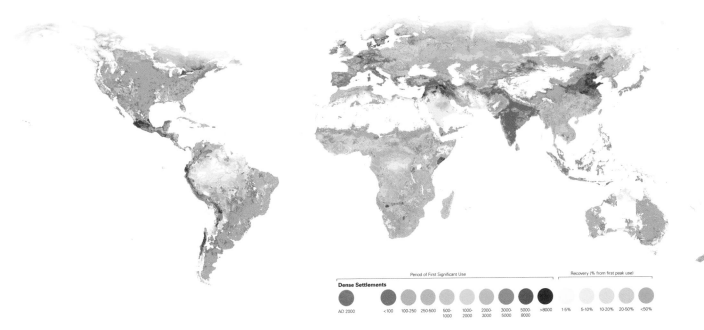

Period of First Significant Use

Dense Settlements

AD 2000   <100   100-250   250-500   500-1000   1000-2000   2000-3000   3000-5000   5000-8000   >8000

Recovery (% from first peak use)

1-5%   5-10%   10-20%   20-50%   <50%

and suitability, barriers to technology adoption and availability, and the potential for intensive use of land to degrade its productivity over time. As a result, a general trend toward increasing social-ecological upscaling of land productivity has been generated not by a smooth and continuous process but through a complex succession of land-use system regime shifts, some of them regressive, subjecting populations to both surplus production and productivity crises.[19]

Social-ecological upscaling accelerated with the emergence of urban and industrial societies.[20] Increasingly productive agricultural systems produced greater potential for extractable surpluses, supporting growth in nonagricultural populations and ultimately the first cities.[21] The growing demands of urban populations have been supported by ever-larger scales of farming operations and commercial networks, ultimately leading to widespread adoption of high-yielding industrial "green revolution" land-use systems by the 1950s and continuing today, sustained by fossil energy and other industrial inputs. These industrial technologies, especially mechanization, have increasingly decoupled human labor from productivity growth in agriculture, driving a growing proportion of humanity into urban areas while focusing agricultural production in regions most favorable to large-scale agriculture. Continued increases in land system productivity have also largely compensated for the increasing demands of growing human populations and progressively richer diets.[22] As a result, lands less suitable for large-scale agriculture are being abandoned in regions

where governance supports this, leading to "forest transitions" as woodlands recover, as in the eastern United States, parts of Europe, and even China.[23]

Anthropocene Ecologies, Anthropogenic Landscapes

Recovering temperate woodlands are just one legacy of global social-ecological upscaling. The ecologies of the Anthropocene are rich and diverse, shaped by the varied agricultural and urban infrastructures that sustain humanity and dispersed widely across the anthromes that extend over most of Earth's ice-free land [**Figures 01, 03**].[24] Most important, anthromes are mosaic landscapes composed both of lands used directly for agriculture and settlements and the ecosystems left embedded within them as remnant, recovering, and less directly used novel ecosystems.[25] Less than one-quarter of Earth's ice-free land remains as wildlands, and mostly in remote areas too cold or too dry to attract humans. The novel ecosystems embedded within anthromes now cover a substantially greater extent than that of wildlands (greater than 35 percent of Earth's ice-free land), and are dispersed across the biosphere in some of its most productive and diverse regions.[26]

The global significance of novel ecosystems is helping to drive a wholesale rethinking of ecological science and conservation, though this is not without controversy.[27]

Figure 01.   Human ecologies of the Anthropocene: a global map of anthromes in year 2000.
Figure 02.   A global history of land use as a force transforming the terrestrial biosphere.

Erle C. Ellis

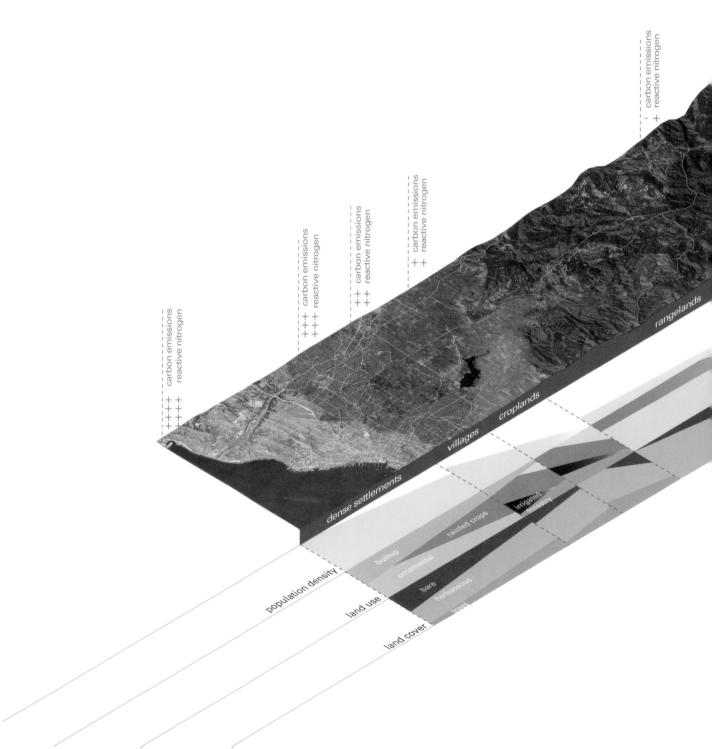

carbon emissions
reactive nitrogen

+++ carbon emissions
+++ reactive nitrogen

++ carbon emissions
++ reactive nitrogen

+ carbon emissions
+ reactive nitrogen

+ carbon emissions
+ reactive nitrogen

+++++ carbon emissions
+++++ reactive nitrogen

rangelands

croplands

villages

dense settlements

population density

land use

land cover

builtup

ornamental

rainfed crops

irrigated

forestry

bare

herbaceous

trees

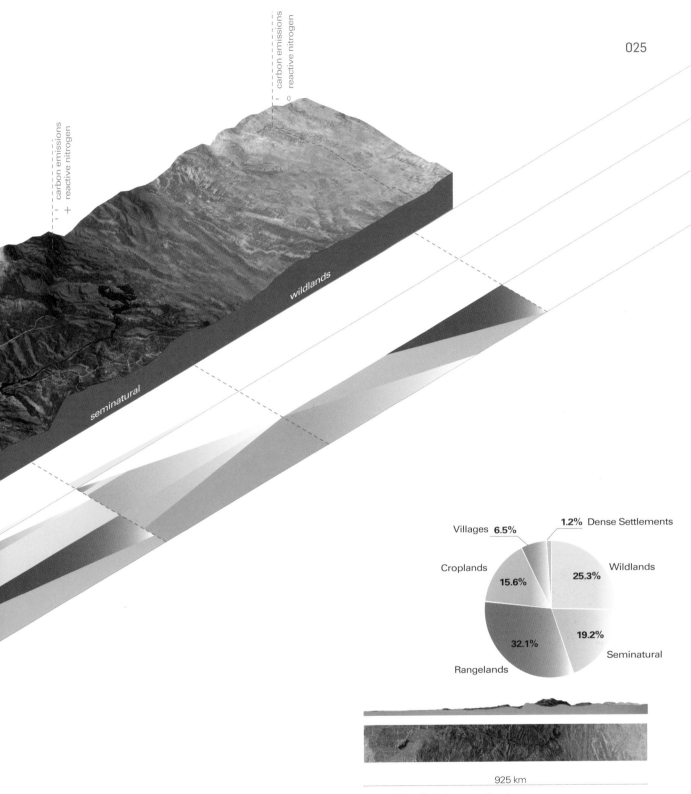

Figure 03a. A guide to anthropogenic biomes of the world: integrating human systems into ecology.
Social-ecological patterning of anthrome landscapes. Anthromes are mosaics of used and novel ecosystems shaped by human populations and their use of land, which in turn shape biodiversity and ecosystem function.

Figure 03b. Global extent of anthromes.

Erle C. Ellis

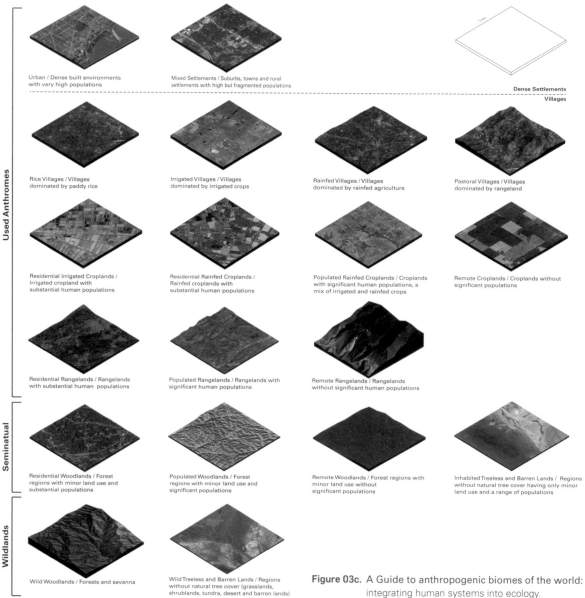

Urban / Dense built environments with very high populations

Mixed Settlements / Suburbs, towns and rural settlements with high but fragmented populations

Dense Settlements
Villages

Rice Villages / Villages dominated by paddy rice

Irrigated Villages / Villages dominated by irrigated crops

Rainfed Villages / Villages dominated by rainfed agriculture

Pastoral Villages / Villages dominated by rangeland

Residential Irrigated Croplands / Irrigated cropland with substantial human populations

Residential Rainfed Croplands / Rainfed croplands with substantial human populations

Populated Rainfed Croplands / Croplands with significant human populations, a mix of irrigated and rainfed crops

Remote Croplands / Croplands without significant populations

Residential Rangelands / Rangelands with substantial human populations

Populated Rangelands / Rangelands with significant human populations

Remote Rangelands / Rangelands without significant human populations

Residential Woodlands / Forest regions with minor land use and substantial populations

Populated Woodlands / Forest regions with minor land use and significant populations

Remote Woodlands / Forest regions with minor land use without significant populations

Inhabited Treeless and Barren Lands / Regions without natural tree cover having only minor land use and a range of populations

Wild Woodlands / Forests and savanna

Wild Treeless and Barren Lands / Regions without natural tree cover (grasslands, shrublands, tundra, desert and barren lands)

Used Anthromes

Seminatural

Wildlands

Figure 03c. A Guide to anthropogenic biomes of the world: integrating human systems into ecology.

While the most densely settled and intensively used anthromes tend to be the most altered, even the least intensively used rangelands and seminatural lands tend toward biotic communities and ecosystem processes transformed by exotic species invasions, altered fire regimes, nutrient pollution, extinctions, hunting, fuel-gathering, and other pervasive human influences.[28] Yet even the most transformed novel ecosystems embedded within the most intensively used and densely populated anthromes can retain essential habitats for most native plant species and other taxa and can maintain ecological functions and services at levels similar to those of native ecosystems.[29]

Can these novel human ecologies be engaged to shape a better Anthropocene for both humanity and nonhuman nature? There should be little doubt that human societies will continue to depend on the global upscaling of social-ecological systems to survive and to thrive. It would be no more possible to sustain 7 billion people by a return to traditional organic farming than to sustain them by hunting and gathering. The human niche has expanded across the planet over millennia of technological inno-vation, social learning, and ecosystem transformation toward the industrial technologies, urban settlements, and global networks of exchange that now sustain most of humanity. Yet the continued global upscaling of social-ecological infrastructures may still offer the greatest planetary opportunity of the Anthropocene—a design space for guiding social-ecological transformation of the biosphere toward more desirable outcomes. As migration to cities depopulates rural landscapes and agriculture continues to scale up, new spaces are opening up for ecosystems to recover or be conserved as social-ecological heritage. As the geosocial powers of cities grow, so have demands for more desirable environments and ecologies, both urban and elsewhere.

Can denser human settlements become increasingly attractive to human populations and ever more desirable to live in? Can our used lands and infrastructures be made more productive while at the same time more permeable to flows of water and wildlife and less conductive of disease, pollutants, and exotic species? Can we restrain the forces of engineering and domestication enough to allow evolutionary freedom in the species we choose to live with? To join with these opportunities is to empower a post-natural view of the human role in shaping nature and to become part of a more desirable future for both nature and humanity in the Anthropocene.

Notes

01. Marina Fischer-Kowalski, Fridolin Krausmann, and Irene Pallua, "A Sociometabolic Reading of the Anthropocene: Modes of Subsistence, Population Size and Human Impact on Earth," Anthropocene Review 1 (2014): 8-33.

02. Donella H. Meadows et al., The Limits to Growth: A Report for the Club of Rome's Project on the Predicament of Mankind (New York: Potomac Associates, 1972); Paul R. Ehrlich and Anne H. Ehrlich, "Can a Collapse of Global Civilization Be Avoided?" Proceedings of the Royal Society B: Biological Sciences (9 Jan. 2013): 280; Paul R. Ehrlich, The Population Bomb (New York: Ballantine Books, New York, 1968); Rockström et al., "A Safe Operating Space for Humanity," Nature 461 (2009): 472–475.

03. Ciara Raudsepp-Hearne et al., "Untangling the Environmentalist's Paradox: Why is Human Well-Being Increasing as Ecosystem Services Degrade?" BioScience 60, no. 8 (2010): 576–589.

04. Fischer-Kowalski, Krausmann, and Pallua, "A Sociometabolic Reading"; Ellis et al., "Used Planet: A Global History," Proceedings of the National Academy of Sciences 110 (2013): 7978–7985; Vaclav Smil, "Harvesting the Biosphere," Population and Development Review 37 (Dec 2011): 613–636.

05. Ruth DeFries et al., "Planetary Opportunities: A Social Contract for Global Change Science to Contribute to a Sustainable Future," BioScience 62 (2012): 603–606.

06. Erle C. Ellis and Navin Ramankutty, "Putting People in the Map: Anthropogenic Biomes of the World," Frontiers in Ecology and the Environment 6 (2008): 439–447; Erle C. Ellis et al., "Anthropogenic Transformation of the Biomes, 1700 to 2000," Global Ecol Biogeogr 19 (Sept 2010): 589–606.

07. Will Steffen et al., "The Anthropocene: Conceptual and Historical Perspectives," Philosophical Transactions of the Royal Society A: Mathematical, Physical and Engineering Sciences 369 (Jan 2011): 842–867; Erle C. Ellis, "Anthropogenic Transformation of the Terrestrial Biospehere," Proceedings of the Royal Society A: Mathematical, Physical and Engineering Science 369 (Jan 2011): 1010–1035; Will Steffen, Paul J. Crutzen and John R. McNeill, "The Anthropocene: Are Humans Now Overwhelming the Great Forces of Nature?" AMBIO: A Journal of the Human Environment 36 (Dec. 2007): 614–621; Erle C. Ellis and Peter K. Haff, "Earth Science in the Anthropocene: New Epoch, New Paradigm, New Responsibilities," EOS Transactions 90 (Dec 2009): 473.

08. Rockström et al., "A Safe Operating Space for Humanity"; Steffen et al., "The Anthropocene."

09. J.R. McNeill, Something New Under the Sun: An Environmental History of the Twentieth-century World (New York: W.W. Norton, 2001).

10. Ellis et al., "Used Planet"; Ellis, "Anthropogenic Transformation of the Terrestrial Biospehere"; Bruce D. Smith and Melinda A. Zeder, "The Onset of the Anthropocene," Anthropocene (June 2013): 2213–3054; William F. Ruddiman, "The Anthropocene," Annual Review of Earth and Planetary Sciences 41 (2013): 45–68.

11. Ellis et al., "Used Planet"; Ellis, "Anthropogenic Transformation of the Terrestrial Biospehere"; Smith and Zeder, "The Onset of the Anthropocene"; Ruddiman, "The Anthropocene"; Patrick V. Kirch, "Archaeology and Global Change: The Holocene Record," Annual Review of Environment and Resources 30 (2005): 409–440.

12. Kirch, "Archaeology and Global Change."

13. Kim Sterelny, "From Hominins to Humans: How Sapiens Became Behaviourally Modern," Philosophical Transactions of the Royal Society B: Biological Sciences 366 (Mar 2011): 809–822.

14. McNeill, Something New Under the Sun.

15. Sterelny, "From Hominins to Humans."

16. Ibid.

17. Kirch, "Archaeology and Global Change."

18. Ellis et al., "Used Planet"; Ester Boserup, The Conditions of Agricultural Growth: The Economics of Agrarian Change under Population Pressure (London: Allen & Unwin, 1965).

19. Ellis et al., "Used Planet."

20. Ibid.

21. Luc-Normand Tellier, Urban World History: An Economic and Geographical Perspective (Québec: Presses de l'Université du Québec, 2009).

22. Ellis et al., "Used Planet."

23. Patrick Meyfroidt and Eric F. Lambin, "Global Forest Transition: Prospects for an End to Deforestation," Annual Review of Environment and Resources 36 (2011), 343–371.

24. Ellis and Ramankutty, "Putting People in the Map"; Ellis et al., "Anthropogenic Transformation of the Biomes."

25. Ibid.

26. Ellis et al., "Anthropogenic Transformation of the Biomes."

27. Richard J. Hobbs, Eric S. Higgs, and Carol Hall, eds., Novel Ecosystems: Intervening in the New Ecological World Order (Oxford: Wiley, 2013).

28. Ellis, "Anthropogenic Transformation of the Terrestrial Biospehere"; Hobbs, Higgs, and Hall, Novel Ecosystems.

29. Hobbs, Higgs, and Hall, Novel Ecosystems; Ellis, "Sustaining Biodiversity and People."

Image Credits

All images courtesy of the author.

Figure 03: drawn by Noam Dvir.

Erle C. Ellis

Peter Baccini

Understanding and Designing the Metabolism of Urban Systems

Systematic investigation revealing the potential of quantitative analysis for comprehending and managing the dimensions and dynamics of metabolic systems.

Peter Baccini is Full Professor of Resource and Waste Management at ETH Zurich (1991-2004) and Emeritus since 2004. He holds a Ph.D. in Chemistry (1968) from ETHZ. Other stations along the way: Research & Development in the Chemical Industry in Basel (1968-1974); associate Professor of Environmental Chemistry at the University of Neuchatel (1974-1991); transdisciplinary research in the regional metabolism of urban systems (1983-2004); visiting Professor at the Universities of Goettingen, California Riverside, TU Vienna, and KTH Stockholm, Dean of Engineering and Geodetic Sciences at ETH Zurich (1994-96). From 2001 to 2006 he was President of the Swiss Academy of Sciences.

There is a long cultural evolution from small groups operating within a subsistence economy on a local scale to a market economy of an industrialized nation acting on a global scale. The common denominator of these two economies is the aim to satisfy the basic needs of *Homo sapiens*: to nourish, clean, reside, work, transport, and communicate. The complexity of the economic system has increased considerably, however, from simple, direct, and slow trade by bartering to a sophisticated financial system superimposed on the exchange of goods. The simple system's "gross domestic product" was based on the production and exchange of physical goods. Today less than 10 percent of the world's GDP is based on the purely physical part of the economy. The big leap, about 3,000 to 4,000 years ago, was the invention of money, which accelerated and extended production and trade by orders of magnitude. Money is the great equalizer, an ingenious abstraction that hides the essences of the physical differences of goods.[01] Contemporary economies wrap their metabolic processes in a package showing balance sheets with monetary units. People in affluent societies know the stocks and flows of their money, giving them ready access to the goods of their daily lives. Production and distribution of these goods, however, are based on sophisticated technical equipment and are changing continually, emerging from a cultural evolution of urban lifestyles.

The notion of metabolism is introduced to comprehend all physical flows and stocks of energy and matter within and between the entities of the system Earth.[02] During the last 200 years, exponentially growing urban systems have become the dominant metabolic actors that are changing the physiological properties of the Earth. Designing the metabolic properties of urban systems is an essential part of a strategy for "sustainable development." It must be based on the understanding of metabolic processes, first of the geogenic group—namely the earth's crust (e.g., volcanic activity, erosion, formation of specific

material stocks) and natural ecosystems, both serving as sources and sinks (e.g., rocks, oceans, rivers, forests)—and second of the colonized ecosystems that serve as biological production sites (e.g., agricultural territory, forests, lakes) and man-made settlements (the anthropogenic group) that are the main sites for producing, refining, and distributing physical goods for consumption. From a scientific point of view, metabolic phenomena have to be grasped on different scales in space (global, regional, and local) and time (from hours to millions of years).

Focusing here on urban systems, here I address the following questions: What metabolic changes took and are still taking place in the cultural process of urbanization? With which scientific methods do we investigate and interpret metabolic properties of urban systems linked with selected colonized and geogenic subsystems? How can we integrate metabolic aspects in the design process of urban systems?

From Cities to Urban Systems

The city as a dense settlement of *Homo sapiens* has existed for thousands of years. Libraries are full of scientific analyses, philosophical treatises, and narratives addressing the phenomenon of urban life. Lewis Mumford coined one of the shortest descriptions, defining the city as "a point of maximum concentration for the power and culture of a community."[03] **Table 01** gives an overview of cultural development, grouped within four periods. From a metabolic point of view, cities of the agrarian period were sites importing high energy and material flows from a large rural area around them to maintain their activities "intra muros." In framing an ecological analog, antique and medieval anthropogenic ecosystems consisted of a large area of primary producers in sparsely populated areas surrounding a densely populated center with secondary and tertiary producers and consumers. The city was the driver of the whole system (via political power and religious authority)

	Hunter and Gatherer	Agrarian Society	Transition Period	Urban Society
Type of Settlement	nomadic	settled 80% rural 20% urban	rural -> urban	urban > 80%
Time Period in Years *before present b.p.* *after present a.p.*	> 12,000 - 7000 b.p.	7000 - 200 b.p.	200 b.p. - 100 a.p.	100 a.p. - ?
Global Population Size *(order of magnitude,* *in billion capita)*	0.001 - 0.005	0.005 - 0.5	0.5 - 9	9 - ?
Societal Organization	egalitarian small groups	feudal invention and expansion of the city	human rights »dissolution of the city« formation of urban systems	democratic regional urban systems
Type of Economy	subsistence economy	planned and market economy	mainly market economy growth oriented	»sustainable economy«
Energy Supply	solar	solar, partly cultivated biomass	mainly fossil fuels	new solar technology
Energy Flow *(in GJ/capita & year)*	10	20 - 100	150 – 300	50 – 100
Material Flow *(in 1000 kg/capita & year)*	0.006	1 -10	50 – 100	50
Material Stock *(in 1000 kg/capita)*	0.001	0.1 - 1	200 - 50	200

Table 01. Cultural periods and their metabolic properties. Defined anthropologically after Dieter Groh, Anthropologische Dimensionen der Geschichte (Frankfurt: Suhrkamp, 1991). Data from Baccini and Brunner, Metabolism of the Anthroposphere.[02]

and the site of trade and technological innovation. From this center the systematic colonization of the environment evolved. Technical modifications of the hydrosphere secured water for irrigation (food production), cleaning (sewage transport), and kinetic energy (e.g., operating mills). Ingenious new building structures optimized indoor and outdoor temperatures. Large-scale territorial management developed, modifying the soil (the pedosphere) for better yields in food and timber production.

The combination of cities and colonized ecosystems formed cultural landscapes (a notion chosen to distinguish them from natural or purely geogenic landscapes). Within these landscapes, the interaction of social and technical innovations led to new anthropogenic systems. During the medieval period in Europe, for example, new political institutions emerged from urban development, establishing a balance between economy (craftsmanship and trade) and dual oligarchic rule (of a secular king and a religious leader).[04] These systems gained

more metabolic independence from naturally given boundary conditions. The morphological pattern of the city and its surrounding territory was transferred smoothly into modern times and still guides contemporary urban planning.

Five hundred years ago, various states in Western Europe started a process now called "globalization." It was based on a combination of political, engineering (civil and military), and economic skills. To become a world power, an imperial institution aimed to control global metabolism—that is, worldwide resource holdings. The first "Great World Exhibition" was held in 1851 in London. It presented the "Works of Industry of All Nations" and gave an overview the anthroposphere. Affluent societies emerging in a world of transition [**Table 01**] were turning toward a new urbanity. At the end of the twentieth century about 2 billion people, a third of the global population, had reached the "life of plenty."[05] One third was about to copy the metabolic pattern of this lifestyle, and the last third was still in a state of chronic shortage ("societies of scarcity").

What were the main reasons for the formation of new urban systems? Historians define "modern times" as a cultural period in which the following properties were combined: industrialization, urbanization, high literacy, general education, complex and highly diversified professional structures, social mobility, and prosperity.[06] This process started slowly in Europe in medieval times and experienced an accelerated development during the last 200 years. The exponential metabolic growth from a "world of scarcity" to a "world of plenty" can be explained with reference to four decisive factors, emerging from the process of modernization: 1) secure property rights (for physical and intellectual property, for civil liberties of the individual), 2) the scientific method (a systematic procedure for examining and interpreting the world), 3) the capital marketplace (a widely available and open source of funding inventions and their application in the production and distribution of innovations), and 4) highly efficient logistics (the ability to rapidly communicate vital information and to transport people and goods).

What are the idiosyncrasies of these new urban systems? Urbanization in affluent societies led to a "dilution" of urban settlement from a dense center into a network, with a variety of nodes and connections.[07] The once concentric and regional "hinterland" diffused into a global set of "hinterlands." Today the majority of the urban population lives in settlements outside of the classical centers that were still present in the nineteenth century. The new urbanity is defined by access to goods and services within half an hour of travel time (whether by foot or private or public vehicle). Therefore the term "urban system" is introduced. The model that I have developed to qualify and quantify an urban system is "Netzstadt." It is defined as follows:

> An urban system is composed of open geogenic and anthropogenic networks that are connected with each other. The nodes of these networks are places of high densities of people, physical goods (geogenic included) and information. These nodes are connected by flows of people, goods and information. The system's boundary is given by political conventions in the case of anthropogenic subsystems and by climatic properties for geogenic subsystems.[08]

In affluent societies the difference between rural and urban life has disappeared, from a metabolic point of view. The reason is the elimination of the metabolic disparity between settlements of low and high densities. All households are attached to an equivalent infrastructure that satisfies the four basic needs: to nourish, to clean, to reside and work, and to transport and communicate.[09] The new urban systems are the physical and institutional products of a globalization that asks increasingly for a frictionless flow of goods (and persons and information), to guarantee the needed supply. The "needed supply," however, is stimulated by an economy that needs to grow. Even a short interruption (weeks to months) could endanger the "world economy."[10] The flow of goods is possible only if the flow of money is not hindered. It follows that all urban systems formed during the last century experience a constant tension between regional needs and global economic constraints. Nations based on these types of urban systems are about to lose aspects of their metabolic sovereignty.

An extrapolation of the metabolic pattern of affluent societies led to the hypothesis that the combination of pollution and limited basic resources ends in a collapse of the growing anthroposphere and in severe damage to the biosphere.[11] An ecologically oriented political movement started. New strategies were drafted "to change the course" to avoid the burnout of the new urban systems.[12]

Great Disparity at the Beginning of the Twenty-First Century

Between 1950 and 1980, most nations enacted environmental protection laws. From a scientific point of view, clarification was needed to answer the question: What are environmental problems? "They are anthropogenic changes in nature that are rated negatively."[13] Based on this definition, the concepts of the natural sciences with regard to ecological processes are dominant. "Sustainability norms" are limited to an ecosystem (e.g., a forest, lake, or ocean). Scientific parameters define the optimal metabolic state of the ecosystem. Yet the world consists of two spheres, the biosphere and the anthroposphere. It is possible to develop urban systems without disturbing nature. It is a question of technical ingenuity to develop the anthroposphere separately from the huge area of natural systems that are conserved or evolve in their own way. At the end of the 1980s, the concept of "sustainable development"

Peter Baccini

(a notion already familiar in forest management) was introduced to describe a "global change that is rated positively in the broadest sense."[14] The target is an aggregated norm for the whole living space. The concepts of social science become dominant. In political practice, however, the new strategy leads to diverse norms regarding resource management, within the frame of a "magic triangle" formed by three adjectives: social-economic-environmental.

From this it is evident that, on a global scale, there is a huge diversity of starting positions and boundary conditions. A comparison of two extreme cases is illustrated in **Table 02**: an agrarian society in Nicaragua[15] and an urban society in the Swiss Lowlands.[16] The distinct differences in the execution of the activity "to nourish" are shown.[17] The agrarian society A consists mainly of farmers, grouped in families, operating within a subsistence economy. Their region is among the poorest on earth. In contrast, the urban society **U** is rooted in one of the world's richest countries. The total energy consumption of **U** is approximately tenfold that of **A**. For the activity "to nourish" (including agricultural production, distribution, and consumption), **A** uses roughly 90 percent of its total energy demand, whereas **U** can manage with only 20 percent of its total. **A**'s energy source is from local forests (80 percent self-sufficiency). **U**'s energy sources are mainly imported fossil fuels.

	Agrar A		Urban U	
	GJ/cap&y	Self-Sufficiency %	GJ/cap&y	Self-Sufficiency %
Energy Total	19	80	180	10
Energy to Nourish	17		30	
Regional Supply		>90		60
Ratio of Total Income	> 80 %		10 %	

Table 02. Comparison of an agricultural society (**A**) in Nicaragua and an urban society **U** in Western Europe with regard to their energy demand for the activity "to nourish" and to their economic effort (energy flows in gigajoules per capita annually). After Pfister, "Resource Potentials and Limitations of a Nicaraguan Agricultural Region," 2005[15]; and after Faist, Ressourceneffizienz in der Aktivität Ernähren, 2000[16].

U uses 80 percent of its energy demand for the activities "to reside and work" and "to transport and communicate." **A**'s food is mainly produced within the region (90 percent self-sufficiency). **U** needs (taking import/export flows into account) a "global hinterland" to supply approximately 40 percent of its food demand. In **A** the farmer household has to spend roughly 90 percent of its income for food, whereas the average urban household can manage this activity with only 10 percent of its total income. In comparing these two cases, the following additional points must be made:

01. The farmers in **A** have a strategy for their agricultural production. Due to their increasing population, however, their system is neither economically nor ecologically sustainable. They need a "hinterland" where they can sell their labor. But their national "hinterland" does not offer sufficient employment. A second source of income is the cash crop coffee, a product sold on the global market that is mostly out of reach for poor farmers. Their main problems are thus population growth and the lack of a strong complementary region offering employment and good prices for agricultural products.

02. The people in **U** are economically successful in a global market, mostly due to their products in the second and tertiary sectors. Because of their strong dependence on nonrenewable energy sources, however, their system is not sustainable over the long term. Unless they convert their energy infrastructure from fossil fuel to solar power within the next two to three generations, **U** will collapse.

These two societies approach sustainable development from completely different ecological and economic starting points, even before considering differences in political and social culture. Since the developed countries with their new urbanity consume about 80 percent of the resources of the worldwide anthroposphere, the focus for sustainable development is on these urban systems. Meanwhile, the developing countries aim to reach the same metabolic level within the twenty-first century (see scheme in **Figure 01** as they build new urban systems. It follows that the dominant environmental protection paradigm within the two separate spheres is superseded by a paradigm promoting the design of cultural landscapes, a procedure that asks for differentiated knowledge of metabolic processes.

Investigating and Evaluating Metabolic Processes in Urban Systems

On a regional scale an urban system, on its way to a sustainable status, has to develop a customized metabolism. Metabolic studies are based on material flow analysis (MFA), which draws on simple chemistry (stoichiometry) and basic physics (flow dynamics). Two material case studies illustrate the great diversity of regional resource management with regard to stocks and flows, the dependence of hinterlands, and the long-term potential of secondary resources within the region. The region chosen is an affluent urban system with 500 people/km2.[18]

Phosphorus

Phosphorus (P) is one of the key elements for sustaining life, without substitutes. It has reached the headlines in public debates, first as a "polluter" of aquatic systems (via eutrophication), then as a potentially scarce nutrient in the future. Affluent societies in moderate climate zones show the following characteristics [Figure 02]: (1) P is mostly imported (5 kilograms per capita annually) from remote mining areas (as phosphates); (2) The export of P is marginal—that is, 90 percent are accumulated in the anthroposphere. (3) The largest P stock, steadily increasing (0.5 percent per year) is in agricultural soil (content roughly 800 kilograms of P per capita); in second place, ten times less, are in waste management landfills. It follows that a large global redistribution of P is taking place. P is extracted as phosphate mineral from concentrated spots and subsequently distributed in the soils of the anthroposphere, building up a long-term eutrophication risk for surface water. For human nutrition, only 11 percent of the total P input is needed (about 0.6 kilograms per capita annually). In other words, the efficiency of anthropogenic P management is relatively low. This is mainly due to the two key processes within the metabolic P system, namely plant production and animal production.

If the contemporary anthropogenic P consumption of affluent societies (about 20 percent of the global population) is extended on a global scale, a P scarcity for food production could pose a problem in approximately 100 to 200 years. What are the consequences for the design of a P management strategy? The first focus must be to change the production of food. The net P-efficiency of agriculture is much too low (output per input is only 28 percent). New ways of growing plants and animals have to be invented, perhaps apart from soil. It is a huge challenge that overturns thousands of years of human culture, with a transformation period lasting at least five human generations.

Copper

Metals such as iron, aluminum, zinc, and copper form a group of widely applied construction materials. Their mean concentration in the anthropogenic stock is less than 2 percent. Their energy and economic value is usually higher than in their original sources, ores in the Earth's crust. In large-scale technical processes demanding energy, they are chemically transformed into the metallic state. Copper metal (Cu), the most expensive among the four mentioned above (between U.S. $5 and $10 per kilogram), has a mean concentration in the anthropogenic stock of only 1 gram per kilogram. However, 99 percent of Cu is installed in "clusters" of high metal concentration (electric wires, roof coverings, heating, water pipes, etc.). In developed countries the present copper stock varies between 200 and 300 kilograms per capita [Figure 03]. This stock is still growing at an annual rate of 1 percent to 2 percent.

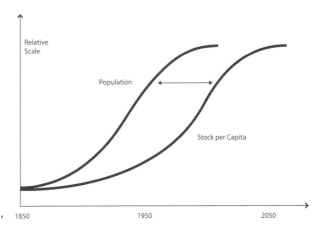

Figure 01. Growth of urban populations and of urban stocks per capita. Affluent societies (about 30 percent of the global population) show the following growth characteristics: a logistic pattern of population growth from the nineteenth century to a nearly steady state at the end of the twentieth century. A similar growth of the material stock per capita (with a time shift of about thirty years) takes place. The developing countries (70 percent of the global population) are about to repeat this process, taking off at the end of the twentieth century.

Peter Baccini

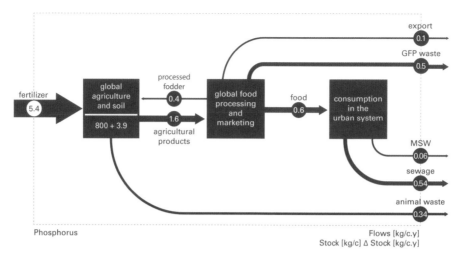

Figure 02. Phosphorus stocks and flows in urban systems.[08] The boxes within the system boundary indicate the processes through which the chosen material fulfills a metabolic function. The processes are entities of material balances. Each process has inputs and outputs, indicated by arrows and flow quantity, and a stock. The urban system, represented by the process "Consumption in the urban system," gets only 11 percent of the total **P** put into the food production. The dominant actors are agricultural production and food processing. The main sink is the soil, storing and immobilizing more than half of the invested fertilizer, increasing annually the total P content by approximately 0.5 percent. The current agricultural technique is not efficient with regard to **P** management.

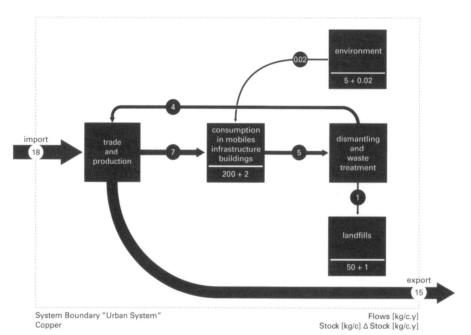

Figure 03. Copper flows in urban systems.[08] The boxes within the system boundary indicate the processes through which the chosen material fulfills a metabolic function. The boxes are entities of material balances. Each process has inputs and outputs, indicated by arrows and flow quantity, and a stock. The presented urban system imports all of its copper, refining and inserting it in various commodities, then exporting most of it (80 percent) to external markets. The losses to the environment are very small (approximately 1 per mille), the recycling rate is highly developed (80 percent of consumption waste). The main stock accumulated in the last 100 years amounts to 200 kilograms per capita and is growing annually by 1 percent. This reservoir has a high reuse potential. Stocks in landfills are smaller yet also growing, but the copper is highly diluted, mixed with a complex variety of other substances and not suited for reuse from an economic and energy-use point of view.

In developing countries the copper stock is an order of magnitude lower, but growing at higher rates. Comparing the present **Cu** stock in affluent societies with the explored copper ore stock in the Earth's crust, divided by the global population, we obtain the same stock of 300 kilograms per capita that is left for the future.[19] If we extrapolate the present copper input flow of affluent societies to a global scale, namely 10 to 20 kilograms per capita each year, a copper scarcity based on "primary copper in ores" could show up as soon as the second half of the twenty-first century. Only a small fraction of copper is "diluted" in a chemically and physically complex ecosystem (such as agricultural soil). Copper maintains, due to its chemical "robustness," its physical quality.

It follows that copper is a good candidate for urban mining, a combination of urban geology and urban engineering. At present this possibility has two major shortcomings. First, the built infrastructure has, with few exceptions, no systematic information available about the amount and location of copper in a building. Second, we do not know enough about the dynamics of the built-up stocks.[20] Some copper-containing goods (e.g., electronic devices such as computers and mobile phones) have brief usage periods—months to a few years. Long-term usage goods (e.g., grids for electricity and information, piping systems for water and waste water in buildings) stay for many decades in the stocks. If the urban system approaches a steady state with regard to copper holdings, very little additional input of **Cu** will be necessary.

In comparison with P, there is another important difference with **Cu**. This metal has substitutes in other materials. From a physiological point of view, it is only essential in trace quantities for nourishment. From a global perspective, it is reasonable to assume that urban exploration is an option for developed countries, which transform their constructed environment rather than expand it, for economic and demographic reasons. Regional metabolic analyses show clearly that there are no "sustainable goods" or "sustainable processes." The sustainability concept should be reserved for regional urban systems. With respect to long-term resource management and urban development, metabolic modeling and simulation based on urban exploration will support scenarios for the sustainable development of large cultural landscapes.

Designing the Metabolic Properties of Urban Systems

To work with the metabolic properties of urban systems, a transdisciplinary approach was chosen to account for the complexity of urban life.[21] The urban system is modeled as a Netzstadt and its design is based on the Netzstadt Method.[22] It consists of a limited set of elements that enable morphological and physiological analysis and synthesis. It can be extended to socioeconomic properties [**Figure 04**]. The urban system is analyzed using the following instruments: The urban system is characterized with three network elements and a scale hierarchy; its metabolic and territorial properties are structured with regard to the four basic life activities; it is evaluated according to five quality criteria.

The quality goals for a concrete urban project have to be elaborated by a participative political process and should not be given a priori by urban designers. Urban design in the Netzstadt Method consists of three steps[23]:

01. The analysis elucidates the essential properties of the urban system in question, helping inhabitants to formulate the strengths, weaknesses, opportunities, and threats (SWOT) of their urbanity.

02. Inhabitants sketch long-term urban goals.

03. The design for reconstructing urban systems meets the goals of [**Step 02**], starting from the state defined in [**Step 01**].

It is necessary to apply the "concept of constant time of safe practice."[24] The development of alternative strategies (e.g., replacing nonrenewable resources and inefficient technical processes and subsystems) should at least keep pace with the exploitation of the nonrenewable resources and with the transformation of indispensable infrastructures (furnishing water, food, construction materials, and communication networks). For the urban system "Swiss Lowland," the time of safe practice was assessed. It comprises the whole twenty-first century or roughly three human generations. The bottleneck for metabolic design, or its rate-determining factor, is energy policy.[25]

It follows from this that proposals for reconstructing urban systems have to allow for customized design work for a concrete regional project. The evaluation of the results of a regional metabolic analysis challenges

Peter Baccini

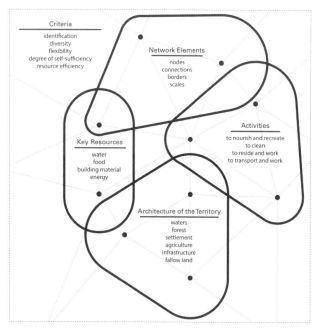

Figure 04. Designing urban systems: summary of the components of the Netzstadt Model (after Oswald and Baccini, Netzstadt, 2003[08]).

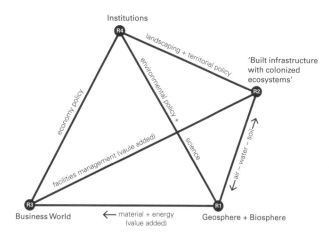

Figure 05. The R-tetrahedron: Scheme of resource correlations within a regional urban system (after Baccini and Brunner, Metabolism of the Anthroposphere[02]).

our understanding of resources for urban systems. Resources are cultural constructs. In metabolic studies we define four groups of resources [**Figure 05**]. The tetrahedron illustrates their relationships within an anthropogenic system: the resources **R1—R4** at the corners indicate their equivalence.[26] Each type of resource is interdependent with the other three. If we study a metabolic (or a material) system, we oriente ourselves on the face defined by [**R1**], [**R2**], and [**R3**]. The connections between them (or three of the six tetrahedron edges) indicate the formation of systems with processes, goods, materials, energy, and substances structured with the instrument material flow analysis. It is the metabolic face of the tetrahedron "anthropogenic system." It is evident that the connections with [**R3**] are partly coupled with monetary flows, but they are always coupled with physical flows. It means that the "value added," formed by transformation of matter and energy within the metabolic face, is always based on physical properties.

The three other faces share edges with [**R4**]. They have two "ruling edges" and one "metabolic edge." Documents from various phases of cultural evolution contain reports on the rules for using land, water, nourishment, etc. Metabolic boundary conditions trigger political control. Political measures stimulate innovations to overcome metabolic bottlenecks. The face defined by [**R2**], [**R3**], and [**R4**] is the "economic triangle" in which enterprises make profits. The face [**R1**]—[**R3**]—[**R4**] is the "engineering triangle" where technological innovation takes place. The fourth face, defined by the corners [**R1**]—[**R2**]—[**R4**], is the "ecological triangle" where all scientific activities (natural sciences and humanities) are resident, where all our knowledge (*logos*) about our house ("eco," from the Greek *oikos*, synonym here for "houses" on all scales) is developed and stored for coming generations. The four basic activities are the driving forces that convert the static scaffolding of the tetrahedron into a dynamic anthropogenic system.

Summary

The aim of "sustainable development" asks for a redesign of urban systems built in the twentieth century. It is evident that a metabolic design is restricted to the metabolic face shown in **Figure 05**. Such a design, however, depends on policies enacted by political institutions. These are based on the values of a society and its individuals, as reflected in religious doctrines, constitutions, laws, human rights charters, and the cultural heritage of the arts. Despite economic globalization, we still have a high degree of national and regional diversity. Each urban system has its specific **R**-tetrahedron. In practice, urban design is regional. The first applications of the chosen method show its strengths in the analysis.[27] Its limitation is given by the existing governance pattern that conditions the participation of the population.

"Anthrodiversity" offers a strategic advantage on continental and global scales. It allows the development of robust urban systems on relatively small scales, comprising between 10 and 100 million inhabitants in an area with a population density of between 300 and 600 people/km2. Small-scale errors have small effects on the large scale, while small-scale improvements stimulate neighbors to do better. Metabolic design for urban systems is a creative process operating between societal changes, technological innovations, and limited physical resources on a regional and global scale.

Notes

01. Peter Baccini and Paul H. Brunner, "Do You Know the Stocks and Flows of Your Real Economy?" European Financial Review (Aug–Sept 2012).
02. Peter Baccini and Paul H. Brunner, Metabolism of the Anthroposphere, 2nd ed. (Cambridge, MA: MIT Press, 2012).
03. Lewis Mumford, The City in History (1961; New York: Peregrine Books, 1987).
04. Britta Padberg, Die Oase aus Stein (Berlin: Akademie Verlag, 1994).
05. William Bernstein, The Birth of Plenty (New York: McGraw-Hill, 2004).
06. Samuel Huntington, The Clash of Civilizations (New York: Simon & Schuster, 1996).
07. Peter Baccini and Franz Oswald, Netzstadt: Transdisziplinäre Methoden zum Umbau urbaner Systeme (Zürich: vdf Hochschulverlag, 1998).
08. Peter Baccini and Franz Oswald, Netzstadt: Designing the Urban (Basel: Birkhäuser, 2003).
09. Ibid.
10. Eric Hobsbawm, Globalisation, Democracy, and Terrorism (London: Little, Brown, 2007).
11. Donella H. Meadows et al., The Limits to Growth (New York: Universe Books, 1972).
12. Stephan Schmidheiny, Changing Course (Cambridge, MA: MIT Press, 1992).
13. Gertrude Hirsch, "Beziehungen zwischen Umweltforschung und disziplinärer Forschung," GAIA 4, no. 5–6 (1995): 302–314.
14. Gertrude Hirsch and Georg Brun, "Ethische Probleme nachhaltiger Entwicklung, In Schweizerische Akademie der Geistes- und Sozialwissenschaften," ed. Kaufmann [-Hayoz], R., Burger, P., Stoffel, M., Nachhaltige Entwicklung: Nachhaltigkeitsforschung. Perspektiven der Sozial- und Geisteswissenschaften (Bern: Schweizerische Akademie der Geistes und Sozialwissenschaften, 2007): 235–253.
15. Franziska Pfister and Peter Baccini, "Resource Potentials and Limitations of a Nicaraguan Agricultural Region," Environment, Development, and Sustainability 7 (2005): 331–361.
16. Mireille Faist, Ressourceneffizienz in der Aktivität Ernähren (PhD diss., ETH Zurich, 2000).
17. Oswald and Baccini, Netzstadt.
18. Peter Baccini, "A City's Metabolism: Towards the Sustainable Development of Urban Systems," Journal of Urban Technology 4, no. 2 (1997): 27–39.
19. Baccini and Brunner, Metabolism of the Anthroposphere.
20. Thomas Lichtensteiger and Peter Baccini, "Exploration of Urban Stocks," Journal of Environmental and Engineering Management 18, no. 1 (2008): 41–48.
21. Herbert Simon, The Sciences of the Artificial (Cambridge, MA: MIT Press, 1981); Christian Pohl and Gertrude Hirsch Hadorn, Principles for Designing Transdisciplinary Research, Proposed by the Swiss Academies of Arts and Sciences (Munich: Oekom, 2009).
22. Oswald and Baccini, Netzstadt.
23. The methodological history of the Netzstadt project is described in Oswald and Baccini, Netzstadt.
24. Dieter M. Imboden, "The Energy Needs of Today are the Prejudices of Tomorrow," GAIA 2 (1993): 330–337.
25. Baccini, "A City's Metabolism: Towards the Sustainable Development of Urban Systems."
26. Baccini and Brunner, Metabolism of the Anthroposphere.
27. Oswald and Baccini, Netzstadt.

Image Credits

Table 01: adapted from Peter Baccini, "Designing Urban Systems: Ecological Strategies with Stocks and Flows of Energy and Material," in Applied Urban Ecology, ed. Matthias Richter and Ulrike Weiland (Chichester, UK: Wiley-Blackwell, 2011). Reprinted with permission.

Figures 01–02: adapted from Baccini and Brunner, "Do You Know the Stocks and Flows of Your Real Economy?" European Financial Review (Aug–Sept 2012). Reprinted with permission.

Figure 03: adapted from Oswald and Baccini, "Designing the Urban: Summary of the Components of the Netzstadt Model," in Netzstadt. Reprinted with permission.

Figure 04: adapted from Baccini and Brunner, Metabolism of the Anthroposphere. Reprinted with permission.

Peter Baccini

Timothy W. Luke

Urbanism as Cyborganicity

Tracking the
Materialities of the
Anthropocene

*Critical investigation of the
disciplinary, conceptual,
and even etymological
challenges of understanding
the geographic imprints
of the metabolic process
of an increasingly
planetary urbanization.*

Timothy W. Luke is University Distinguished Professor
and Chair in the Department of Political Science in the
College of Liberal Arts and Human Sciences at Virginia
Polytechnic Institute and State University in Blacksburg,
Virginia. He also serves as Program Chair for
Government and International Affairs for Virginia Tech's
School of Public and International Affairs in the College
of Architecture and Urban Studies, and was founding
Director of the interdisciplinary Alliance for Social,
Political, Ethical, and Social Thought (ASPECT) doctoral
program in both of these colleges at Virginia Tech. He
also is the co-editor of Fast Capitalism and book line
editor for Telos Press Publishing. His research interests
include modern cultural, social, and political theory
as well as the materiality of contemporary urbanism,
politics of environmental movements, international
politics, museum politics, and material culture.

To articulate here a provisional understanding of certain concepts rooted in my ecocritiques of urbanism, I explore how alternative notions tied to the cyborganic ecologies beneath, beside, and behind urbanization could better disclose key aspects of modernity not yet well understood. By using "arcology" unconventionally to track cybernetic organisms and machinic formations, my goal is to get beyond city-centric notions of urbanization, modernization, and globalization.[01] Instead one must trace the multiple materialities maintaining the metrometabolisms of energy, labor, money, and resources created by citification across time, which can be, or are now in fact, embedded in built, unbuilt, and yet-to-be-built spaces, and confusing the social designs of architectural structures and the natural wilds of terrestrial environments.[02]

Today's increasingly popular notion of "the Anthropocene"[03] provides a foreground for detailing the aesthetic, formal, material, and symbolic imprints left by modern materialities, as spatial processes and structures, that are associated with citified metabolic exchanges across a wide array of sites with divergent scale, speed, and scope. The idea of the Anthropocene, as the age of anthropogenic ecological destruction, could be respecified more accurately as "the Urbanthropocene" inasmuch as many of its most environmentally degrading outcomes flow from the transport, sanitation, manufacturing, habitation, energy, consumption, or agronomic systems engineered along with modern urbanization. To acknowledge the synthetic environments sustaining global urbanization'which material flow analysis, life-cycle assessment, biomimic design, or environmental services accounting track, in part, through the disciplines of industrial ecology—raises the challenge of how to appraise their operations. Understanding the ways in which designed and nondesigned sociotechnical formations intertwine in concentrated urban built environments as unique variants of complex cyborganic biomes, or "metrometabolomes," must be a project for mapping out today's "third

nature."[04] Machinic and organic analogues to cellular metabolic catabolism and anabolism exist, and they also release energy, recode information, reassemble matter, and reorder activity on multiple scales for humans and nonhumans alike in citification's urbiformative processes. To the degree that mapping such humachinic assemblages can be done, one must track how they emerge from the dynamic creation and accretion of immaterial and material metabolites as citifying masses, communities, or regions all continue to inhabit these increasingly global metrometabolomes.

My conceptual probes are meant to be suggestive efforts at mobilizing ecocritique as a tool to unpack the planetary upscaling of contemporary metabolic processes at play now in global citification. Biosphere II, as an experiment for "terraforming" other planets (such as Mars, for example, to become something like Earth[05]), ignores the scales of complexity that already make our world—Biosphere I—something like Biosphere II by diverting each visitor's attention away from the megacities that send tourists to Tucson on such eco-tours to behold stylized ecologies under glass. Human individuals and collectives with their varying modes of urban technics, complex agricultures, and dense trade networks already have, in actuality, transformed Terra—along with their companion species of domesticated animals and plants (and undomesticated but equally coevolutionary microbiota)—by "urbiforming" this planet's land, water, and air. Developing and then sustaining the metrometabolisms of these humans, animals, plants, and microbiota to sustain modernity rests at the core of urbiformative processes, and their metromorphoses cannot begin without the acts and artifacts that fuse ecologies and economies with different scales, speeds, and sizes into cyborganicity.[06]

Not yet fully legible agrarian, informational, and industrial ecologies pose major questions for political economy. To turn to more comprehensive critical analyses of their logistic grids, links, and nets, using

Figure 01. **Interstitialities:** global energy grids. Major electricity transmission networks and pipelines.

the insights of cyborg-driven assessment, could initiate a key inflection.[07] Despite the long lineage of past approaches to local, regional, or national studies of economic exchange in relation to urban design, much is still missing.[08] An arcological ecocritique of metrometabolisms also might better capture insights into the dark corners, unknown areas, or blind spots of citification. These sites are there, and new discoveries are waiting to be mapped to write new geographies animated by the theories and practices of new urbanistic discourses, disciplines, or designs, which can be forged from reappraising urbanism in this light.

New Nomenclatures for the Yet Not Recognizable

Provisional notions like "cyborganicity," "humachines," and/or "urbanatura," as I previously have deployed them, track many socio-spatial transformations unfolding around the world.[09] Whether or not one accepts their designation as being the constitutive forces behind the Anthropocene thesis,[10] as Brenner and Schmid argue, many unusual curiosities now must be confronted: new scales of urbanization, fuzzy rearticulations of urbanized territories, degradation of disintegrating hinterlands, and an end to wilderness.[11] They agree that "we need first of all new theoretical categories through which to investigate the relentless production and transformation of socio-spatial organization across scales and territories. To this end, a new conceptual lexicon must be created for identifying the

wide variety of urbanization processes that are currently shaping the urban world and, relatedly, for deciphering the new emergent landscapes of socio-spatial difference that have been crystallizing in recent decades."[12]

To a degree, ecocritique responds to these analytical and conceptual needs with third nature-based notions like urbanatura, humachines, and cyborganicity.[13] Conceptual explorations of the flux in urban metabolisms during the Anthropocene essentially force us to launch into etymological excess, linguistic legerdemain, subversive semiosis. Otherwise, the disciplinarities of already always in-use diction will reimpose existing terms behind language's cognitive contracts in an older, fixed, or empty manner. These enforcement actions inevitably block fresher, more fluid, fuller precategorical resources for bringing greater meaning with yet-to-be-signified referents into many ongoing debates.

Cyborganicity and Humachines

Using essentially biocentric images, Haraway's depiction of "the cyborg"—as complex cybernetic organisms coevolving in man-machine fusions—helps one envision new worlds.[14] Still, her cyborganic speculations speak mainly to natural organisms, inhabiting those hemispheres near the pole of naturalistic organism, while the alternate world of cyborg life arguably also address the less observed machinic hemisphere centered around the pole of socio-technical formations. For now nearly two centuries,

Figure 02   Nodality: major airports and air routes of the world.

advanced industrial societies have set themselves and their human inhabitants apart from Nature's organic economies in distinctively urbanized habitats, which are so artificially powered, mechanically maintained, and scientifically constructed that the once evenly balanced equilibria between "the historical" and "the biological" tip strongly toward greater human historical freedoms and away from deadly biological necessities.[15]

By pushing hard against anthropocentric readings of man and nature with her theses on cyborg life, Haraway clearly has, however, downplayed other less obvious new life forms in advancing her biocentrically biased analysis of cyborg life to play up the human, animal, physical lineage of cyborg descent groups. If cyborgs enact once unnoticed modes of agency in the metabolisms of modernity (as discretely individualized subjects forming along the brittle borders of man/machine interfaces), then what are the much more collectivized subjectivities flowing in the fusion of machine/human, animal/human, nonphysical/physical forces? Without being non-biocentric, where do these families—borne by machinic, humane, and nonphysical lineages in cyborg descent groups—gather in the metabolisms of modernity?

The metropolitanizing metabolisms of modernity plainly foster the generation and evolution of more than one major life form. Beyond the organic, what about the once unacknowledged cyborganic fusions of humans/machines—steam-driven railroads, profit-centered enterprises, gasoline-fueled automobiles, nuclear-powered cities, solar-energized computing grids—that spark powerful catabolic and anabolic reactions, making possible fresh layerings of physical and nonphysical being in the less, or even not, mapped domains of the first and second natures' modes of cyborganization.[16] Individual cyborgs appear, at the same time, to be always branching off in different directions. Certain cyborgs in Germany compose various collectives of gasoline-burning, Audi-driving, smartphone-using, vaccine-getting humachines that differ considerably from wood-burning, burro-riding, telephone-lacking, vaccination-needing cyborgs in Guatemala. Both communities coexist in our globalized grids of urbiformative metrometabolism, but one niche might tend to be made from high-end designer condos, and the other often rests in patchwork barrios of tin sheets and scrap lumber. One might tidy up its rooms with little domestic robots, and the other sits under the watch of surveillance drones.

If our theoretical scans profile cyborgs as quasi-objects (on one scale) in particular figurations, the presences of cyborgs as syncretic organisms must be counterpoised in object-oriented ontologies (on another scale) against parallel representations of the humachines as quasi-subjects to balance the equations of cyborganic existence.[17] When taken together, these peculiar agents—which are simultaneously

Timothy W. Luke

quasi-objects and quasi-subjects—now fabricate their own complex synthetic environments in mega-technic structures. That is, humachines could rightly be regarded as machinic ensembles of power, space, production, energy, reproduction, matter, organization, and information that constitute operational settings, survival environments, or sustainable lifeworlds where the urbanistics of global flows sustain humans and nonhumans alike in globalizing cyborganicity.

Weber plainly sensed the stirrings of such humachinic evolution in his theoretical musings about the volatility of capitalist modernization. Indeed, the purposive rationalization brought out of industrial modernity appears to require complex machinic metrometabolisms simply to take hold. Once the fusion of symbolic iconomies and material economies ignite at the interfaces of urban-industrial exchange, "it did its part in building the tremendous cosmos of the modern economic order. This order is now bound to the technical and economic conditions of machine production which today determine the lives of all individuals who are born into this mechanism, not only those directly concerned with economic acquisition, with irresistible force. Perhaps it will so determine them until the last ton of fossilized coal is burnt."[18] Without saying so, Weber entreats us to entertain a fully humachinic construction of the Earth as Gaia; yet Gaia's life is now metromorphing through nano/bio/info/cogno (NBIC) technics with their forms and functions.

The planet is, in fact, alive on many scales, for not only are the Earth and its living organic systems "alive" as a planetary life form, but so too are its diverse coevolving machinic systems "alive" within human economies and societies. Their global commodity chains, pipeline webs, electrical grids, gas lines, fiber networks, wireless footprints, and transport lanes are still neither fully made nor mapped. Moreover, these new humachinic life forms increasingly determine the ecological fate of all other natural and artificial life. Until their last reserves of consumable energy are ingested, metabolized, and excreted by the humachinic infrastructures of cities, economies, and industries sustaining the development of cyborg beings, cyborganicity will evolve. Humachines, as DeLanda hints, are out there anywhere in "any process in which order emerges spontaneously out of chaos: the non-organic life represented by the machinic phylum."[19]

Metrometabolisms pull through the roots of all these urbiformative processes in which many more geographically detached and distant places are caught in the same branches—infiltrated by, and then imbricated into, deep machinic metromorphogenetic processes. Casinopolitan urbanism in Macau and Vegas perhaps are sustainably developed by the toxic energies entombed within the thanatopolitan urbanism of Chernobyl's Pripyat and Fukushima Daiichi's Okuma. Systemic forces of meaning, power, and money reframe locality and globality as glocalities, redirect discourse and discipline in metromorphic power/knowledge regimes, and revalorize capital and labor in various metrometabolomes.[20] Such restless landscapes continuously metromorphose widely dispersed and different city regions, whose transplant regions, subsistence regions, clearance regions, supply regions, and abandoned regions all rise and fall in new metrometabolic logistical linkages.[21]

Ironically, today's urbiformative practices can guarantee that Chernobyl is everywhere, but what happens at The Venetian stays in Vegas or Macau. Speed, structure, and size once kept detached and distinct certain sites—the core and periphery, heartland and hinterland, metropolis and wilderness. The evolving fusions of humans and machines, organisms and mechanisms, informatics and biospherics in the urbanatura of third nature are imploding urbanistics with coaligned biospheres, technospheres, cyberspheres. The gas-pump hose put into every Audi in Berlin extends around the world. The machinic formations behind oil refineries, fracked fields, crude trains, modular factories, utopian ads, state legalities, personal taste, and corporate offices oversee this web of industrial and informational ecology growing in Europe, and overlook the dusty roads of Barberena that typify how Central America remains much less well connected to the sources of fossil-fueled modernity.

Metromorphosis is tracked implicitly by Jacobs's suggestive analysis of upscaling concentrated human and nonhuman populations whose expansive quantitative growth launches qualitative intensive qualitative shifts. Urbiformative forces arise as localized humachinic contrivances such as markets, bureaucracies, networks, enterprises, grids, technics, or currencies, and then focalize labor and capital in varying operational scales to draw together an organization of production, consumption, accumulation, and circulation.

Each artifactant produced amid such diverse artifacticity exerts its own productive powers and iconomic influences. Dynamic metrometabolisms reshape the pace and space of everyday life's operations, whose citifying practices create self-organizing, self-regulating, self-steering, and self-correcting stabilities out of energy, materials, labor, and ideas. Material flow analysis is one step toward mapping them, but those analyses frequently make few moves of material significance.

The scale and size of metrometabolisms then recontour regions as far and wide as any given city's networks, grids, currencies, enterprises, and technics carry under many enterprises' and bureaucracies' guidance. Urbiforms zone out and away subsistence regions unable to link into their metrometabolizing development. Supply regions are contacted and/or captured to feed energy, food, materials, livestock, and workers into the metro-morphosis of cityscaped and countrysided spaces.[22] Concentrated technics under citified command, control, and communication accelerate many citified exports, lessen some rural imports, and enlarge intra-and-extraurban exchange, whose economic demands and iconomic directives generate abandoned regions where people move from and into cities as well as transplant regions where citifying technics, enterprises, currencies, and bureaucracies become more embedded as part and parcel of the modernity emerging as metromorphosis.

Settlements and unsettling, embeddedness and extraction, concentration and dispersion, internaliza-tion and externalization, growth and decline are all produced out of humachinic workings. Citification is a metrometabolic transformation that leaves many regions remade and unmade as metromorphosed transplant, supply, abandoned, clearance, or subsis-tence regions bring localizable technics into play for export work to focalize the transplants of outmoded technologies, increase in new, different, and richer jobs, accumulate financial, intellectual, and social capital, and circulate needed imports from elsewhere as urbiformativity exerts its now "urbinorma-tive" powers and knowledges. The push and pull of metrometabolizing humachines thereby citify more and more places as their layered spaces fill with the human and nonhuman populations inhabiting them.

The quest for new geographies even might begin peeling apart human and nonhuman bodies to identify how metromorphogenic spaces commodify and control their somatic utility and behavioral normality

with genetic testing, brain mapping, tissue cultivation, and DNA databanking. To assure maximal efficiencies for metrometabolism, both the individual body and each body of population are being reappraised as sites for greater nanotech, biotech, infotech, or cognotech production and consumption. Indeed, these artifactants of citification are becoming recognized as having police powers in the new micro/meso/macro environments laid open in human and nonhuman bodies by NBIC techniques. Humachinic existence, once experienced mostly in bigger public spaces, is in turn becoming interpolated into smaller private places to intrude into, and then capture, biogenic materials.

Metabolic Mazeways of Urbanism

In departing from Marx,[23] urbanism must plainly be seen as the space of places where enduring sites and mutable systems assure that "a change in form [*Formwechsel*] and a change in matter [*Stoffwechsel*] take place simultaneously" as the cyborganic fusions of time and labor, production and consumption, mate-rial and information, circulation and accumulation explode as citified modernity.[24] The metrometabolic cycles of machinic objects and anthropic subjects, nonhuman being and human being, collectives and individuals literally collaborate, transposing the pro-ductive force of energy, material, information, and labor into more frozen polymorphic fluxes. From Aldi to Tesco to Walmart, the logistics of metromorphosis repetitiously mediate these cycles, concentrating and accelerating their multiscalar externalization of labor as capital, capital as stock, stock as structure, struc-ture as service in, of, and as the sites and systems of third nature. Metrometabolisms, on one level, channel flows from disparate pools of money, power, and ideas, enabling a social economy and industrial ecology to subsist in flows to-and-from each other. These machinic ecologies also spin up modes of putative autonomy dressed up as plutonomy and/or iconomy, which urban design all too often flattens in the conventional eco-nomics of master builders and iconified starchitects.[25]

[continued on p. 048]

Figure 03. Plasticulture: greenhouse agriculture in Almeria
[p. 044]   region, Spain.

Figure 04. Metrometabolisms I: Large-scale industrial livestock
[p. 045]   farming. Tascosa Feedlot, Bushland, Texas.

Figure 05. Metrometabolisms II: Copper mine in
[p. 046]   Chuquicamata, Chile.

Figure 06. Metrometabolisms III: Les Toules Dam near Bourg-
[p. 047]   St-Pierre, Switzerland.

Timothy W. Luke

Timothy W. Luke

NG06—Grounding Metabolism

Timothy W. Luke

Mumford, therefore, basically gets it backward when he opines, "Our age is passing from the primeval state of man, marked by his invention of tools and weapons for the purpose of achieving mastery over the forces of nature, to a radically different condition, in which he will have not only conquered nature, but detached himself as far as possible from the organic habitat."[26] Without seeing it, Mumford actually detected that material modernization has become completely embedded in the respective nature/culture environments of urbanatura, and tying together the different registers tracking the machinic and the organic via the embedded governance engines of subpolis beneath/behind/beside today's arcological articulations. At this juncture, man/machine interfaces crackle and spark along the conjunctures of *Kraft/Kultur/Kommerz* in urbanism's cyborganicity. Soleri's Cosanti is not the roots of Phoenix's urbiformativity; instead, the Valley of Sun's iconomy keeps Soleri's utopian arcology imprisoned in a tiny time warp where 1972 still struggles to become actually existing ecologism at Arcosanti outside Cordes Junction on the high desert many miles away. It is not yet mummified as Arizona's "Casa Grande II," but its once liberatory hippie urbanity is nearly as lost as the Southwest's long-gone Anasazi.

Machinic ensembles, in the last analysis, refunction human forms and rematerialize non-human substances in new environmentalized concretions of animal and apparatus.[27] Cyborganic life forms embody traces of becoming within, but also against the substances of autochthonous being. Mumford captures bits and pieces of this hybridizing drift in his reading of machines as "space capsules" whose encapsulated spatialities are

> the attempt to modify the environment in such a way as to fortify and sustain the human organism: the effort to extend the powers of the otherwise unarmed organism, or to manufacture outside of the body a set of conditions more favorable toward maintaining its equilibrium and ensuring its survival. Instead of a physiological adaptation to the cold, like the growth of hair or the habit of hibernation, there is an environmental adaptation, such as that made possible by the use of clothes and the erection of shelters.[28]

By fixating on comparatively low-tech innovation, like "the City in History" as the permanent site of agrarian dwellings made enduring by domesticated grasses, priestly bureaucracies, and war-making monarchs, he understates how extreme newer environmental adaptations, at the rates or on the scales of modern megamachineries, are indeed essentially unprecedented. In remanufacturing technically the bodies of human organisms, and by totally readapting physiologically the tools of human machines, that environment and organism become one complex aggregate nanotech/biotech/infotech/cognotech body to know, control, and exploit as the technified *terra nullis* of urbanatura.

Cyborganizing dynamics behind artificializing habitats/naturalizing techniques then compound the identities of nature and culture to the point of confusing the differences of animal and apparatus in metrometabolic metamorphoses. They mingle luminescent jellyfish DNA with pigs to track them better as transgenic bioreactors for special drugs, while building robotic jellyfish to float complex environmental sensors on the currents of the world's warming, acidifying, and dying oceans. No longer wholly nature, but not yet totally urbanized, urbanatura's artifactive environments are the primal soup brimming with new metamorphoses for all life forms, hybridizing animals and apparatuses, humans and machines, physical and nonphysical entities in new humachinic constellations at the local roots of the global market's *Formwechsel* and *Stoffwechsel*.

Cyborganicity forms the zones of urbanatura. Crude oil lifted out of West Texas soon becomes the plastic particulates swirling in the Pacific Ocean's Great Plastic Gyres. Fossil-fueled work accumulates in the grandiose bronze and marble edifices for the World War II Memorial in Washington, D..C., while innumerable detrital flows of solid, liquid, and gaseous wastes from the cities, towns, and farms burned from 1939 to 1945 still linger aloft in carbon dioxide molecules dispersed all around the planet's multilayered atmosphere, lithosphere, and hydrosphere—material markers for a degraded biosphere being wrenched into the Anthropocene. What lies behind us in the distant past probably is less significant than what is being produced and consumed today, because the scale, scope, and severity of change in the planet's arcologies are unprecedented. Nonetheless, the CO2 of the Gilded Age remains high overhead melting Greenland, killing the corals around Guadalcanal, and thawing the glaciers beyond Gorno-Altaysk.

Artifactivity matters, and matter's artifactive expressions in built environments, building forms, and builder goals gives rise to human and nonhuman artifactants whose metabolisms unfold behind, beneath, beside the intended specifications of designers, architects, or craftspeople in cyborganicity. Sustaining artifactivity with energy, materials, information, users, location, and providers, to call out only a few elements of survival, creates embedded artifacticities that constrain and enable new powers and knowledges. Only now after decades of agitation for extracting more negawatts out of fewer megawatts are LEDs, CFLs, and halogens displacing Mr. Edison's incandescents in the United States.

Design presumes to give form, take command, lend shape to all of these influences, but it misses as much as it makes in the metrometabolisms of urbiformativity. Citification, therefore, coordinates and concretizes the material kinematics of logistics past, the megamechanics of logistics present, and the ontographies of logistics future.[29] While triggered by the command, control, and communication of big nodal "Global Cities," the networks of cyborganic flows exceed the boundaries once drawn around a few metropoli, exploding in the general omnipolitanization of urbinormative living in huge sprawling "global cities."[30]

When Exxon takes out a full two-page spread advertisement, looking down Michigan Avenue, Chicago, at twilight from above with its skyscrapers and suburbs all alit to the horizon, it celebrates its (ours, Chicago's, Earth's) humachinic cyborganicity, by declaring, "Energy lives here."[31] Moreover, this enterprise promises to still be on the job, serving this quasi-subject a generation ahead. In 2040 with 2 billion more humans, a 130 percent larger global economy, and 40 percent better energy efficiency, Exxon will still be reminding all "the real challenge is supplying the energy needed for progress while reducing greenhouse gas emissions."[32] What 80,000 Exxon employees, in fact, work to achieve is sustaining the agentic capacities that "Energy" drives as well as the metrometabolic forms living energy assumes in such sprawling planetarian urbiformations.

Not unlike the current discussion of "the Anthropocene" in new scientific terms, this preliminary analysis is only provisional. It surveys material, operational, and symbolic forces, which are creating the constitutive contrivances and distinctive detritus accumulating in the anthropoceneries that now allegedly mark the advent of the Anthropocene. It focuses attention on the scale and permanence of humanity's and nonhumanity's actions when fused into humachinic collectives in which "human machine interaction" (HCI) becomes the existential order linking first, second, and third nature.[33]

Of course, efforts by social ecological system (SES) managers to calibrate some return to a set of mapped-and-measured coordinates in the spatialities of 1990, 1970, or 1950 are likely to fail, even if there were nearly trustworthy tools to use for making that return.[34] What is not fully understood cannot be managed, and little of it will become more discernible for designers and managers, without heeding the call by Brenner and Schmid to find new concepts. These new terrains are uncertain, but also they are becoming less unfamiliar. They are our anthropoceneries: corporate owned seed and genetically engineered fish, plastic-laden oceans and soil-burdened rivers, disappearing animal beings and evolving machine intelligence, rising seas and retreating ice fields, drought-stricken regions and inundated coastal zones, last gasps of going-extinct charismatic megafauna and rapid blooms of post-antibiotic microbial diseases, continental urban sprawls and miniscule remote wildernesses, light-polluted night and exhaust-polluted day.

Glossary

Arcology: Paolo Soleri's (1974) fusion of "architecture" with "ecology," this term is used more critically to trace deep urbanistic forces and deep technic forces in play with urbiformative, metrometabolic, and artifactive practices and policies either intended, or unanticipated, by design.

Artifactivity: If culture (*pace* Robert Redfield) expresses the common understandings of the acts and artifacts of any given human group, then artifactivity seeks to understand artifacts as cultured acts, as technocultural facticity, as founded/discovered acts whose technics, techniques, and technologies are active and inactive amalgams of quasi-objectivity/quasi-subjectivity.

Artifactants: Latour (1993) sees more than human actors at work in the world; nonhumans, things, institutions all can be actants. Specifying actancy as intended via discovery or invention is the intention of seeking artifactants at work in metrometabolism or urbiformativity.

Citification: Meaning more than urbanization, citification fuses "city" and "reification" to express citified programs, practices, and powers at work in cities as spatialities, technics, structures, and populations of multiscalar, expansive, and intensive thing powers.

Timothy W. Luke

Citificates: Citification as a metrometabolizing change regime generates products and by-products. These ideational and material flows of products and by-products rise from the iconomic and economic practices of urbiformative processes.

Cyborg: First proposed to describe the encapsulated terrestrial spatiality for cybernetic organisms in extraterrestrial space capsules, ships, sites, etc. Donna Haraway (1991) expands its ambit to account for any complex man-machine, man-animal, man-plant, animal/plant-machine fusions.

Cyborganicity: As urbiformative processes advance, all of the cyborg species can be seen as the cyborganicity of our processed world (Luke 1996). The Anthropocene is a recent effort to conceptualize the Earth as transformed by animate and machinic coevolution whose cyborganic effects (e.g., anthropogenic greenhouse gassing, radioactive manufactures and waste, plastic detritus, bioengineered ecologies, genetically modified biota, and nanotechnical inventions are altering the planet on a geological time scale.

Iconomy: A fusion of "icon" and "nomos," this idea seeks to track how images, ideas, concepts, memes begin to direct individuals and collectives not unlike the order of the "oikos" (household) and "nomos" (order, rule, law) of economy.

Metromorphosis: Multiple metamorphic alterations stem from citification's urbiformative forces as human and nonhuman life is captured more and more to be continuously transformed in and by cities.

Metrometabolism: Cities are founded, grow, decline, and die out for only awhile or forever. Their metrometabolisms sustain them and their resident populations with material flows, environmental services, and growth regimens.

Metrometabolomes: Concentrated built environments blend together uneasily urban and natural agents, forces, and sites that constitute their own complex biomes for cyborganic and organic beings.

Terraform: Aerospace science and geoscience imagine how extraterrestrial environments (e.g., Mars, Luna, other planets and moons) can become made artificially into Earth-like ("Terra") environments. Ironically, the Earth itself has been in continuous terra formation since the Neolithic Revolution. Hence one has the logic of "the Anthropocene" being changed to the "Urbanthropocene."

Third Nature: A speculative ontographic conceptualization of space in terms of its scale, scope, site, and speed (Luke 1996, 1997, 1998). Playing off Aristotle and Marx, "first nature" is sited in the biosphere's terrestriality with its "organic" aero/bio/enviro/geo/hydro-scapes tied to pre-industrial antiquity and agrarian or pastoral economy, while "second nature" emerges from modernity, manufacturing, and mechanistic formations. Its machinic technospheres stress governmentality over population as well as security in territorialities woven around the ethno/ideo/metro/pluto/socio-scapes of nation-states. Now a "third nature" of informationalization stresses the nano/bio/info/cogno technics whose infostructures encompass the telemetricality of cyber/media/icono-scapes.

Urbiform: Rampant citification with its multiple metromorphoses is urbiformative as the ironically terraformed Earth becomes predominantly a mostly urbanized human, nonhuman, and machinic environment made and remade by successive urbiformations.

Notes

01. Paolo Soleri, Arcology: The City in the Image of Man (Cambridge, MA: MIT Press, 1974).
02. Timothy W. Luke, Ecocritique: Contesting the Politics of Nature, Economy, and Culture (Minneapolis: University of Minnesota Press, 1997).
03. Paul Crutzen and Eugene F. Stoermer, "Have We Entered the "Anthropocene?" Global Change 41 (International Geophysical-Biosphere Programme, Oct 2000), http://www.igbp.net/news/opinion/opinion/haveweenteredtheanthropocene.5.d8b4c3c12bf3be638a8000578.html.
04. Timothy W. Luke, "Running Flat Out on the Road Ahead: Nationality, Sovereignty, and Territoriality in the World of the Information Superhighway," in Rethinking Geopolitics, ed. Gearóid Ó Tuathail and Simon Dalby (London: Routledge, 1998), 274–294.
05. Luke, Ecocritique.
06. Matthew Gandy, Concrete and Clay: Reworking Nature in New York City (Cambridge, MA: MIT Press, 2003).
07. Donna Haraway, Simians, Cyborgs, and Women: The Reinvention of Nature (New York: Routledge, 1991).
08. Lewis Mumford, Technics and Civilization (New York: Harcourt, Brace, 1963); Jane Jacobs, Cities and the Wealth of Nations: Principles of Economic Life (New York: Vintage, 1985); Soleri, Arcology.
09. Timothy W. Luke, "Liberal Society and Cyborgs Subjectivity: The Politics of Environments, Bodies, and Nature," Alternatives: A Journal of World Policy 21, no. 1 (1996): 1–30; Luke, Ecocritique; Timothy W. Luke, "Property Boundaries/Boundary Properties in Technonature Studies: Inventing the Future," in Environments, Technologies, Spaces, and Places in the Twenty-First Century, ed. Damian F. White and Chris Wilbert (Waterloo, ON: Wilfrid Laurier University Press, 2009), 173–213.
10. Paul J. Crutzen, "The 'Anthropocene'," in Earth System Science in the Anthropocene: Emerging Issues and Problems, ed. Eckart Ehlers and Thomas Krafft (Berlin: Springer Verlag, 2010).
11. Neil Brenner and Christian Schmid, "Planetary Urbanization," Urban Constellations, ed. Matthew Gandy (Berlin: Jovis Verlag GmbH, 2011), 11–12.
12. Ibid., 13.
13. This meditation on questions of urban scale, scope, and system underscores why and how "reality" does not just exist. Its theoretical tones and textures always must be made, and then continuously remade in use. Once wrought in speculating writings, disruptive ontographic wrighting also inscribes its (re)cognitions in all who read those right writings. Every day, in all of the ways that language captures, contours, and contains meaning, textual totalities stabilize what people believe actually "is" and ideally "ought to be" through the discursive representations for writing realities in nuanced ontographies. Who makes these representations? For whom? Deploying what processes of production? Any means that can be found to shake/shock/stop the logic of their workings would disclose a great deal about the ontocratic reach of prevailing regimes of thought and action.

To push Edmund Burke up against the conservative current of his concepts, language must be regarded, in many ways, as a cognitive contract between the living, the dead, and the yet to be born. Its stipulations always carry traces of presence, and already reveal marks of absence, in the multiplicitous contact of linguistic signifiers with all of that is regarded as the real world's referents when they are captured and contained, to whatever measure, as language's ontic signifieds. With words, one always already (re)cognizes the world in some determinate historicized fashion. And, language's old word order sustains, in some sense, the speech and language of its entire old world order.

To rework these cognitive contracts, semantic subversion becomes essential. As filters of feeling, diction groups together, and apart, the (in)significance spinning through mazeways of meaning from the past, present, or future in the cites of language. Conceptual ver/diction, or truth-giving speech, should always be subjected to subversion, particularly now as the new world ordering of "third nature" informational networks with its new materialities remakes the older "second nature" industrial world order with new connective circuitries, which cannot be disembedded from "first nature" itself. This initial study, in turn, draws strongly from prior analyses found in Alternatives, Environment & Planning A, Telos, and Platypus Review.

14. Haraway, Simians, Cyborgs, and Women.
15. Michel Foucault, Power/Knowledge: Selected Interviews and Other Writings, 1972–1977 (New York: Random House, 1980).
16. Luke, "Liberal Society and Cyborgs Subjectivity," 1–30.
17. Bruno Latour, We Never Have Been Modern (London: Harvester Wheatsheaf, 1993).
18. Max Weber, The Protestant Ethic and the Spirit of Capitalism (New York: Scribners, 1958), 181.
19. Manuel DeLanda, War in the Age of Intelligent Machines (New York: Zone Books, 1991), 10.
20. Jane Jacobs, The Economy of Cities (New York: Vintage, 1970).
21. Jacobs, Cities and the Wealth of Nations.
22. Ibid.
23. Timothy W. Luke, Capitalism, Democracy, and Ecology: Departing from Marx (Urbana: University of Illinois Press, 1999).
24. Karl Marx, "Capital as a Revolutionary, but Limited, Force," chap. 13 in Grundrisse (New York: Harper and Row, 1972).
25. Mumford's machinic family trees of man/machine hybrids ought not, then, to occlude the equally significant organismic genealogy of these beings. Instead of calling the fusion of animal and apparatus "a power complex" or "human machine," its metrometabolisms show the citificate forces of cyborganism. Humachines are, on one level, "a machine composed of a multitude of uniform, specialized, interchangeable, but functionally differentiated parts, rigorously marshalled together and coordinated in a process centrally organized and centrally directed: each part behaving as a mechanical component of the mechanized whole: unmoved by an internal impulse that would interfere with the working of the mechanism." On another level, humachines also are cyborganicity aggregating large populations of diverse, generalized, unique, but substantively identical wholes, loosely working apart and uncoordinated in any structures that are peripherally organized and marginally directed. Lewis Mumford, The Lewis Mumford Reader, ed. Donald Miller (New York: Pantheon, 1986), 318.
26. Ibid., 304.
27. Sigfried Giedion, Mechanization Takes Command: A Contribution to Anonymous History (New York: Norton, 1948).
28. Mumford, Technics and Civilization, 10.
29. More obviously now, urbanism increasingly expresses its metromorphoses in the cyborganic materialities of citificates, ranging from sentient infrastructures, like smart grids, autonomous vehicles, robotic factories, wired buildings, and surveillant streets to humachinic subjectivities, ranging from online social movements, real-time virtual artistic performances, prosthetic cardiac, or endocrinal devices embedded for constant client care, new literacies in/as/ of digital discourses, and civic agency as automobility/ biometric identity/telecommuting/online voting. Urbanism is megamachinics-in-action, but its global articulations in real-time face-to-face or online only now are bringing out its cyborganic powers that essentially were more "invisible, unthinkable, and unrepresentable" (Latour, 34) before urbanization's quantitative acceleration over the past century adduced these qualitative accentuations of the planet's urbiformative turn. Bruno Latour, We Never Have Been Modern (Cambridge, MA: Harvard University Press, 1993); R. Buckminster Fuller, Untitled Epic Poem on the History of Industrialization (New York: Simon & Schuster, 1962).
30. Timothy W. Luke, "Global Cities vs. 'Global Cities': Rethinking Contemporary Urbanism as Public Ecology," Studies in Political Economy 71 (2003): 11–22.
31. Wall Street Journal, 29 Nov 2013, A10–11.
32. Ibid.
33. Once these metrometabolic flows and concretions are accepted and identified, the challenge of mapping their origins and operations begins. Some, for example, will identify spe- cific urbiformative sites as points of interest for environmental history, as Cronon begins to document in a close rereading of Chicago as "nature's metropolis." Others take on the iconomic, economic, and plutonomic dimensions of metrometabolism by tracing the impact of its many stylistic, commercial, and financial products remaking architectures, industries, and markets through cinematography, photography, or telegraphy. And, still others track the sum of the corporate-sourced carbon citificates of big oil, like Exxon, in anthropogenic carbon dioxide and methane emissions to understand the intended and unintended effects of such industrial designs. While the methodology needs refinement, Exxon alone appears to have caused 3.2 percent all greenhouse gas emissions from 1854 to 2010 to ensure that "energy lives here." William Cronon, Nature's Metropolis: Chicago and the Great West (New York: Norton, 1992); Richard Heede, "Tracing Anthropogenic Carbon Dioxide and Methane Emissions to Fossil Fuel and Cement Producers, 1854–2010," Climate Change (2013); Donald L. Miller, City of the Century: The Epic of Chicago and the Making of America (New York: Simon & Schuster, 1997).
34. Eckart Ehlers and Thomas Krafft, eds., Earth System Science in the Anthropocene: Emerging Issues and Problems (Berlin: Springer Verlag, 2010).

Image Credits

Figure 01: Cartography by Nikos Katsikis. Based on the VMap0 dataset, released by the United States National Imagery and Mapping Agency (NIMA) in 1997.

Figure 02: Cartography by Nikos Katsikis. Based on flight and airport data from www.openflights.org.

Figure 03–06: Google Earth.

Timothy W. Luke

Roi Salgueiro Barrio,
Aanya Chugh and
Maynard León

Petrified Metabolism as Urban Artifact

Tells and Artificial Topographies in the Khabur Basin, Syria

Roi Salgueiro Barrio is a Spanish architect and urbanist. His research focuses on the relation between geography, the spatial typologies of contemporary urbanization, and architectural production. In addition to his degree in architecture and to his specialization in urbanism, Roi Salgueiro holds an Advanced Studies Diploma in Architecture from the School of Architecture of Barcelona. From 2007 to 2013 he was the chief architect and director of the Office of Architecture and Urbanism of the University of A Coruña. Since 2007 he has been a founding partner of Salgueiro-Rosell Architects.

Revealing the material palimpsest of a historical, long-lasting, and geographically confined urban metabolism in the Crescent Valley and exploring its implications for design.

Aanya Chugh is a masters candidate at the Harvard University Graduate School of Design. She graduated from Barnard College in 2009 with distinction and has since worked in architectural offices in Bangalore, India, and New York City. Her design work at the GSD has explored issues of urbanization in China, Turkey, and the US-Mexico border.

Maynard León is a dual masters candidate in architecture and urban planning at the Harvard University Graduate School of Design. He received a B.S. in Architecture from the University of Michigan and has worked professionally for a number of architecture firms in New York and California. His design research has explored topics such as multi-unit housing typologies in South America, the evolution of zoning code in the United States and projective maritime urbanism in extreme northern territories.

In 1972 Vittorio Gregotti extended his thesis about the forms of architectural intervention on the territory, as presented six years earlier in a short essay titled "La Forme du Territoire" in his Il Territorio dell' architettura.[01] Gregotti proposed a four-step methodology of formal interpretation of the territory as a possible basis for the conjunction between the architectural and the geographic, which he considered essential for the meaningful organization of the expanded scale of post–World War II urbanization. Gregotti aimed to reverse the negativities of the up-scaling of the city, which settled geography as the inevitable destiny of urbanization, positing a geographical grounding of the architectural and urban project. The proposed four steps—the reading and classification of "formal typologies of anthropogeographical structures," the implementation of a "formal cartography of the formal values of the territory," the reading and representation of "formal transformations generated by the introduction of planning structures," and the definition of "criteria for the repertory of forms"— pointed to the necessity of a structural or formal consistency between the geographic and the man-made. Presiding over the system was an entirely hybrid category, the anthropogeographical, which recognized the role of humanity as a geographical agent. The classification of anthropogeographical elements clarified the structure of the territory, setting parameters for any contemporary intervention.

More than fifty years after the publication of Il Territorio dell'architettura, the territorial expansion of the urban that motivated Greggotti's description of a geographically inflected urban project has become a constantly increasing planetary reality. His insistence on the necessity of finding the forms in which the geographic and the urban can be considered together has therefore become all the more relevant. Yet any possible recovery of a geographical project must acknowledge that the contemporary geographical scale of urbanization is strongly linked to the temporal dimension of an economy of networks, fluxes, and mobility that, in imposing variable dynamics of deterritorialization and reterritorialization, requires both an extended geography of detachment and specific geographical groundings. In this sense, to recover Gregotti's project—which, treating anthropological structures from a descriptive, typological point of view, analytically dissociates time and form—a clearer incorporation of the temporal dimension is needed. This, in our view, means adding to the formal comprehension of existing structures a study of how dynamic processes of interchange construct anthropogeographical formations and how these can be turned into elements of territorial order.

In this light, the formalization and cultural appropriation of metabolic processes can be seen as triggers for the creation of anthropogeographical structures of order for the contemporary urban nebula. Far from being a novel project, this approach tries to explore the new forms of the connected chain of metabolism, anthropogeography, and territorial order that has informed the urban phenomenon since its origins. We would like to deploy this approach through an investigation of how natural geography was redefined, in the beginning of the urban phenomenon, by the first sedentary settlements in Mesopotamia. As is well known, the most distinctive feature of this geographic redefinition are the man-made mounds, called tells, which were constructed as places for settlement from the Neolithic era onward. These tells constitute clear anthropogeographical structures. They are entirely artificial topographies—a sort of vertical urbanism that resulted from the accumulation of successive layers of occupation of the same, delimited place. The iteration of this process over millennia generated huge artificial mountains, reaching 40 meters in height. Their geographical dimension, in the flat landscape of Mesopotamia, turned them into structural elements for the organization of the territory: the diverse civilizations that occupied various areas of Mesopotamia, even after prolonged periods of abandonment, tended to reoccupy the tells or their surroundings.

The significance of the tells as landscape markers and their apparent confinement were behind Aldo Rossi's geographic metaphor of the tells as "islands of brick." Rossi considered them primal "urban artifacts" and original human modifications of the environment. Yet pointing to the environment, Rossi relativized their condition as islands. This is entirely the case: the construction of the tells was based in the organization of metabolic dynamics that connected the demands of construction and agricultural production with cycles of material extraction and recuperation, culturally managed processes of soil creation, and natural processes of erosion/sedimentation. The scale of these processes defined hinterlands and, eventually, an entire regional system. Accordingly, anthropogeographical modifications are not limited to the tells themselves. They expand from them in a range of sectional and thick-2D modifications of the natural ground that, together with the tells, formed the organizational landscape infrastructure of the territory. It is this complex system, and not only the tells, that determined successive patterns of occupations.

In this sense, the analysis of the sectional anthropogeography of tells and, more important, its conceptual reappropriation, requires a shift toward the study of their regional metabolism. This does not mean denying the primary value of any a priori cultural intentionality behind the process of elevation or the morphological value of the result. It means, rather, that the lesson of the tells for today resides in how to create territorial structures elaborating—culturally—purely metabolic processes.

The analysis of this cultural elaboration of metabolism is of course regionally and temporarily specific. For our purposes, it is especially perceptible in one of the best- preserved landscapes of tells: the Khabur basin. A former part of northern Mesopotamia, now within the Syrian Jazira, the Khabur basin saw the emergence of one of the first proto-urban systems during the Early Bronze Age (EBA).[02] In this moment of demographic growth and intensification of land use and construction, high tells were built with surfaces greater than 100 hectares to house between 10,000 and 20,000 people. These main, "urban" nuclei—as Tell

Brak, Tell Leilan, or Tell Mozan—loosely governed minor tells distributed roughly every 10 kilometers.[03] At the apex of the period, the totality of the region, of about 140 x 70 kilometers, was covered by this pattern of tells.

The metabolism of this proto-urban system had to combine available material resources with the necessities of agricultural production, itself determined by the availability of water and the quality of soil. In the Jazira, annual precipitation diminishes from 500 millimeters per year in the north to 250 millimeters annually in the south, the limit for sustainable rain-fed cultivation.[04] Thus agricultural exploitation has been conducted historically as dry farming: a regime of low productivity per hectare that demands extensive use of the land and the preservation of soil moisture through annual fallows.[05] The combination of dry farming with the abundance of clay in relation to other resources informed the essential metabolism of the EBA development of the region. The necessity of maximizing agricultural land was behind a regime of rotational land tenure that prohibited the construction of houses on agricultural land, limiting the options of inhabitants and the size of settlements, consequently increasing the tendency to vertically overlap.[06] These confined settlements took for their construction the most available material: mud-brick.

In its confinement and elevation, the tell internalized its external material constraints. Within its limits, construction was deployed, essentially, in iterative cycles of material (re)distributions.[07] As mud-brick is vulnerable to water, attention to decay and erosion was a primary factor in its manipulation. The need to secure drainage contributed to the process of elevation of the settlement, which mobilized three layers. Formally, the tells were originally defined by a cultural, structural layer that comprised the architectural fabric of the city and infrastructural elements such as moats, terraces, towers, city walls, and ramparts. This structural level was supported by a primary matrix produced, essentially, through the artificial sedimentation of mud-brick. The decay of both layers, both by natural and cultural factors, generated a secondary matrix that added to the cultural level's organo-cultural refuse and natural sediments of aeolian or alluvial origin.

The cyclical interconnection between these three layers was culturally managed. Existing infrastructural elements such as ramparts or glacis complemented their defensive purpose with an intentional limitation

Figure 01. Location of the main tells of the Middle-East and Anatolia.

Figure 02. Location of the main tells of the Khabur basin, Syrian Jazira, and of their agricultural hinterland.

Roi Salgueiro Barrio, Aanya Chugh and Maynard León

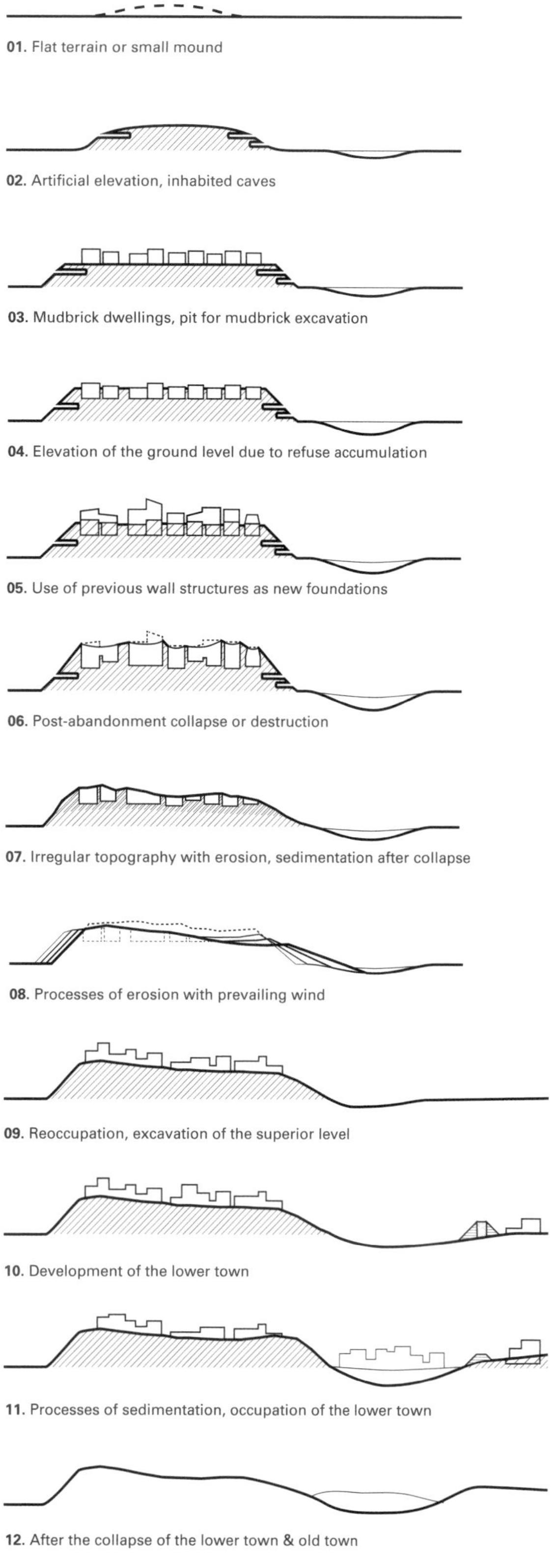

01. Flat terrain or small mound

02. Artificial elevation, inhabited caves

03. Mudbrick dwellings, pit for mudbrick excavation

04. Elevation of the ground level due to refuse accumulation

05. Use of previous wall structures as new foundations

06. Post-abandonment collapse or destruction

07. Irregular topography with erosion, sedimentation after collapse

08. Processes of erosion with prevailing wind

09. Reoccupation, excavation of the superior level

10. Development of the lower town

11. Processes of sedimentation, occupation of the lower town

12. After the collapse of the lower town & old town

Figure 03. Main steps and metabolic relations in the process of tell construction.

and confinement of the processes of erosion of the tell and with the facilitation of its drainage.[08] Inside the settlements, the quotidian removal of street debris to use as fertilizer was not total, leading to the continuous deposition of secondary matrix.[09] In response, buildings were originally, and successively, adapted to the increasing external level. Later, new floors or new constructions had to be built. But these constructions were not, in any case, entirely new: former structures were only partially demolished; previous parts of walls and foundations were reused; and collapsed rubble remained in place as a new, elevated soil. When structural necessities required the construction of a new resistant soil, a new layer of the primary matrix was created, filling the collapsed remains with more mud-brick.[10]

During the phases of occupation these processes of soil elevation were iterative. In the phases of abandonment, natural processes of decay, sedimentation, and erosion altered the cultural layers to create a new topography. The different post-decay heights of the structural features of the tell determined its later topographic conditions; where high parts, gullies, or draining areas were located.[11] The resulting topography was then an index of former cultural activity and also a new functional, determining matrix for new occupations. The original artificiality was hybridized with nature when water- or wind-deposited particles consolidated the soils that resulted from decay and when, during prolonged periods of abandonment, the natural generation of new soils occurred.[12] Finally, erosion shaped the tell: northern prevailing winds caused the parallel retreat of the original slope on the north side of the tell, while, along the south, they caused the decline of its original slope and the sedimentation of parts of the top of the tell in its base.[13]

Post-abandonment occupations of the tells reacted to the resulting functional topography. The distribution of monuments, dwellings, or points of access was adapted to sectional differences and to draining or water-collecting areas. If the high mound was neglected for inhabitation—either because it was assigned a specific functional purpose or because it became insufficient to shelter an increasing population—the extension of the tell took place, whether by widening the former mound, keeping its total height, or developing a system of adjacent lower mounds.[14]

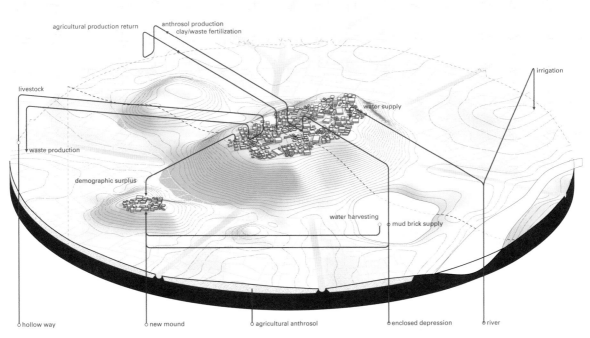

agricultural production return

anthrosol production
clay/waste fertilization

irrigation

livestock

water supply

waste production

demographic surplus

water harvesting

mud brick supply

hollow way

new mound

agricultural anthrosol

enclosed depression

river

Figure 04. Main metabolic relations required for the reciprocal
construction of the tell and its immediate hinterland.

Figure 05. Tell Brak.

Roi Salgueiro Barrio, Aanya Chugh and Maynard León

Yet this elaborated cycle between construction, waste, and reuse did not eliminate the necessity of material extraction. The elevation of the EBA high tells was accompanied by neighboring enclosed depressions; pits from which the clay was extracted and whose volume roughly corresponded to the material deposited in the tell.[15] The remainders of these depressions joined the tells in the generation of a functional landscape infrastructure attractive to later occupations. The low mounds constructed adjacent to the EBA high tells benefited from the moisture retained in the depressions—which facilitated material extraction—or by its possible use for water harvesting.[16] Combining high tells, depressions, and low mounds, the evolution of the EBA tells resulted in a complex functional topography that gave form to metabolic dynamics of the extraction, construction, reuse, degradation, and erosion of clay.

The movement of clay also helps us to understand a second metabolic scale, linked now to the organization of a modular functional landscape around the tell and to its regionalization. Archeologists are analyzing the set of sectional and thick-2D markers of geographical modification that surround the EBA tells as indexes of regional land uses and of different forms and rhythms of human presence.[17] Around the tells, clay appears in the form of dense "field scatters," or pottery shards deposited on the ground. These remains result from a practice of fertilization based on a quotidian flux of waste from the tell to the agricultural fields, designed to maximize agricultural return. This waste contained street debris with fragments of shard, compost, and ash.[18] Its deposit created a human-modified soil—an anthrosol—that delimited a maximum radius of 5 kilometers of agricultural production around the tell.[19] Beyond this ring were grazing areas.

This sequence agricultural field-grazing area is reiterated by a third anthropogeographical modification. From the EBA tells emanates a series of paths, called "hollow ways," which are huge erosional incisions of the ground, extending from 20 meters to more than 100 meters wide and from 1 to 2 meters deep. These ways were caused by another flux, the iterative round trip of flocks from the tells to the grazing areas, which eroded the ground during the 4 or 5 kilometers where the path was restricted by surrounding agricultural land.[20] Consequently, the form of operation of this network is essentially local. Although occasionally the hollow ways may reach

another tell, direct trans-local connections are almost nonexistent.[21] EBA connectivity tends to be at most from tell to tell, pointing to local exchange networks between similar entities and to corresponding barely hierarchical administrative or political organizations—possibly conglomerates of city-states with administrative control and frequent commercial interchange with a range of close secondary tells.[22]

Yet originally, high tells with low mounds, enclosed depressions, field scatters, and hollow ways constituted a modular landscape of potentially self-sufficient units.[23] The 5-kilometer of associated agricultural terrain was at the basis of a regional system where the distance between secondary tells was roughly 10 kilometers and where grazing was limited to the areas between agricultural fields. As a complement, third level, peripheral satellites were occasionally built to minimize times of displacement in agricultural exploitation.[24] This pattern was continuously repeated, including even the nucleus of governance. Despite its formal similarity with Christaller's administrative central place model, archeologists discard any organizational equivalence, in the same manner than they differentiate the densities of the system of hollow ways from the market demands of the gravity mode. Instead, they see the constitution of this proto-urban regional system as a derivative of the internal expanse of agricultural production prior to market interchange. The original EBA modular landscape would conform then to a sort of simplified Von Thünen's model.[25] Metabolic processes would have had originally an almost monadic character in which cyclical phases of material production, agricultural cultivation, and animal farming would have been replicated by the aforementioned material returns for construction and agricultural intensification.

The processes of interchange within the modular landscapes, however, tended to increase because of the limits to evolution and growth of the system itself. The 5-kilometer distance corresponded to the two-hour round trip that limited profitable daily access to agricultural and grazing lands.[26] This radius imposed a maximum surface of agricultural cultivation linked to each tell, with the consequent limitation of agricultural production and of population fed by it. In a first moment, this limit could be surpassed using processes of intensification of agricultural production, mainly substituting the rotational dynamics of fallow

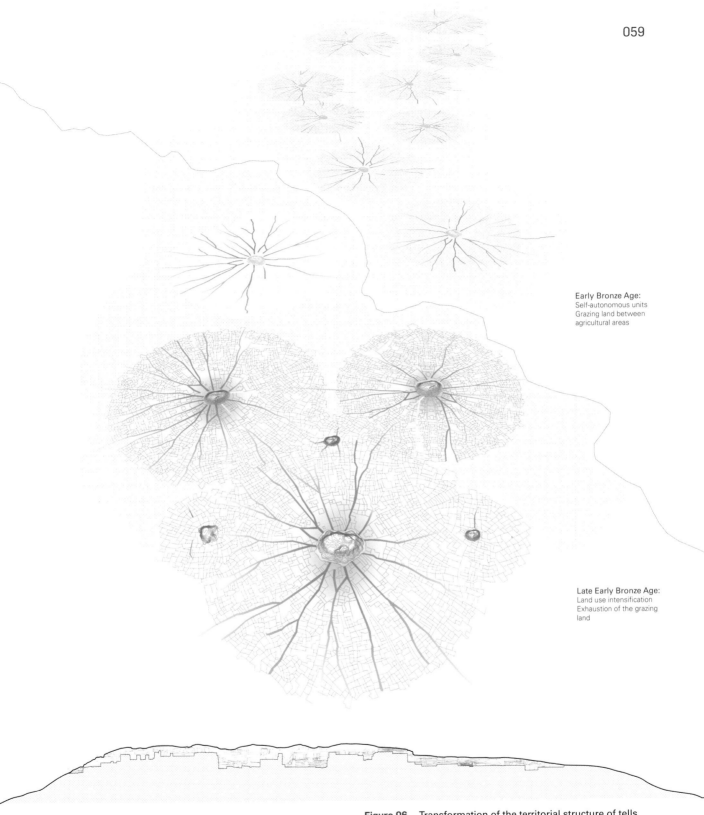

Early Bronze Age:
Self-autonomous units
Grazing land between
agricultural areas

Late Early Bronze Age:
Land use intensification
Exhaustion of the grazing
land

Figure 06. Transformation of the territorial structure of tells
between Early Bronze Age and Late Bronze Age.

Figure 07. Overlapping of archaeological strata.

Roi Salgueiro Barrio, Aanya Chugh and Maynard León

land demanded by the dry-farming system with annual cultivation in terrains improved by manure. But intensification did not displace the limits to growth of the system, at the same time that it led to soil exhaustion.[27] In this sense, the size and population of the major tells would have required first agricultural intensification and then importation of food, leading to the creation of areas of regional interchange. This first phase of land-use intensification may have resulted, however, in an intensification of the secondary tells. In addition, a reduction of grazing land would follow when the number of tells augmented for sheltering exceeded population. In this sense, the processes of land-use intensification revealed a fragile regional pattern in which momentary perturbations, such as droughts or political turmoil, may lead to collapse.[28]

And collapse in fact took place in the whole region during various moments of the Late Bronze Age, when the proto-urban system of high tells was replaced by a dispersed landscape of smaller agricultural mounds. The structural character of anthropogeography became then again apparent. Although neglected for inhabitation, high tells retained their cultural, symbolic value. Orbiting around them, new mounds avoided, when necessary, the anthrosols created and exhausted by the previous settlers.[29] Valued as routes for communication or as spaces for water harvesting, the hollow ways determined the location of new mounds. In this sense, the modular landscape of tells, a landscape of agricultural and "urban" intensification, is far from being an example of a past ecological order. It is rather an example of a landscape of persistence in which the intentional formalization of metabolic processes has created a cultural and functional landscape that is still susceptible of contributing to a contemporary territorial order. Indeed, this is now the case of the Khabur basin. The area was populated uniquely by nomads for more than a millennium, before sedentary settlements were again constructed in the region after World War II as a result of Syrian government programs of agricultural intensification. As a norm, most new settlements reoccupied the tells or placed themselves adjacent to them. Now, when agricultural villages and infrastructures have notably proliferated, they are completely overtaken by the scale of the tells that still provide the most significant, visible territorial structure. The former urban artifacts, turned entirely into geography, turned again into urban artifacts.

Let us return to Gregotti and Rossi. Following Rossi, we take up the necessity of creating urban artifacts that may structure our urban space. From him we also grasp the pressing necessity of understanding which are the urban artifacts of the diluted realms of extended urbanization—artifacts that carry with them, as Rossi intended, the history, culture, and politics of our time. From Gregotti we absorb the need to acknowledge the structural role of geography and the role of humanity as a geological agent. It is in this intersection of urban artifacts and anthropogeography where we see a cultural and territorial project for the formalization of metabolic processes through the practices of architecture and landscape. In regions strongly subjected to metabolic cycles of material extraction and deposition—such as mining regions from Johannesburg to the Ruhr Valley—the legibility of the territorial order of urbanization is already constructed more through the sectional evidence of human geological action than through the built fabric per se. Certainly this was the result of a process informed exclusively by economical vectors, the very vectors that globally determine the metabolic processes that unceasingly construct the territorial fabric of extended urbanization. The cultural territorial project resides in a critique of economic rationales and in a denial of the condition of these metabolic processes as mere externalities to the urban phenomenon, demanding and designing instead their meaningful organization as a part of the urban. The project resides, in short, in the elaboration of their anthropogeographical dimension as a territorial urban artifact.

Acknowledgments

This essay is the result of previous research on Territorial Tropes conducted at GSD's New Geographies Lab. We would like to thank Hashim Sarkis for his continuous support of this work and for his valuable insights. Victor Manuel Rico Espinola has greatly contributed to the primary phase of this research. We would also like to thank Santiago Orbea for his collaboration. Finally we would like to thank Jason Ur for his interest in this work and for allowing us to use his image of Tell Brak.

Notes

01. Vittorio Gregotti, "La forme du territoire" (originally published in Edilizia Moderna [1966] and in L'Architecture d'Aujourd'hui, no. 218 [1980]); Vittorio Gregotti, Il Territorio dell' architettura (Milano: Feltrinelli, 1972).
02. Although this essay describes the specific regional conditions of the Khabur basin and of the system of tells that populated it, most of its considerations are applicable to neighboring areas of the Syrian and Iraqi Jazira. Correspondingly, some of the bibliographic references relate

to those areas. The expression "landscape of tells" comes from Tony J. Wilkinson, <u>Archaeological Landscapes of the Near East</u> (Tucson: University of Arizona Press, 2003),100–127. For the emergence of this urban system, see Joan and Davis Oates, "An Open Gate: Cities of the Fourth Millennium BC (Tell Brak 1997)," <u>Cambridge Archaeological Journal</u> 7 (Oct 1997): 287–297; Joan Oates et al.,"Early Mesopotamian Urbanism: A New View from the North," <u>Antiquity</u> 81 (2007): 585–600; and Mette Marie Hald, <u>A Thousand Years of Farming: Late Chalcolithic Agricultural Practices at Tell Brak in Northern Mesopotamia</u> (Oxford: Archaeopress, 2008), 1–3.

03. Wilkinson, <u>Archaeological Landscapes of the Near East</u>, 108–109; Tony J. Wilkinson and D.J. Tucker, <u>Settlement Development in the North Jazira, Iraq: A Study of the Archaeological Landscape</u> (Warminster, Wiltshire: British School of Archaeology in Iraq and Baghdad, Department of Antiquities and Heritage, 1995), 81.

04. Jason A. Ur, <u>Urbanism and Cultural Landscapes in Northeastern Syria: The Tell Hamoukar Survey, 1999–2001</u> (Chicago: Oriental Institute of the University of Chicago, 2010), 10, fig. 2.7; and Wilkinson, <u>Archaeological Landscapes of the Near East</u>, 100.

05. Wilkinson, <u>Archaeological Landscapes of the Near East</u>, 100; and Ur, <u>Urbanism and Cultural Landscapes in Northeastern Syria</u>, 6,11.

06. T.J. Wilkinson, Jason Ur, and Jesse Casan, "From Nucleation to Dispersal: Trends in Settlement Pattern in the Northern Fertile Crescent," in <u>Side-by-Side: Comparative Regional Studies in the Mediterranean World</u>, ed. Susan Alcock and John Cherry (Oxford: Oxford Books, 2004), 202–203.

07. The following principles of tell construction are generally common to the tells of the Middle East, as described in Arlene Miller Rosen, <u>Cities of Clay</u> (Chicago: University of Chicago Press, 1986).

08. Ibid., 14.

09. According to Karl W. Butzer, quoted in Rosen, <u>Cities of Clay</u>, 10. In the same sense, for the southern Mesopotamian tells, see Spiro Kostof, <u>Historia de La Arquitectura</u> I (Madrid: Alianza, 1988), 97.

10. Seton Lloyd, <u>Mounds of the Near East</u> (Edinburgh: Edinburgh University Press, 1963), 26–28; and Kostof, <u>Historia de la arquitectura</u>, 97–99,102–104.

11. Rosen, <u>Cities of Clay</u>, 14–15.

12. As studied by Karl W. Mutzer and Reuben Bullard, both quoted in Rosen, <u>Cities of Clay</u>, 13.

13. Rosen, <u>Cities of Clay</u>, 25–35, fig. 9.

14. See Lloyd, <u>Mounds of the Near East</u>, 18–21, and for an example of the contiguous distribution of Bronze Age lower towns, see Ur, <u>Urbanism and Cultural Landscapes in Northeastern Syria</u>, 104–107.

15. Wilkinson, <u>Archaeological Landscapes of the Near East</u>, 110.

16. Wilkinson, Ur, and Casan, "From Nucleation to Dispersal," 202.

17. Within this frame, Tony J. Wilkinson has elaborated in <u>Archaeological Landscapes of the Near East</u> (48) a catalogue of archeological references to gradients of settlement that, together with the tells, incorporate low mounds, nonmounded sites, soil coloration, cut features, and nomad settlements that, with infrastructural and agricultural facilities, trace the different organizations of the regional system of the Jazira.

18. Ibid., 117.

19. Ibid., and Bjoern H. Menze and Jason A. Ur, "Mapping Patterns of Long-term Settlement in Northern Mesopotamia at a Large Scale," <u>Proceedings of the National Academy of Sciences</u> 109, no. 14 (2012): 778

20. Wilkinson, <u>Archaeological Landscapes of the Near East</u>,111; Jason A. Ur, "Emergent Landscapes of Movement in Early Bronze Age Northern Mesopotamia," in <u>Landscapes of Movement</u>, ed. James Snead (Philadelphia: University of Pennsylvania Press), 192.

21. Menze and Jason Ur, "Mapping Patterns," 785; Jason A. Ur, "Emergent Landscapes," 192.

22. Ur, "Emergent Landscapes of Movement," 197-201; Wilkinson and Tucker, <u>Settlement Development in the North Jazira</u>, 81.

23. Wilkinson, <u>Archaeological Landscapes of the Near East</u>, 109.

24. Wilkinson and Tucker, <u>Settlement Development in the North Jazira</u>, 85.

25. Ibid., 27, 85.

26. Ibid.

27. Ibid.

28. Ibid., 88.

29. Jason A. Ur, "Spatial Scale and Urban Collapse at Tell Brak and Tell Hamoukar at the End of the Third Millennium BC," in <u>Looking North: The Socio-Economic Dynamics of the Northern Mesopotamian and Anatolian Regions during the Late Third and Early Second Millennium BC</u>, ed. Nicola Laneri, Peter Pfälzner, and Stefano Valentini (Wiesbaden: Studien zur Urbanisierung Nordmesopotamiens, 2012), 25–35.

Image Credits

All images courtesy of the authors.

Figure 05: drawn by Jason Ur.

Roi Salgueiro Barrio, Aanya Chugh and Maynard León

Sabine Barles

Urban Metabolism

Persistent Questions and Current Developments

Overview of seminal studies of urban metabolism, positioning contemporary analytical methodologies to modeling and quantifying metabolic systems in historical perspective.

Sabine Barles is Professor of Urban Planning at Université Paris 1 Panthéon-Sorbonne. Trained as a civil engineer, she holds a masters in history of technology and a PhD in urban planning. The focus of her research concerns the urban environment, urban technology, and the interactions between societies (especially cities) and nature in both contemporary and historical (from the eighteenth century onward) terms. In particular, her research addresses the questions of supply, the management of excreta (solid and liquid waste), urban metabolism, environmental imprints, and territorial ecology.

Societies and the biosphere can be considered two interdependent systems in co-evolution, resulting in a socio-ecological system. The most tangible expression of their interactions is the energy and materials they exchange. Societies, and cities in particular, are significant consumers of materials and energy, either directly within their limits or indirectly through the goods and services they import. Urban metabolism—the various processes involving energy and material flows in urban functioning—has both upstream and downstream consequences in terms of the removal of resources and the discharge of waste materials (to the atmosphere, water, and soils), with multiple impacts on ecosystems and the biosphere.

The present socio-ecological regime is characterized by the linearization of material flows—societies taking resources from the biosphere and returning waste (i.e., transformed materials often incompatible with the receiving area)—and the establishment of biogeochemical cycles. Although the natural functioning of the biosphere features substance cycles (carbon, nitrogen, etc.), anthropogenic activity not only intensifies their flows but also linearizes them, since the materials do not return to their place of origin and therefore accumulate in other parts the biosphere. If the materials somehow return to their origin, they do so in a different chemical form. Many of the environmental problems encountered today can be attributed to these abundant and linear flows: resource depletion, climate change, eutrophication, proliferation of solid waste, dispersion of toxic material, and loss of biodiversity, just to name a few. These complex situations call for thoughtful solutions, such as dematerialization, decarbonization, and dewatering as an alternative to the "end-of-pipe" approaches long used to address environmental problems.

Some researchers use the term Anthropocene for the current geological epoch, marked by the emergence of anthropogenic drivers alongside natural drivers that previously conditioned the planet. Better understanding society's metabolism is essential to confronting these problems.[01] Considering the leading role of cities in the industrial socio-ecological regime, a focus on urban areas seems particularly important, as their metabolism is directly or indirectly responsible for the Anthropocenization of the world. Managing urban metabolism, an activity that could seem relatively new on the urban agenda, has in fact long been a major issue for scientists and urban stakeholders.

My aim here is to give an overview of the origins and developments of urban metabolism studies since the nineteenth century and an indication of their varying motivations, and to present current trends of research in this field: urban material balances, substance flow analyses, energy balances, and urban environmental imprints.

Urban, Industrial, Territorial, and Social Ecologies
Supply, Urban Excreta, and Urban Chemistry

Concerns about urban metabolism are not new. European scientific, intellectual, and political communities have addressed the question of supplying cities with energy and materials since the beginning of the nineteenth century. This issue provoked many thoughts and actions on the scope of urban supply (often associated with the notion of hinterland) and the amelioration of soil. The development of transport systems and the turn to fossil energy were two particularly significant responses. Urban metabolism (a term not used at the time) primarily involved the work of chemists concerned with food production and agricultural fertilizers. Indeed, population growth in conjunction with the limitations of rural organic fertilizer sources led to fears of soil depletion and food shortages. With growing populations, cities began to be considered as both centers of consumption and, through their abundant output of excreta, new sources of fertilizers: human and animal urine and excrement, organic mud produced on streets, household and preindustrial refuse, butcher shop and slaughter (later, slaughterhouse) by-products, etc. Quantification of potential fertilizers and development of effective collection and conversion techniques became major issues, as important as hygiene, in the management of urban excreta.

This resulted in the birth of a true urban chemistry— which was not biochemistry before Pasteur's work—that sought to understand the cycle of organic matter and nutrients (nitrogen, then phosphorus and potash). Jean-Baptiste Dumas, Jean-Baptiste Boussingault, and Justus von Liebig were the most famous European urban chemists. These chemists, and the manufacturers and engineers who followed, fought against the linear flow of materials, favoring exchanges between the city and agriculture. Similarly, many industrial activities in the nineteenth century depended on urban by-products. The fertilizer revolution and the mobilization of new raw materials that made urban excreta useless led to the death of urban chemistry and sparked interest in urban metabolism.[02]

The Urbs Ecosystem: Heterotrophic and Parasitic
Several decades elapsed before renewed interest in urban metabolism was expressed within the context of two emerging worries: the capacity of the planet to feed and maintain a growing population, and the destructive power of humans given the Earth's finite characteristics. This was an idea particularly brought forward at the Intergovernmental Conference of Experts on the Scientific Basis for the Rational Use and Conservation of the Resources of the Biosphere, sometimes called the Biosphere Conference, held in Paris in 1968.[03] In addition to these planetary worries, severe criticism of the industrial town was frequently expressed. To cite one example, in The City in History, Lewis Mumford denounced the "myth of megalopolis" and forecast, like many contemporaries, the decline of industrial towns.[04]

The resulting urban ecology, developed from the 1960s onward, fell within the scope of scientific ecology and, in particular, of ecosystem theory as brought forward by Eugene Odum. In 1965, the engineer Abel Wolman introduced the notion of urban metabolism. He defined metabolic needs ("all the materials and commodities needed to sustain the city's inhabitants at home, at work and at play"), the metabolic

cycle, and urban metabolic problems.[05] Shortly after, Odum described the city as a heterotrophic system[06] and later as a parasitic ecosystem.[07] The Belgian ecologist Paul Duvigneaud, who played an important role in the implementation of international environmental research programs, closely followed him and gave the urbs ecosystem significant coverage in his popular Synthèse écologique. Duvigneaud wrote: "Scientific knowledge ... is required to ensure proper urban planning of the areas where most people live."[08] These first texts on urban ecology of naturalistic origin were well received internationally and their ideas promoted through the UNESCO Man and Biosphere program, launched in 1971. In this framework, the cities of Rome, Barcelona, and Hong Kong have been the subject of detailed analyses.[09]

Nevertheless, this research did not lead to the anticipated opportunities and received fierce criticism during the 1980s. Indeed, some urban ecologists wanted to make ecology a division of science of its own, with social sciences constituting only a part, an idea tolerated with difficulty by social scientists. Furthermore, these urban ecologists stuck to an energy determinism and anti-urban views—characterizing the city as a parasite—that prevented them from considering approaches to controling the environmental impact of cities. Finally, the methods developed to analyze urban metabolism remained quite rough.

Industrial Ecology, Territorial Ecology, and Social Ecology
Industrial ecology appeared at the same time as urban ecology, but in a different scientific sphere: chemistry, chemical engineering, and physics. Its first interest was the industrial sector (i.e., production), and it focused on industrial metabolism and industrial symbiosis, or how to use waste from one industry as raw material for another, to minimize resource consumption and waste and pollutant emissions. In contrast to urban ecology, industrial ecology actively pursued its disciplinary development, with the founding of the Journal of Industrial Ecology in 1997 and the International Society for Industrial Ecology in 2000 contributing to the structuring of the field.[10]

Although cities were initially largely absent in industrial ecology because the approaches were generally poorly spatialized, urban issues eventually gained in importance. In 2007 and 2012, issues of the Journal of Industrial Ecology were devoted to

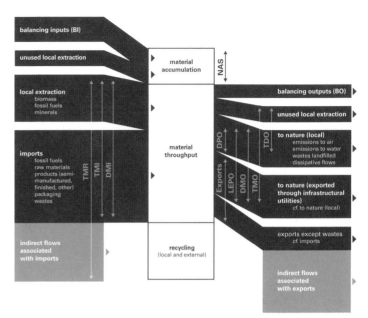

the city,[11] and in 2008 the ConAccount conference held in Prague specifically addressed urban metabolism.[12] Simultaneously, some scholars emphasized the need for a broader view in metabolic studies, involving not only industrial production but industrial society as a whole. Some, such as members of the Institute of Social Ecology in Vienna (Austria), referred to the notion of society's or social metabolism to express this new challenge.

This trend gave rise to a new expression: territorial ecology. This field of research is based on the accomplishments of both industrial ecology and urban ecology as defined above; it brings together scholars from industrial ecology, urban planning, urban engineering, urban biogeochemistry, and ecological economics. Territorial ecology emphasizes the importance of the spatial dimension in socio-ecological interactions; it studies territorial metabolism considered as the result of two sets of intertwined processes: natural (biogeochemical, physical) and anthropogenic (social, technological, political, cultural). It stresses the fact that both the natural functioning and the social dimension of the territory under study have to be taken into account to understand (and transform) the territorial metabolism.

Figure 01.   Schematic of local material flow analysis. Adapted from the National Balance Method of the Statistical Office of the European Community (EUROSTAT). Total Material Requirement (TMR); Total Material Input (TMI); Direct Material Input (DMI); Net Addition to Stock (NAS); Direct Processed Output (DPO); Local and Exported Processed Output (LEPO); Total Domestic Output (TDO); Direct Material Output (DMO); Total Material Output (TMO).

Learning from Urban Metabolism

In this context, research projects were recently launched that fell, implicitly or explicitly, within the fields of urban ecology, industrial ecology (when focused on cities or parts of cities), territorial ecology or social ecology, or biogeochemistry applied to urbanized systems.

Material Flow Analyses and Urban Materials Balances

In the last few years, material flow analysis (MFA) has become more refined and precise, although studies of this type remain rare at the urban level. Different methods exist today to characterize urban metabolism, some of them derived from the Eurostat method for national material flow accounting [**Figure 01**].[13]

These material balances aim at characterizing the material needs of cities and their impact on the biosphere on a local and global scale. They allow weighting the urban operation, in the full sense of the term. In the case of Île-de-France region (which comprises the Paris metropolitan area and includes

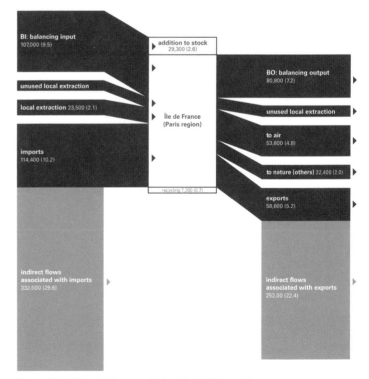

Figure 02.   Material flow analysis of Paris Metropolitan Region (Île-de-France), 2003. kt (t/inhab.)

Sabine Barles

11.5 million inhabitants), **Figure 02** shows the huge material flows involved in urban functioning. Looking at the direct flows shows that emissions to nature (air, water, soil) represent more than half of the total material inputs and are consequently more significant than conventional exports (i.e., those linked to monetary flows). These numbers reveal the stakes involved in dematerialization. Indirect flows represent another important aspect of urban metabolism; their remote impact is much more important than their local one because cities, especially in developed countries, import products more than raw materials, so the extraction and transformation processes have taken place outside of the city boundaries.

Material balances can also be broken down into product categories. The results, presented in **Figure 03** for the Paris metropolitan area, show these balances to reflect the metropolitan operation: much is eaten in Paris because of the large number of jobs and tourists; many construction materials are consumed in the outer suburbs due to urban sprawl (especially for linear infrastructure construction related to new housing). The link between land use and urban metabolism is seen here. Thus material balances can be used to define targets for dematerialization and, more generally, for improvements to the ecologic performance of cities.

Another telling activity would be to compare urban metabolic profiles and analyze the differences. Preliminary comparisons suggest that these differences can be important and could be explained

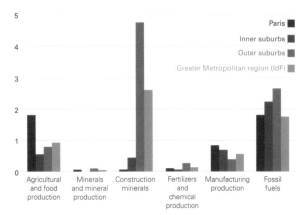

Figure 03. Direct material consumption (DMC) for Paris, its inner suburbs, outer suburbs, and Greater Metropolitan Region (Île-de-France), 2003. Rail transportation excluded. t/inhab.

by the level of development (in fast urbanizing countries, the material stock increases much more than in long-industrialized countries), the way cities expand (urban sprawl meaning a greater material consumption), the level of consumption and the main economic activities characterizing the city (production sector versus service sector).[14]

Substance Flows

Substance flow analysis (SFA) is used to address more specific questions (like water, air, or soil contamination), or to understand the role of cities in global biogeochemistry. In view of the broad diversity of natural and anthropogenic processes being considered, there is no standardized SFA method such as the one used for material flows.

SFA concerns biogenic elements such as carbon, nitrogen, and phosphorus. The carbon cycle is altered by fossil fuel consumption, food (especially meat) production, and forestry; the city is a direct and indirect contributor to this alteration with its consequences for resource exhaustion and climate change. The same can be said about nitrogen and the city: as shown in **Figure 04**, the amounts of nitrogen directly involved in a metropolitan area (in this case Paris) are considerable and have consequences for air, water, and soil. They are even greater if indirect flows are taken into account, especially in the food system (to produce the 7.5 kgN contained in the food consumed by a Parisian during one year, 25 gN have been required by the food production system). This raises the question of urban diets and nitrogen recovery.[15] Phosphorus is also a matter of concern because it is a limited fossil resource and is responsible for eutrophication. In the future, its recovery will be crucial to food production, so it is crucial to better analyze urban phosphorus consumption and discharge.[16]

Because of their high toxicity, heavy metals are the subject of numerous studies; see, for instance, the Swedish research program Metals in the Urban and Forest Environment—Ecocycles and Critical Loads, directed by Bo Bergbäck and Kjell Johansson at the end of the 1990s, and the related special issue of Water, Air, and Soil Pollution.[17] The management problem associated with heavy metals is different from that related to food. The consumption of metal is either directly linked to its use in industry and other human activities (for example, zinc on roofs or lead in accumulators) or a side effect of the consumption of other materials in which it may be present as an impurity (for example, in coal). Furthermore, the life of these substances, in society as in ecosystems, can be much longer. Consequently, the evaluation of both stocks and flows is necessary and, beyond the substance's general circulation, dissipative losses (wear) and various fugitive emissions must be identified and quantified. This is emphasized by the fact that these substances are often toxic at very low doses; minor flows can thus have significant consequences on the environment and public health.[18]

Energy Balances

Although the notion of metabolism refers to both the energy and the material required for the operation of a given system, studies of urban metabolism have long favored the material balance rather than the energy balance. One reason for this is that the questions raised by interactions between human societies and nature stem more from material than energy issues—though they do involve large amounts of energy as well. For example, climate change is due, at least partially, to energy consumption, but it can be analyzed as a particular case of the prompting of biogeochemical cycles. It is a case of excess material—greenhouse gases—in the atmosphere, and the exploitation of certain material resources, particularly hydrocarbons, are at the origin of the problem, even if these resources are used for their energetic qualities. Another reason is that urban energy issues are often addressed by engineers specialized in this field and belonging to scientific communities different from the one dealing with urban metabolism.

Nevertheless, it is also possible to qualify urban metabolism in terms of energy instead of material balance. Examples of such approaches are found in research conducted at the Institute of Social Ecology in Vienna, especially by Fridolin Krausmann[19] and Helmut Haberl.[20] These researchers compare the metabolism of societies to their total energy consumption, both technical and nontechnical, and on this basis develop a set of indicators that characterize the impact of human societies on the biosphere (especially human appropriation of net primary productivity, or HANPP).[21]

Together with material balances, energy balances, when they involve a long-term approach, contribute to address the questions of socio-ecological trajectory, socio-ecological regime, and socio-ecological transition, whether observed in the past or desired for the

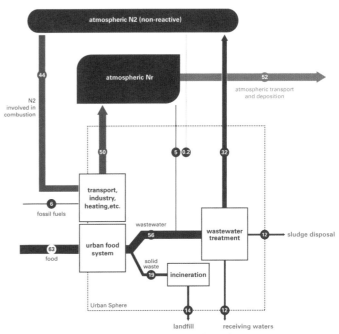

Figure 04. Nitrogen Budget, Paris Metropolitan Area. GgN/year.

future.[22] We know that nineteenth-century cities experienced a major energy transition from firewood to coal and fossil fuels that resulted in a tremendous change in cities' shape and life and in city-nature relationships: a socio-ecological transition. Today many scholars, urban planners, architects, and landscape designers call for another transition to a more circular metabolism, based on renewable energy and resources. Studies of material and energy balances can help us to understand to what extent the transition is actually occurring.

The Environmental Imprints of Cities

Whereas the notion of socio-ecological trajectory is an invitation to consider time in urban metabolism studies, the notion of imprint is a way to address the question of space and of the remote impact of cities. The idea of footprint has been widely disseminated thanks to William Rees and Mathis Wackernagel's concept of an ecological footprint.[23] The ecological footprint represents the amount of biologically productive land surface needed to sustainably maintain a human society given its living standard and lifestyle, compared to the carrying capacity of the area under study and of the biosphere. A number of criticisms have been aimed at the concept.[24]

The concept of environmental imprints is, however, particularly important for characterizing the impacts of metabolism (urban in the context of this essay) on the biosphere. The term imprint (or footprint) is used to designate both the spatial dimension of the impacts

Sabine Barles

		Beginning 19th	End 19th	Beginning 21st
Population	thousands	700	3,340	Spatial imprint
Spatial Imprint	ha/inhab	0.59	0.56	0.13
		4,130	4,130	15,364	11,900
Quantitative Water Imprint	m³/inhab	2,508	2,307	495
	Mm3	1,755	7,706	5,705
Nitrogen Imprint	kgN/inhab	25	22	tN
		17,360	17,360	73,480	199,504
Local Water Consumption	m³/inhab	5	150	4
	Mm³	366	366	1,684

Table 01. Imprints of meat and milk consumption, Paris, nineteenth to twenty-first centuries.

(in three dimensions, the third being its depth, or the intensity of its environmental impact) and their varying severity. Each city has a set of imprints whose size, shape, localization, and depth changes over time, but accurately reflects the city's metabolism, the lifestyle of its citizens and its urban (national and international) socio-economic, political, and technical systems.[25]

Examples include studies on the water footprint: cities import goods whose development required the consumption of a certain quantity of water elsewhere and also led to an impairment of the resource in the drainage basin concerned.[26] Similarly, studies on the food imprint (or "food-print") have shown that it has decreased in area because the agricultural yield has increased since World War II in developed countries [**Table 01**].[27] Its depth, however, has increased as a result of the growing use of synthetic fertilizers and phytosanitary products. In addition, the food-print is increasingly discontinuous and distant from the cities supplied. Furthermore, the concept of environmental imprints allows spatial limits to be placed where human and urban activities develop, while emphasizing the critical issue of land use and its competing allocations.[28]

Conclusion: Consolidating the Field

Although it is a relatively new field of research, urban metabolism in its wide sense, as suggested by the French territorial ecology, has a bisecular past and its epistemology must still be refined.[29] Future progress, both in the scope of research and in action taken, can be expected if the city begins to be considered not as an unsustainable parasite but as a source of physical, energy, social, and intellectual resources.

It would be useful to consolidate the theoretical basis of urban metabolism studies, in particular by going beyond the problems that arise from using analogies and metaphors, which all too often characterize it. Methods should be improved to better understand urban metabolism. Special attention should be paid to the identification of the latent and remote effects of cities in time and space. It is also important to link urban structures, lifestyles, and urban metabolism.[30] Another issue that remains to be addressed is the creation of a stronger link between energy and material approaches, one not being reducible to the other.

Taking things a step further, urban metabolism studies must also go beyond energy and material accounting. The analyses must consider the spatial, ecological, and social contexts as well as the agriculture– industry– city triptych. They should not limit themselves to the quantification of material and energy flows but favor a more interdisciplinary approach that does not reduce urban management to an engineering issue. To date, this field of interdisciplinary research is fragmentary.

Notes

01. Paul J. Crutzen, "Geology of Mankind," Nature 415 (2002): 23.
02. Sabine Barles, "A Metabolic Approach to the City: Nineteenth and Twentieth Century Paris," in Resources of the City: Contributions to an Environmental History of Modern Europe, ed. Bill Luckin, Geneviève Massard-Guilbaud, and Dieter Schott (Aldershot: Ashgate, 2005), 28–47.
03. Use and Conservation of the Resources of the Biosphere (Paris: UNESCO, 1969).
04. Lewis Mumford, The City in History (New York: Harcourt, Brace, 1961).
05. Abel Wolman, "The Metabolism of Cities," Scientific American 213, no. 3 (1965): 179–190.
06. Eugene Odum, Ecology: The Link between the Natural and the Social Sciences, 2nd ed. (New York: Holt, Reinhart & Winston, 1975).
07. Eugene Odum, Ecology and Our Endangered Life-Support Systems (Sunderland: Sinauer Associated, 1989).
08. Paul Duvigneaud, La synthèse écologique: populations, communautés, écosystèmes, biosphère, noosphère (Paris: Doin, 1974), 245. Author's translation.
09. Stephen Boyden et al., The Ecology of a City and Its People: The Case of Hong Kong (Canberra: Australian National University Press, 1981).
10. Suren Erkman, Vers une écologie industrielle, 2d ed. (Paris: Ed. Charles Léopold Mayer & la Librairie FPH, 2004).
11. "Industrial Ecology and the Global Impact of Cities," special issue, Journal of Industrial Ecology 11, no. 2 (2007); and "Sustainable Urban System," special issue, Journal of Industrial Ecology 16, no. 6 (2012).
12. Miroslav Havranek, ed., "Urban Metabolism: Measuring the Ecological City" (Proceedings of the ConAccount Conference, Charles University Environment Centre, Prague, 11–12 Sept 2008).

13. EUROSTAT, Economy Wide Material Flow Accounts: Compilation Guidelines for Reporting to the 2009 Eurostat Questionnaire, 2009; Yan Zhang, "Urban Metabolism: A Review of Research Methodologies," Environmental Pollution 178 (2013): 473–473.

14. See, for instance, Mark Swilling, Blake Robinson, Simon Marvin, and Mike Hodson, eds., City-Level Decoupling: Urban Resource Flows and the Governance of Infrastructure Transitions. A Report of the Working Group on Cities of the International Resource Panel (Nairobi: UNEP, 2013). See also, for other case studies: Mark Hammer et al., "Die ökologische Nachhaltigkeit regionaler Metabolismen: Materialflussanalysen der Regionen Hamburg, Wien und Leipzig [Ecological sustainability or regional metabolisms: material flow analyses of the regions of Hamburg, Vienna, and Leipzig]," Natur und Kultur 7, no. 2 (2006): 62–78; Samuel Niza, Leonardo Rosado, and Paulo Ferrao, "Methodological Advances in Urban Material Flow Acounting Based on the Lisbon Case Study," Journal of Industrial Ecology 13, no. 3 (2009): 384–405.

15. See, for instance, Jennifer Forkes, "Nitrogen Balance for the Urban Food Metabolism of Toronto, Canada," Resources, Conservation, and Recycling 52 (2007): 74–94.

16. Tina Schmid Neset, et al., "The Flow of Phosphorus in Food Production and Consumption—Linköping, Sweden, 1870–2000," The Science of the Total Environment 396 (2008): 111–120; Yuliya Kalmykova et al., "Pathways and Management of Phosphorus in Urban Areas," Journal of Industrial Ecology 16, no. 6 (2012): 928–939; Jens Færge et al., "Urban Nutrient Balance for Bangkok," Ecological Modelling 139, no. 1 (2001): 63–74.

17. Water, Air and Soil Pollution: Focus 1, no. 3–4 (2001).

18. Laurence Lestel, Michel Meybeck, and Daniel Thévenot, "Metal Contamination Budget at the River Basin Scale: An Original Flux-Flow Analysis (F2A) for the Seine River," Hydrology and Earth System Sciences 11 (2007): 1771–1781; J. Sviden and A. Jonsson, "Urban Metabolism of Mercury Turnover, Emissions, and Stock in Stockholm 1795–1995," Water, Air, and Soil Pollution: Focus 1, no. 3–4 (2001): 179–196.

19. Fridolin Krausmann, "A City and Its Hinterland: The Social Metabolism of Vienna 1800–2000," in Third ESEH Conference: History and Sustainability, Florence, 17–19 February 2005.

20. Helmut Haberl, "The Global Socioeconomic Energetic Metabolism as a Sustainability Problem," Energy 31 (2006): 87–99.

21. Helmut Haberl et al., "Quantifying and mapping the human appropriation of net primary production in earth's terrestrial ecosystems," Proceedings of the National Academy of Sciences of the United States of America 104 (2006): 12942-12947.

22. Marina Fischer-Kowalski and Helmut Haberl, eds., Socioecological Transitions and Global Change: Trajectories of Social Metabolism and Land Use (Cheltenham, UK: Edward Elgar, 2007); Sabine Barles, "Socio-ecological Trajectories: The Urban Dimension. Paris, Eighteenth–Twentieth Centuries" (Proceedings of the European Society for Ecological Economics Conference, Lille, France, Jun 2013).

23. William Rees and Matthis Wackernagel, Our Ecological Footprint: Reducing Human Impact on the Earth (Gabriola Island, Canada: New Society, 1996); Rees and Wackernagel, "Urban Ecological Footprints: Why Cities Cannot Be Sustainable—and Why They Are Key to Sustainability," Environmental Impact Assessment Review 16 (1996): 223–248.

24. Nathan Fiala, "Measuring Sustainability: Why the Ecological Footprint Is Bad Economics and Bad Environmental Science," Ecological Economics 67, no. 4 (2008): 519–525.

25. Gilles Billen, Josette Garnier, and Sabine Barles, eds., "History of the Urban Environmental Imprint," special issue, Regional Environmental Change 12, no. 2 (2012).

26. Arjen Y. Hoekstra, and Mesfin M. Mekonnen, "The Water Footprint of Humanity," Proceedings of the National Academy of Sciences 109, no. 9 (2012): 3232–3237; Petros Chatzimpiros and Sabine Barles, "Nitrogen, Land, and Water Inputs in Changing Cattle Farming Systems : An Historical Comparison for France, Nineteenth–Twenty-first Centuries," The Science of the Total Environment 408, no. 20 (2010): 4644–4653.

27. Gilles Billen et al., "The Food-print of Paris: Long-Term Reconstruction of the Nitrogen Flows Imported into the City from Its Rural Hinterland," Regional Environmental Change 9, no. 1 (2009): 13–24.

28. Fridolin Krausmann, "Land Use and Industrial Modernisation: An Empirical Analysis of Human Influence on the Functioning of Ecosystems in Austria, 1830–1995," Land Use Policy 18, no. 1 (2001): 17–26.

29. Marina Fischer-Kowalski, "Society's Metabolism: The Intellectual History of Material Flow Analysis, Part I, 1860–1970," Journal of Industrial Ecology 2, no. 1 (1999): 61–78; Marina Fischer-Kowalski and Walter Hüttler, "Society's Metabolism: The Intellectual History of Material Flow Analysis, Part II, 1970–1988," Journal of Industrial Ecology 2, no. 4 (1999): 107–135.

30. Chris Kennedy, Stephanie Pincetl, and Paul Bunje, "The Study of Urban Metabolism and Its Applications to Urban Planning and Design," Environmental Pollution 159, no. 8–9 (2011): 1965–1973.

Image Credits

Figure 01: Adapted from Sabine Barles, "Urban Metabolism of Paris and Its Region," Journal of Industrial Ecology 13, no. 6 (2009): 898–913; corrected according to EUROSTAT, "Economy Wide Material Flow Accounts: Compilation Guidelines for Reporting to the 2009 Eurostat Questionnaire."

Figure 02: Adapted from Sabine Barles, "Urban Metabolism of Paris and Its Region," Journal of Industrial Ecology 13, no. 6 (2009): 898–913; corrected according to EUROSTAT, "Economy Wide Material Flow Accounts: Compilation Guidelines for Reporting to the 2009 Eurostat Questionnaire."

Figure 03: Adapted from Sabine Barles, "Urban Metabolism of Paris and Its Region," Journal of Industrial Ecology 13, no. 6 (2009): 898–913.

Figure 04: Adapted from Anastasia Svirejeva-Hopkins and Stefan Reis et al., "Nitrogen Flows and Fate in Urban Landscapes," in The European Nitrogen Assessment: Sources, Effects, and Policy Perspectives, edited by Mark A. Sutton et al. (Cambridge: Cambridge University Press, 2011), 259.

Table 01: Adapted from: Petros Chatzimpiros, Les empreintes environnementales de l'approvisionnement alimentaire: Paris ses viandes et lait, XIXe–XXIe siècles" (PhD thesis, Université Paris-Est, 2011).

Sabine Barles

Matthew Gandy
in Conversation with
Daniel Ibañez and
Nikos Katsikis

On Circulations and Metabolisms

Challenges and Prospects

*Questioning dominant
paradigms in design and
urban studies around
the metabolism of urban
environments, in light of
developments in the field
of urban political ecology.*

Matthew Gandy is Professor of Geography at
University College London (UCL) and was Director
of the UCL Urban Laboratory from 2005 to 2011.
His books include Concrete and Clay: Reworking
Nature in New York City (MIT Press, 2002), The
Acoustic City (JOVIS, 2014, co-editor), and The
Fabric of Space: Water, Modernity, and the Urban
Imagination (MIT Press, 2014), along with essays
in Architectural Design, International Journal
of Urban and Regional Research, New Left
Review, Society and Space, and many other journals.

New Geographies: Both in the "Projective Views on Urban Metabolism" conference (see **pp. 188–189**) and in this publication, the concept of urban metabolism has been central because of its promising capacity to grasp complex social, technical, and ecological dynamics of urbanization processes and thus allow design to position itself in relation to a broader and redefined context. It remains, however, a very loosely defined concept. We would like to discuss its nature and potential for grasping the complexities of urbanization processes.

Mathew Gandy: Urban metabolism is not a unified field but rather a range of different approaches. It could be argued that in some respects the discussion about urban metabolism is really about how scientific metaphors are used for the understanding of human societies. There is a tension here between conceptions of cities as produced through contested historical processes, which is closer to neo-Marxian understandings of metabolism, and the more universalist or positivist aura that often surrounds the use of scientific metaphors when transferred to the urban arena. It is the transformative dimension to metabolism that links these different theoretical domains. The idea of urban metabolism relates not only to the production of space but also to its ongoing functional dynamics. One of the interesting questions is how we conceptualize changing relations between the body and the city. We can extend the idea of urban metabolism to consider the city as a complex hybrid entity comprising different kinds of socio-technological entanglements. The connections between urban metabolism and the idea of cyborg urbanization moves us beyond a focus on augmented human bodies toward an interest in different kinds of connectivities and vulnerabilities.

NG: One of the challenges both in the organization of the conference and in the structure of this volume has been the creative and critical merging of analytical frameworks and theoretical approaches to urban metabolism with more projective design attempts to reshape the contemporary urban environment. We would like to discuss how you perceive this tension and how it could more productively inform design interventions.

MG: I think that during the conference, there was a movement from theory to practice marked by a shift from analytical debates toward the showcasing of different design approaches. What I noticed across a number of the presentations is that the modeling of complexity or the aesthetic refinement of the presentations began to predominate over analytical themes, so that in some cases the political implications of different projects became effectively occluded. The conference was really useful in foregrounding these tensions by putting together a range of very different perspectives. And in a school like the GSD, one might say at a superficial level that this tension exists between architecture and planning, but I think it is more accurate to identify these tensions between theory and practice within disciplines rather than at the scale of disciplinary fields themselves. These types of tensions are inherent to any critical intervention in urban space, and in this respect the conference was quite provocative by enabling some of these themes to be openly debated.

NG: We would like to return to this emphasis and the associated challenges of modeling and the aesthetics of representing complex metabolic processes. We feel that these have been prominent directions in which design has looked to redefine its agency by visualizing metabolic flows and processes that are normally either too complex or largely concealed. How do you react to this recent preoccupation of design with mapping and visualizing metabolic processes through innovative indexing, diagramming, and cartographic representations?

MG: One of the interesting developments in recent years has been the increasing sophistication of modeling and various forms of cartographic representation. Within the discipline of geography, for example, the fields of GIS and remote sensing have grown enormously by offering new creative and technical capacities to represent space. In this respect one of the most intriguing contributions to the conference was Chris Reed's presentation on "Projective Ecologies" that combined theoretical aspects of ecological science with an extremely interesting sense of the aesthetic and sensory experience of space [**Figure 01**]. This work combines a very sophisticated visual representation of socio-ecological relations with a critically reflexive approach toward the human sensory realm. A particularly interesting example used in Reed's lecture was a study of an individual fire escape and the attempt to depict the specific ecological niches associated with a small piece of physical infrastructure [**Figure 02**]. This project connects with different forms of "attentive observation" in urban space: by looking at socio-ecological processes in closer detail, we can begin to explore the functional dynamics of urban space in greater analytical depth. This type of art-science interaction can also take on critical political dimensions. In the early 1970s, for example, the

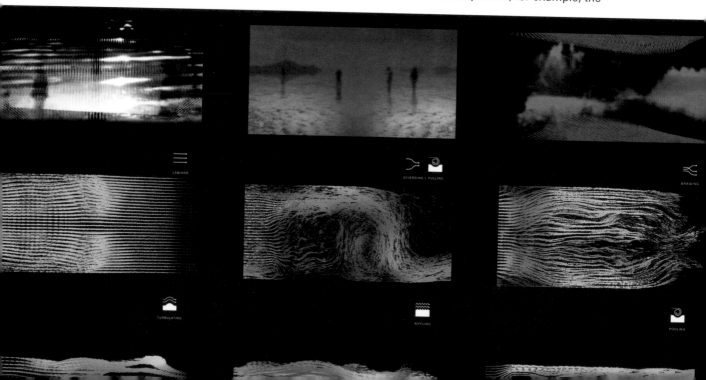

artist Hans Haacke completed a study of Manhattan based on the mapping of ownership patterns for a series of slum tenements [**Figure 03**]. He put together a diagrammatic and cartographic representation of data on ownership, mortgage finance, and property values that proved too controversial to be exhibited in the Guggenheim because some of the museum trustees were themselves landlords implicated in the provision of slum housing. If we consider socio-ecological processes, similar tensions might be revealed by using "radical cartography" to develop more detailed, rigorous, and sophisticated representations of cities.

NG Overall, how do you perceive the increasing effort of designers to redefine and in some respects expand their agency in shaping socio-metabolic processes?

MG: I think that professional fields such as architecture and urban design tend to exaggerate their agency to promote their own disciplinary perspective. There is often an ignorance of how key interventions are facilitated through broader processes of urban change. If we take an ostensibly powerful figure such as Robert Moses, for example, his work mirrored the wider socioeconomic and political dynamics of urban space in a similar fashion to Haussmann in Second Empire Paris. So there is this tension between the idea of individual agency, exemplified by high-profile architects or planners, and broader processes operating in the urban arena. In this sense the question of what happens after design, how these structures and relationships continue to evolve or change, is also really important, including the neglected question of urban maintenance. The significance of maintenance or "urban sustenance" also connects with the concept of cyborg urbanization and emphasizes these complex interrelationships where the city can be conceived as a kind of complex structure that enables human life to flourish, a kind of technological life-support apparatus, but not necessarily in relation to the individual human body but rather as a collectivity of bodies in biopolitical terms.

NG: We would like to expand on the concept of cyborg urbanization, which is of course one of the foundational concepts allowing us to interrogate critically the increasing technological mediation of almost every aspect of contemporary urbanization. We would like to discuss certain contemporary trends that we feel are already largely reshaping or promising to reshape processes of urban metabolism. The first is the various forms of "smart" urbanism claiming to offer more efficient and sustainable technocratic modes of development.

Figure 01. Landscape visualizations by Taehyung Park and Hyemin Choi, "Turbolaria" project as part of "Californa Linmolarium" option studio. Fall 2013, Harvard GSD, Prof. Chris Reed, Teaching Fellow Daniel Ibañez.

MG: The different elements of the contemporary "smart city" relate to a certain mode of technological governmentality under late modernity where an increasing range of logistical and organizational forms of decision making is placed in the realm of digital systems of command and control. At a broader level of analysis there are many worrying issues. Many of these approaches are characterized by a reluctance to recognize the importance of democratic deliberation or political contestation in the urban arena. And of course there are certain issues regarding the storage and manipulation of data, because so many activities can be influenced or controlled through this concentration and manipulation of information. There is a sense that urban development can be portrayed as an automatic process that is separate from human intentionality. There is an enhanced techno-managerial dimension to decision making that appears to lie beyond politics in a reprise of earlier types of technological politics. We can envisage the dystopian scenario of new kinds of digital citizenship that can be switched on and off.

Matthew Gandy, Daniel Ibañez and Nikos Katsikis

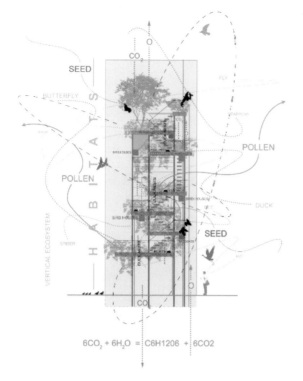

$6CO_2 + 6H_2O = C6H1206 + 6CO2$

Figure 02. GROSS.MAX and Mark Dion, Delirious Piranesi in Bloom.

Figure 03. Hans Haacke, Real-time Social System.

NG: A connected issue then seems to be how this renewed technocratic imperative relates to the continuing privatization of infrastructures and services.

> **MG**: With the retreat of municipal models of urban government and the privatization of public services, there is a niche that has opened up for companies such as CISCO to offer an increasing range of services. This trend might lead to a future scenario in which mayors are more similar to corporate CEOs answerable to shareholders and enmeshed in an array of contract negotiations for urban services. We can imagine a future city characterized by highly diversified forms of digital citizenship that are reminiscent of the complicated voting hierarchies that existed in the nineteenth century. On the other hand, we should counter fatalism with examples of reversibility where people have succeeded in wresting back control over public services including metabolic aspects to urban life such as energy and water supply. There are, however, many barriers to be overcome to achieve this in terms of commercial confidentiality, access to technical information, and the fact that franchises often last for twenty years or more so that opportunities for change are infrequent.

NG: At the same time, several equally promising paradigms of effective environmental governance with emphasis on sustainable development have called for urbanization patterns that would be more self-sufficient, reducing their external metabolic footprints in favor of a social and ecological autarky, often connected to the development of efficiently controlled and selectively enclosed socio-ecological regions.

> **MG**: Interest in forms of social and ecological autarky does have some problematic ideological underpinnings that can extend to culturally homogeneous conceptions of place or authoritarian forms of environmental politics. These tensions also exist in relation to global environmental discourse where we encounter cadres of scientists or specialists who believe that they should be able to control things because of their expertise and are deeply frustrated with the messy uncertainties of democratic politics. Questions of scale in relation to environmental policy making are always very complex. In the case of the

Los Angeles River, for example, we find an administrative tension between LA County and smaller non-incorporated districts and vested interests that oppose a regional approach to managing water resources. Administrative and political fragmentation makes a rational socio-ecological arrangement across a larger scale more difficult to achieve. A key challenge is how an active and informed citizenry can be involved in these discussions and help to develop resolutions to land-use conflict or other challenges facing watersheds or urban floodplains.

NG: The challenge of dealing with the various scales of metabolic processes in terms of both theorization and design intervention seems to be a predominant issue in urban studies and urban design over the past decade. From a theoretical perspective, there are calls for an understanding of urbanization that would be able supersede the city/country, urban/nonurban divide as, for example, the recent agenda of planetary urbanization attempts to do. How do you perceive these developments, and do think that the notion of the city is still relevant as a category for both theoretical analysis and design intervention?

MG: I think that this emerging agenda of planetary urbanization is interesting, especially in relation to the concept of the "operational landscape" and the opportunity to revisit Lefebvrian concerns with cities as just one facet of a wider process of urbanization. The operational landscape helps to illuminate the wider ecological dynamics of capitalist urbanization. An emphasis on specific sites or projects can easily obscure these relationships at a broader scale. If we consider water, for example, cities require elaborate infrastructure systems that can extend hundreds of kilometers away from the built-up spaces of the city. By looking at these circulatory dynamics we can begin to differentiate "the city" as a particular kind of urban form from the broader phenomenon of urbanization. We should not dispense with the idea of the city completely, however, since it also relates to the generation of particular kinds of socio-cultural or political discourses. If we are talking about urban nature, or the urbanization of nature, it is not just a matter of the extension of physical infrastructure into space but also the emergence of new kinds of cultural discourses in relation to nature that we can observe in relation to the edge of the city, the urban hinterland, or even more distant places.

NG: Along the same lines, over the past decade there seems to be a systematic effort to reposition design and its agency in relation to a changing context, grasping the expanding social and environmental influences of urbanization. Such efforts are premised upon an effort to rediscover and redefine regional and ecological design and develop more environmentally informed approaches to urbanism, such as the recent developments in landscape or ecological urbanism.

MG: The recent development of landscape urbanism raises many interesting questions about changing conceptions of nature, landscape, and urban planning. You could argue that the decline of a particular idiom of regional or large-scale planning has coincided with the growth of landscape urbanism since the 1990s. A difficulty with some projects associated with landscape urbanism, however, is that fundamental questions about how urban space is produced can get lost in an implicit aestheticization of land-use planning discourses. There are projects that reclaim post-industrial industrial spaces or so-called brownfield sites by using ecological rhetoric to promote what is essentially a publicly subsidized form of land speculation. The recently opened Olympic Park in London is an example of this process of "ecological speculation."

Matthew Gandy, Daniel Ibañez and Nikos Katsikis

NG: It could be argued that in one way or other many of these cases are characterized by a limited understanding of the social and political complexities inherent in metabolic processes. Over the past two decades the discourse of urban political ecology has specifically tried to foreground and critically assess these issues. We would like to spend some time summarizing the main elements of this agenda and assess its current status.

Figure 04. Nordbahnhof Park, Fugmann-Janotta.

MG: The first wave of urban political ecology, exemplified by the earlier work of Erik Swyngedouw and others, was characterized by the application of a neo-Marxian framework to explore the socio-ecological dynamics behind the production of space, with a particular emphasis on water. I think a second wave of urban political ecology is now opening up a new set of questions related to scale, including micro scales within the city, different types of materials and processes, along with conceptual challenges from post-humanist perspectives, queer theory, and neo-vitalist approaches. Theoretically there is now a moment of what could be termed "vibrant eclecticism": while the neo-Marxian framework is still very present, it is not necessarily the predominant mode of analysis or even the starting point in some cases. There is also scope, although not yet fulfilled, to look very carefully at new developments within the ecological sciences. I think that in some of the literature there has been only a limited engagement with the ecological sciences and what a genuinely interdisciplinary approach might offer for the analysis of urban space. We should not forget that ecology is itself a diverse field of work that has many points of intersection with social, political, and historical questions.

NG: Do you see certain examples from design that already seem to engage creatively with the issues raised by urban political ecology?

MG: I think that there are certain projects that reflect a productive synthesis between urban design discourse, public culture, and scientific inputs from the study of urban ecology and biodiversity. One of the interesting debates has emerged in relation to urban biodiversity and spaces of spontaneous nature or *terrain vague*. There are rare cases where these sites of wild urban nature or *Stadtwildnis* (urban wilderness) have been incorporated into public parks such as Park am Nordbahnhof or Gleisdreieck Park in Berlin as part of a longer-term strategy to enhance the aesthetic diversity and scientific interest of urban nature [**Figure 04**]. A further example is Berlin's former Tempelhof airfield that has been the subject of a public referendum over its future. These extraordinary spaces of urban nature have the potential to produce what I would term "heterotopic alliances" between quite disparate groups of people with different interests who nevertheless come together to protect spontaneous spaces of nature from land speculation or more conventional approaches to urban design. A fascinating example is Atelier Dreiseitl's work on the Bishan-Ang Mo Kio Park in Singapore that allows a more naturalized water flow to produce a new kind of public space. This project reflects hydrological constraints such as effective storm water drainage or flood control, but also shows an awareness of urban epidemiology and natural forms of mosquito control by fish and other predators. A further example is the work of Gilles Clément for Parc Henri Matisse in Lille, France. Clément brings together aspects of scientific understanding of ecological processes with a sophisticated aesthetic agenda for how we might experience cities differently. There is enormous potential to rethink the relationship between urban ecology and urban design, along with the development of more critically engaged aesthetic perspectives on urban space. To achieve this, we need a more rigorous level of critical scrutiny toward ecological rhetoric and the practice of urban planning and design.

Relevant Works by Matthew Gandy

The Fabric of Space: Water, Modernity and the Urban Imagination (Cambridge, MA: The MIT Press, 2014).

"Marginalia: Aesthetics, Ecology, and Urban Wastelands," Annals of the Association of American Geographers 103, no. 6 (2013): 1301–1316.

"Entropy by Design: Gilles Clément, Parc Henri Matisse and the Limits to Avant-Garde Urbanism," International Journal of Urban and Regional Research 37, no. 1 (2013): 259–278.

"Interstitial Landscapes: Reflections on a Berlin Corner" in Urban Constellations (Berlin: JOVIS, 2011), 149–152.

"Urban Nature and the Ecological Imaginary" in In the Nature of Cities: Urban Political Ecology and the Politics of Urban Metabolism, ed. Erik Swyngedouw, Nik Heynan and Maria Kaïka (London: Routledge, 2006), 62–73.

"Cyborg Urbanization: Complexity and Monstrosity in the Contemporary City," International Journal of Urban and Regional Research 29 (2005): 26–49.

Matthew Gandy, "Rethinking Urban Metabolism: Water, Space and the Modern City," City 8, no. 3 (2004): 371–387.

Image Credits

Figure 01: Drawings by Taehyung Park and Hyemin Choi.

Figure 02: Courtesy of GROSS.MAX and Mark Dion.

Figure 03: Courtesy of Hans Haacke / Artists Rights Society (ARS), New York / VG Bild-Kunst, Bonn.

Figure 04: Courtesy of Philip JSF Winkelmeier Landscape Photography.

Matthew Gandy, Daniel Ibañez and Nikos Katsikis

Volker M. Welter

The Valley Region

From Figure of
Thought to Figure
on the Ground

*Historical analysis of
the development of the
regional concept in the early
twentieth century and its
influence as a spatial notion
linking metabolic processes
to geographic settings.*

Volker M. Welter PhD (University of Edinburgh) is
an architectural historian who has lived, studied,
and worked in Germany, Scotland, and England. He
is now Professor at the Department of the History
of Art and Architecture, University of California
at Santa Barbara, where he teaches Californian
and Western modern architectural history and
theory. His publications include Biopolis-Patrick
Geddes and the City of Life (2002), Ernst L. Freud,
Architect: The Case of the Modern Bourgeois
Home (2012), and articles in such journals as Israel
Studies, Oxford Art Journal, Cabinet, Manifest,
Bauwelt, Berfrois, Archithese, and many others.

Since 1853, a camera obscura stands high above the city of Edinburgh at the upper end of the Royal Mile, just below the castle. In that year, Short's Observatory was established by extending upward a seventeenth-century tenement building. In 1892 the Scottish biologist, sociologist, and city designer Sir Patrick Geddes (1854–1932) acquired the building, kept the camera obscura at the top, but converted the remaining floors into a new type of regional laboratory for the citizens of Edinburgh.

Rechristened the Outlook Tower [**Figure 01**], the tower's viewing platform on the uppermost level, the camera obscura inside a small turret at its center, and the floor below now formed a comprehensive exhibition on the historic and contemporary conditions of the region around Edinburgh. Yet Geddes's imagination did not stop at the local level. Rather, each of the lower floors was dedicated to a larger geographical entity; a sequence that began with Edinburgh, moved from there to Scotland, the British Empire (euphemistically called the realm of the English language), Europe, and the world at the ground level.

Residents and visitors to Edinburgh were invited to hasten to the highest level; with blood circulation and breathing pattern speeded up, all sense organs were highly perceptive of the visual impressions offered by the camera obscura and the viewing platform. As one walked down the main stair, maps, topographical models, drawings, engravings, photographs, lantern slides, books, and other exhibits illustrated the range of geographical areas. A "thinking cell," a small darkened room with just a chair, enabled reflection on the ideas taken in before the real city was faced again.

Physically, Edinburgh may not have changed much during one's visit to the Outlook Tower. But residents returned to the city newly aware that the local and the global were indissolubly intertwined via a series of widening geographical frames of reference that bridged the distance between Edinburgh as the smallest and the world as the largest entity. At the center of the Outlook Tower stood the reciprocal relationship between the local and the global, or, more philosophically stated, the specific (Edinburgh's region) and the general (the region as a basic building block of the world). The tower invited visitors to look at this relationship from either without or within, to paraphrase an essay title by Geddes.[01] The view from without zooms in downward from the level of the world to that of the smallest unit—in this case Edinburgh in its region. The view from within looks upward from the level of a city toward that of the largest entity. The Outlook Tower made visible what was either too large to be grasped in its entirety by the human gaze or easily overlooked for being too small or too close to the human eye. Despite functioning accordingly as both telescope and microscope, the tower did not require selecting either instrument's point of view, because whichever way one looked, the region entered the viewfinder.

By bringing the region into focus, the Outlook Tower moved it from the level of, by analogy, a Platonic idea to that of reality. The camera obscura, assorted optical instruments on the viewing terrace, and geographical pointers to distant places carved into the terrace's balustrade visually establish the region as the frame of everyday life and the field for interventions by citizens. Accordingly, regions became "real" the moment an Outlook Tower made them phenomenologically visible as units that existed in space and time, in geography and history.

Geddes named the region as a geographical entity the "valley region." Strictly speaking, the word valley should be in the plural because this region encompasses a fan-shaped set of valleys that accommodates a network of human settlements. It begins uphill with isolated dwellings, continues downhill with a series of increasingly larger human

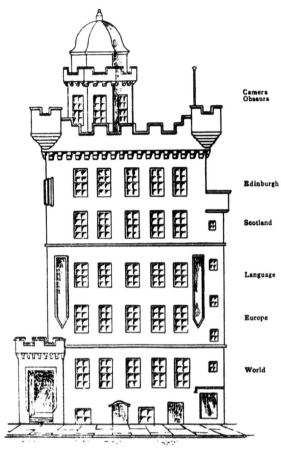

Camera
Obscura

Edinburgh

Scotland

Language

Europe

World

Figure 01. The Outlook Tower.

settlements (villages, foothill towns, market towns, etc.) that follow a river's course, until it culminates in a big city at the river's estuary. The valley region matches closely the region around Edinburgh, though Geddes never defined the physical dimensions of his model other than to the extent of what could be seen from the tower. Occasionally he referred to towns in the middle of the section as being "a day's march" apart, indicating that the spatial expanse of the concept was flexible.[02]

Figure 02 shows an early rendering of the valley section, the diagram Geddes conceived to illustrate the valley region. Geddes published this version in 1909 and used it as late as 1925.[03] It includes all types of human habitation; yet since the mid-1950s the valley section is usually portrayed as an empty hinterland of a big city.[04] While this depiction may help to imagine the valley region as a planning unit, it eliminates many of its important geographical, ecological, and historical characteristics.

A series of pictograms in the lower margin capture the ecological implications of the valley region. They depict what Geddes called "natural occupations." Pickaxe, axe, bow, and crook represent miner, woodman, hunter, and shepherd. Hoe, plow, and spade refer to peasants working the land, while a fishing net closes the sequence at the coast. Each pictogram symbolizes a type of labor best suited for a particular area within the larger region. Geddes borrowed here from the work of French botanist Charles Flahault, who in the 1890s had surveyed the regional distribution of plants by identifying dominant tree species—"social species" that fostered a defined set of subordinated plants, increasing benefits for all plants in the region. Thus botanical regions were hierarchically structured and cooperatively organized to maximize the exploitation of regional conditions.

A comparable thought underpins the valley section because each natural occupation aligns with a particular type of human settlement. For example, to the hunters belong isolated huts, and to the peasants, villages and smaller towns. Ultimately the social organizations of these human settlements derive from the ecological adaptation of their related natural occupation to conditions in the sub-environments. Geddes summarized this train of thought in the triad of Place, Work, and Folk, a shortcut to the ecological reality of the valley section that he had adopted from French engineer and sociologist Frédéric Le Play (1806–1882). Sometimes Geddes substituted environment, function, and organism for Place, Work, and Folk, thereby moving from sociology to biology, specifically Darwin's theory of evolution. Viewed in light of evolutionary biology, the valley region acquires a distinct historical dimension.

The large city at the end of the valley is not aligned with a single natural occupation because "It takes the whole region to make the city … each complex community, as we descend [the valleys], is modified by its predecessors."[05] Geddes thereby described a historical process, for considered collectively the sequence of natural occupations illustrates the progress of human civilizations, from primitive to complex societal stages. Geddes draws here on the Scottish Enlightenment, which had argued that humanity evolved through the stages of hunting and gathering, pastoralism, and agriculture, toward the commercial stage as the highest form of social organization.[06] Philosophers such as John Millar and

Adam Smith equated the last stage with civilized urban life, which depended on a high degree of specialization of labor and, deriving from that, a high degree of cooperation. As a truly enlightened Scot, Geddes claimed that the mixture of professions and types of labor in the commercial streets of a modern city were not only differentiations of the natural occupations but cooperatively created the city. Accordingly, the city could not be assigned a single natural occupation, as it condensed the entire region. It was, symbolically, the heart and head of a region.

Within a region, the city occupied a position comparable to that of a nucleus within a cell, which transmitted biological traits from one generation to the next; that precise mechanism was beginning to be understood within Geddes's lifetime. Cities passed on to citizens the cultural inheritance of a regional civilization; Outlook Tower, museum, and other cultural and educational institutions were some of the means, while current citizens were the agents of this process.

Already in 1895, the anarchist-geographer Elisée Reclus, a close friend of Geddes, had reflected along similar lines on the relationship between cities and regions. Envisioning a coming age of infinite regional growth of towns, Reclus was excited about the expansion's consequences for the historic city. Reclus imagined the historic city, abandoned in favor of suburbs and areas even further out, as the new core of the extended city: The new "heart of the city is the patrimony of all … Every town should have its agora, where all who are animated by a common passion can meet together."[07]

Geddes based his view of a city's central position within a region on a comparably organized hierarchy. When planning a region, Geddes focused on the city. And when planning a city, Geddes concentrated on the cultural acropolis, a dense accumulation of cultural and educational institutions where citizens could cooperatively learn and reenact their city's and region's history while working toward their futures. Visually comparing Edinburgh and Athens [**Figure 03**], Geddes concluded that the cultural acropolis should be located on the highest available ground, making the appeal to the citizens a widely visible call to action.

Even though Geddes remained something of an outsider within his chosen professions of sociology and planning, his ideas about the region spread widely during the 1940s and 1950s. At least two channels of influence can be identified. There were those who knew Geddes personally; most famous among these is probably Lewis Mumford (1895–1990). Second, there were architects and planners such as Jaqueline Tyrwhitt (1905–1983) who became familiar with Geddes's thought as students.

Lewis Mumford's encounter with Geddes's writings from 1915 has been well documented by biographers.[08] A personal meeting furthered Mumford's critical and selective adoption of Geddesian ideas. Still, in The Culture of Cities (1938), Mumford offers a "Regional Framework of Civilization" whose structure recapitulates major stages of Geddes's intellectual progression.[09] From a discussion of the biological origins of life, which recalls Geddes's beginnings as a biologist, Mumford moves to the regional basis of human life, the equivalent of Geddes's valley section. He then looks at region and city as geographical facts, before he considers the earth as the home of man, thus adopting the basic structure of the Outlook Tower with its two outermost poles of region and world.

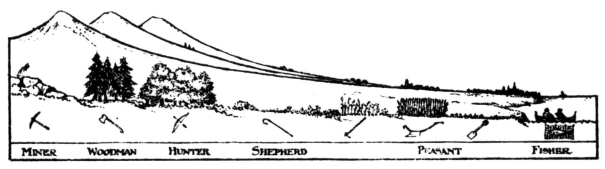

Figure 02. The Valley Section, c. 1909.

Volker M. Welter

Figure 03. Comparison of the urban topography of Athens and Edinburgh.

The Indian social scientist Radhakamal Mukerjee (1889–1968) also belongs in this group. After meeting Geddes around 1914, Mukerjee later explicitly referenced his ideas when writing that regional sociology "will derive support from … the school of Le Play, with its concrete treatment of the interrelations between Place, Work and Folk—an occupational analysis which has been endowed in the hands of Patrick Geddes with rich practical significance in a renewed application of sociological method to social life in definite cities and regions."[10] Like Geddes, Mukerjee refrained from defining absolute dimensions of a region. Nevertheless, he aimed to give it an empirical base in observable ecological facts of the Indian countryside.

Mukerjee's region may have thus been more tangible, but at the cost of losing Geddes's imaginative combination of ecological thought, historical ideas, and a visionary and activist outlook toward the future.

The most prominent disseminator of Geddesian thinking was probably Jaqueline Tyrwhitt.[11] Trained as a horticulturist, Tyrwhitt learned about Geddes when she studied at the School of Planning at the Architectural Association in London in 1933. The school's director was physicist and structural engineer Eric Anthony Ambrose Rowse (1896–1982), who was acquainted with Geddesian ideas from his time at the Edinburgh College of Art where

083

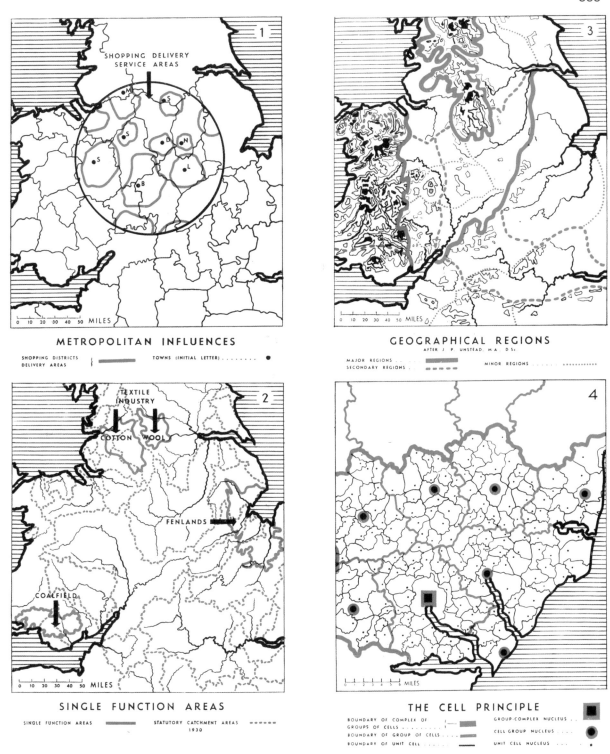

Figure 04. Association for Planning and Regional Reconstruction, <u>Broadsheet 1: The Delimitation of Regions for Planning Purposes</u>, September 1942, reprinted March 1943.

Volker M. Welter

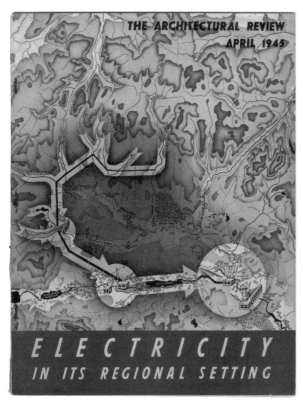

Figure 05. Cover for "Electricity in Its Regional Setting, prepared for the Architectural Review by the Association for Planning and Regional Reconstruction," <u>Architectural Review</u>, April 1945.

Figure 06. Cover for "Gas in the National Plan, a Special Number of the Architectural Review for April 1947 ... produced in collaboration with the Association for Planning and Regional Reconstruction," <u>Architectural Review</u>, April 1947.

Arthur Geddes, a son of Patrick Geddes, was a lecturer in Geography.[12] From 1941 onwards Tyrwhitt directed the Association for Planning and Regional Reconstruction (APRR) while Rowse, its founder, fought in the war. At the request of the War Office, Tyrwhitt organized a correspondence course in town planning for members of Her Majesty's forces and their allies. The importance of this course—allegedly 2,000 students enrolled, of which 170 men and two women completed their studies[13]—for the history of planning in Great Britain and beyond remains to be researched.

Tyrwhitt's importance in making Geddes's ideas known can be gleaned from her 1949 edition of his <u>Cities in Evolution</u>. Tyrwhitt included a text by John [F. C.] Turner (born 1927)—later the author of <u>Housing by People</u> (1976)—and Paffard Keatinge-Clay (born 1926) that analyzes the triad of Place, Work, and Folk as an expression of a holistic "life-motion of a unitary form of thought."[14]

The APRR and Tyrwhitt were among the first to translate Geddes's valley region into a planning figure on the ground. Anticipating large-scale postwar reconstruction, they developed many regional plans that combined surveys of land and resources, analyses of contemporary conditions, and projections of future needs with planning proposals. Their efforts came close to a comprehensive national plan of which numerous aspects were published in beautifully designed <u>Broadsheets</u> [**Figure 04**], special issues of the <u>Architectural Review</u> [**Figures 05, 06**], and essays in the Architects' Year Book and the voluminous <u>Town and Country Planning Textbook</u>.[15] The textbook drew heavily on teaching material from the correspondence course. True to Geddes's preferred methodology of visual analysis, the APRR presented most of its surveys and plans in the form of maps and diagrams. Missing, however, was a contemporary version of the Outlook Tower, the one visual tool with which Geddes had defined the region and invited the active involvement of citizens.

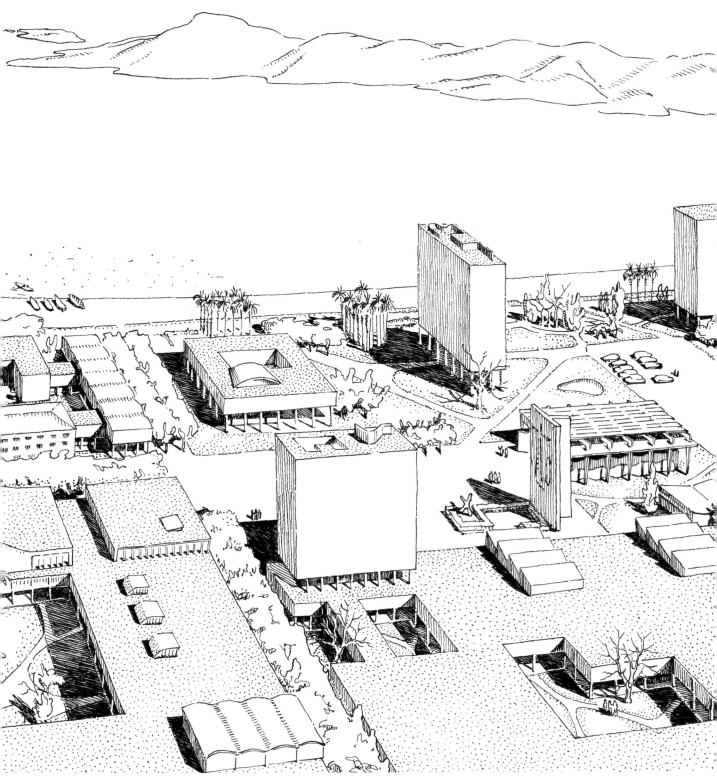

Figure 07. Josep Lluís Sert and Paul Lester Wiener, Civic Core for Chimbote, Peru, 1948.

Volker M. Welter

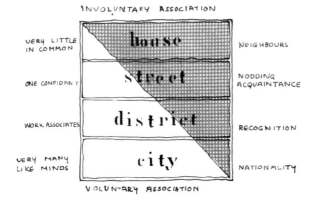

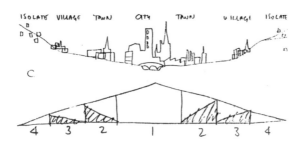

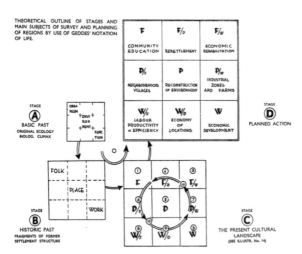

Figure 08. Alison and Peter Smithson, Diagram of Human Association, drafted for CIAM 10, 1953.

Figure 09. Alison and Peter Smithson, for Team 10, CrossSection through the Valley Region, Doorn Manifesto, 1954. The cross section references the types of settlement from Geddes's longitudinal valley section. The diagonal hatching in the sketch indicates levels of human association; see the diagram in **Figure 08**.

Figure 10. Artur Glikson, Theoretical Outline of Stages and Main Subjects of Survey and Planning of Regions by Use of Geddes's Notation of Life, 1953.

By comparison, Geddes's idea of a cultural acropolis fared better, briefly at least, among professional planners and architects. Largely organized by Tyrwhitt, CIAM 8 discussed "The Core of the City" when it met in Hoddesdon, England, in 1951. Geddes's idea resonated with CIAM members, as illustrated by the many modernist cultural city centers that Tyrwhitt included in The Heart of the City, the published proceedings of the meeting [**Figure 07**].[16]

The aim of CIAM 8 was to revitalize the aging organization. Yet to some younger attendees, such as Peter and Alison Smithson, two key figures of the emerging Team 10, the event may have appeared as barely more than a return to traditional city centers. Peter Smithson occasionally recalled that Geddes's urban thought was widely known during the 1940s and 1950s even at Smithson's alma mater, the University of Newcastle/Durham.[17]

Team 10 did not approve of CIAM's attempt to complement the Charter of Athens with an urban core: "CIAM elders no doubt felt they had said all there was to say on the four problems they have tackled in repetition since 1928. That is: the House/the Group/the Community/the Core."[18] As an alternative, Team 10 emphasized the characteristics of communities and human associations specific to place and time, reprising two key elements of Geddes's theory. First, the Smithsons drew up a version of the spatial hierarchy that underpinned Geddes's Outlook Tower, but reinterpreted it as indicating levels of social association among humans. Yet as illustrated in [**Figure 08**], the Smithsons confined their gaze to a realm ranging from the house to the city and back; Geddes's far wider horizon that had connected the region with the world had been lost.

Second, Team 10 illustrated its Doorn Manifesto from 1954—the centenary of Geddes's birth—with a valley region, drawn in cross section rather than longitudinally [**Figure 09**]. The group understood the valley section as a depiction of the social structure of human societies, a model for architectural interventions, and a conceptual tool that directed the architect's gaze away from universal assumptions and toward local specifics. Broadly consistent with the legacy of Geddes, the reinterpretation nevertheless transformed the valley section into a tool for planners rather than a Geddesian call on citizens to act.

True to his anarchist leanings, the valley region and the other elements of his urban theory were for Geddes means to entice citizens to take charge of the future of their cities and regions. In the Outlook Tower the region that could be seen as a figure on the ground was brought together with its counterpart, the region as imagined, a figure of thought. From this union of the world without and the world within, citizens' activism would radiate into their surroundings.

For the APRR, CIAM 8, and Team 10, Geddesian thought became an alternative approach to their own professional work as architects and planners on behalf of the inhabitants of a city or region. Mumford had defined in the 1930s four stages of regional planning that culminated in a "plan proper" that required "intelligent absorption …by the community and … translation into action through the appropriate political and economic agencies."[19] Israeli planner Artur Glikson (1911–1966) emphasized the shift from citizens as their own planners to the profession of planning when he reduced the triad of Place, Work, and Folk and its biological foundation in Environment, Function, and Organism—two pillars of Geddes's valley region—to ingredients in a four-step process of professional regional planning [**Figure 10**].[20]

For Geddes the valley section was a figure on the ground and one of thought. To realize that both existed and had to be cultivated together required an Outlook Tower, with citizens as the agents of this process. Subsequent generations of planners and architects read the valley section as both model and tool for professional regional planning. Most ignored, however, the function of the Outlook Tower, and many of their regional plans and voluminous planning proposals have remained unrealized. They gather dust in archives and libraries, whereas Geddes's valley region continues to inspire, for it lives in the world of ideas.

Notes

01. Patrick Geddes, The World Without and the World Within (Bournville: Saint George Press, 1905).
02. Patrick Geddes, "Civics: As Applied Sociology, Part I," in Sociological Papers (1904): 105.
03. Patrick Geddes, "The Valley Plan of Civilization," Survey Graphic (Jun 1925): 288.
04. For example, Philip Mairet, Pioneer of Sociology: The Life and Letters of Patrick Geddes (London: Lund Humphries, 1957), 124.
05. Geddes, "Civics I," 106.
06. John Millar, The Origin of the Distinction of Ranks, 4th ed. (Edinburgh, 1806; Bristol: Thoemmes, 1990). Geddes owned a copy of the first edition of this book.
07. Elisée Reclus, "The Evolution of Cities," Contemporary Review 67 (1895): 246–264.
08. Lewis Mumford and Patrick Geddes, The Correspondence, ed. Frank G. Novak, Jr. (London: Routledge, 1995); Robert Wojtowicz, Lewis Mumford and American Modernism: Eutopian Theories for Architecture and Urban Planning (Cambridge: Cambridge University Press, 1998).
09. Lewis Mumford, The Culture of Cities (New York: Harcourt, Brace, 1938; London: Secker & Warburg, 1940), 300–347.
10. Radhakamal Mukerjee, Regional Sociology (New York: Century, 1926), 236.
11. Ellen Shoskes, Jaqueline Tyrwhitt: A Transnational Life in Urban Planning and Design (Farnham, UK: Ashgate, 2013).
12. See Mary O. Ashton, "'Tomorrow Town': Patrick Geddes, Walter Gropius, and Le Corbusier," in The City after Patrick Geddes, ed. Volker M. Welter and James Lawson (Bern: Peter Lang, 2000), 191–210.
13. Jaqueline Tyrwhitt, "The School of Planning," unpublished typescript, 3 Mar 1953 (Archives of the Royal Institute of British Architects, London, TyJ/38/2/4).
14. John Turner and W. P. Keating Clay, "Part 2. The Contribution of the Diagrams towards a Synthetic Form of Thought," in Patrick Geddes, Cities in Evolution, ed. Outlook Tower Association and the Association for Planning and Regional Reconstruction (London: Williams & Norgate, 1949), 200–205.
15. "Electricity in Its Regional Setting," Architectural Review 97 (Apr 1945); "Gas in the National Plan," Architectural Review 101 (Apr 1947); Jaqueline Tyrwhitt, "Town Planning," Architects' Year Book 1 (1945): 11–29; APRR, ed., Town and Country Planning Textbook (London: Architectural Press, 1950).
16. CIAM, The Heart of the City: Towards the Humanisation of Urban Life, ed. Jaqueline Tyrwhitt et al. (London: Lund Humphries, 1952).
17. Telephone conversation with Peter Smithson, 29 October 2001.
18. Alison and Peter Smithson, "The Theme of CIAM 10," Architects' Year Book 7 (1956): 28–29.
19. Mumford, Culture of Cities, 379–380.
20. Artur Glikson, Regional Planning and Development (Leiden: A. W. Sijthoff Uitgeersmaatschappij, 1955), 83; Volker M. Welter, "Artur Glikson, Thinking-Machines, and the Planning of Israel," in Welter and Lawson, City after Patrick Geddes, 212–226.

Image Credits

Figure 01: From Patrick Geddes, Cities in Evolution: An Introduction to the Town Planning Movement and to the Study of Civics (London: Williams & Norgate, 1915), 324.

Figure 02: From Patrick Geddes, Country and Town in Development, Deterioration, and Renewal (n.p.: n.d. [ca. 1909]), no pagination.

Figure 03: From Patrick Geddes, The Civic Survey of Edinburgh (Edinburgh: Outlook Tower, 1911), 544–545.

Figure 04: Association for Planning and Regional Reconstruction, Broadsheet 1-The Delimitation of Regions for Planning Purposes (Sep 1942, reprinted Mar 1943), 2–3.

Figures 05, 06: With permission of the Architectural Review.

Figure 07–09: Images courtesy of the Frances Loeb Library, Harvard University Graduate School of Design.

Figure 10: With permission of the International Institute of Social Studies, the Hague.

Volker M. Welter

Hadas A. Steiner

After Habitat, Environment

Historical exploration of key concepts—from habitat to environment—that informed the expanding context of architecture in the first two decades after World War II.

Hadas A. Steiner is an Associate Professor at the University at Buffalo, SUNY, who researches cross-pollinations of technological, scientific and cultural aspects of architectural fabrication in the postwar period. She is at work on a manuscript that will provide an historical analysis of the evolving use of ecological terms in architectural discourse, from the abortive "Charter of Habitat" proposed by Le Corbusier at the seventh meeting of CIAM in 1949, through the work of John McHale in the 1970s.

In 1942, ecological science popularizer Julian Huxley published <u>Evolution: A Modern Synthesis</u>, in which he described biological differentiation in terms of descending ecological scales, from the gross climatological (ecoclimatic) attributes of a region to the topological (ecotopic) conditions and biotic (ecobiotic) associations that define the habitats to which organisms adapt.[01] Habitat, in Huxley's work, was determined by clearly demarcated thresholds relating to each of his ecological scales; differentiation, or the minute evolutionary divergences between closely related species, was a result of variations in habitat caused by the cloistering effects of border conditions. Although migratory patterns and abutting climatological zones may blur the rigid localization of Huxley's model of habitat, the model itself relies on the clear delineation of regions.

Fewer than twenty years later, Huxley's peer Conrad Waddington would describe evolution in vastly different terms—those of the "feed-back or cybernetic system" that pertains between organisms and their "environments."[02] Throughout Waddington's later work, the term "environment" took on an increasingly inclusive role, incorporating not only the immediate physical interactions between ecologies and organisms but also global systems of information exchange and the "human environment."[03] The later were conditioned by a unique technological/biological hybridization, as is apparent in Waddington's assertion of a "socio-genetic" evolutionary model for human development. This shift away from the language of habitat to that of environment, from regional territory and biology to global informational networks, was thus marked by a loss of binary oppositions such as those between natural and social, open and closed systems, city and country.

Ecological and social models of biology such as those advanced by Huxley and Waddington played a crucial role in the reformulation of the built environment as part of a complex system of adaptive interactions.

The intertwining of ideas about form, function, community, and environment beginning in the late 1940s led to a habitat-based model of urbanism that replaced the conception of housing units, or *oikos*, with one that embraced the interdependency of domestic space and its environment: or an *oecology*—"ecology," as the word came to be used.

The territorial ethos of the ecological construct of habitat made its formal debut in postwar architectural culture at the eighth meeting of the Congrès International d'Architecture Moderne (CIAM). It was at that congress held in Bergamo in 1949 that Le Corbusier presented the challenge for a new charter to be drafted for the organization, to be known as the <u>Charte de l'Habitat</u>. Since its foundation in 1928, CIAM had sought solutions for the basic conditions of *habitation*, or dwelling as this goal was translated into English, in the context of the functionalist city. The destruction of World War II raised questions for participants about the sufficiency of functionalism as an approach. Le Corbusier's call for a Habitat Charter was directed at that concern. While habitat was an established concept in the biological fields that governed the interconnectedness of organisms that inhabited a region, as well as the territorial configuration of social activities, what this notion of a physical environment would mean for architecture was less clear.

The British delegation to CIAM, known as the Modern Architectural Research (MARS) group, was chosen to organize the next congress to be held in 1951 and decided against the dedication of the meeting to the building of a new charter. The group did, however, address the concern over the insufficiencies of the old functionalist categories of domestic, work, circulatory, and recreational space. In place of those classifications in the common *grille* (grid) framework used for congress presentations, the MARS group requested that five ascending scales of community—village, neighborhood, city sector, city, and metropolis—be

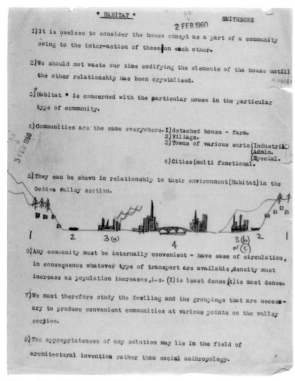

Figure 01. Alison and Peter Smithson, Draft for a statement on Habitat, 1954.

substituted in presentations.[04] Thus despite the rejection of habitat as a theme, the format for the presented work clearly reflected the Geddesian urban ecology of human development, even if the focus remained on formal solutions rather than biological processes.[05] Le Corbusier, undeterred that no progress had been made during CIAM 8 toward drafting a Habitat charter, officially dedicated the ninth congress to the project. CIAM had embarked on a policy of actively encouraging students and graduates to join the organization after the war, and an unexpectedly large contingent of younger members participated in the preparatory sessions for CIAM 9 held in Sigtuna, Sweden, during June 1952.

In an effort to smooth over some of the discord in advance, the executive council issued a statement that acknowledged the varied nuances that the word habitat assumed in the dominant languages of CIAM. Where in French the term denoted "the living conditions of any creature," the statement somewhat misguidingly explained, in English it implied "something larger than 'housing' and smaller than 'neighborhood'—in other words, the setting of daily human life."[06] In the event, the arguments at Sigtuna focused on the ideological

difference implied by the prioritization of the new concept of habitat over the older one of *habitation*, exacerbating the generational rift.[07] Indeed these terms would still be deployed in partisan fashion at the next congress. Although the preliminary meeting may have done nothing to impart a commonly acceptable working definition for habitat as an architectural agenda, it did promote a sense of cohesion among the younger members, who at least could agree that the term suited the desired change in focus from the object to the expanded field of the immediate environment.

At the ninth congress, held in Aix-en-Provence during the summer of 1953, disagreement over the future of CIAM came to a head. This was the largest meeting to date, as well as the last at which the "founding fathers" would be present. It was a chaotic, at times confrontational, event and no charter was drawn up. Instead, a team of the younger members was put in charge of the tenth congress to be broadly based, still, on the search for an "ideal Habitat, fully cognizant of social and climatic conditions."[08] As Alison Smithson would recount, this group, to be known as Team X, recognized its shared concerns first through participation in a CIAM working group (known in the organization as a commission), dedicated to building the new charter.[09] The report of this commission concluded that since achieving even the most basic conditions of dwelling was a luxury unobtainable by most world populations, habitat must serve as a "permanent contract between society and the individual with reciprocal rights and obligations."[10]

As before, the report was vague on the form this contract would assume, but the issue of implementation was more specifically addressed in two appendices submitted by the Dutch and English youth contingents. As indicated by the need for addenda, variance of opinion expressed in terms of national difference would continue even within the most vocal of the pro-habitat crowd. The high stakes of the habitat debate culminated in the collapse of the institutional body that had been formed to promote the tenets of modernism. Thus the debate over of the concept of habitat directly influenced the trajectory of postwar practice. The support of the youngest CIAM generation for the cause of habitat was further instrumental in the shift to the ecosystem model of the city championed by neo-avant-garde practitioners of the 1960s and 1970s.

Figure 02. Alison and Peter Smithson, Diagrammatic section of the Golden Lane housing complex, ca. 1952.

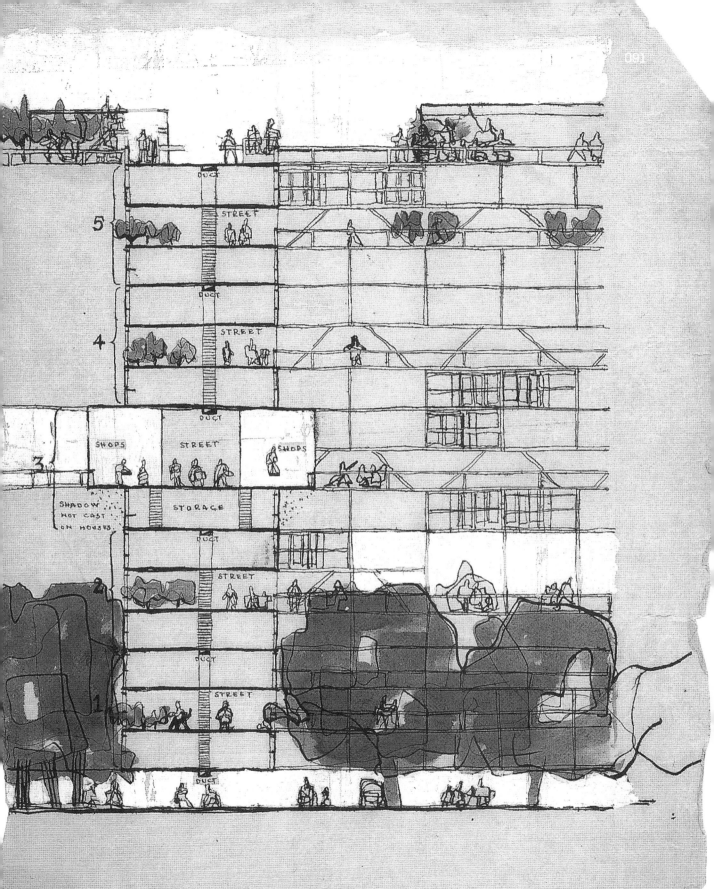

CAP. EMPHASIS ON SITE, CIRCULATION, HABITATION &

HUMAN PRESENCE

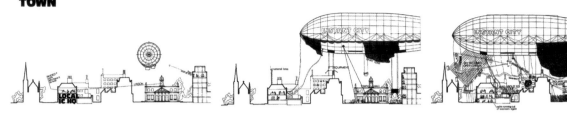

Decades prior to the CIAM debates, Huxley had promoted the cause of building better habitats for animals and humans.[11] Evolutionary biologists such as Huxley recognized a unique advantage of humans among other living things because as a species they consciously affect their surroundings over short durations. Architecture played a large part in this deliberate shaping. In his role as secretary to the Zoological Society of London, Huxley fostered a dialogue with prominent modernists, including Walter Gropius and László Maholy-Nagy, who were in Britain for a time in the 1930s. Moholy-Nagy in particular was an early proponent of the belief that architecture could only be functional in tandem with biology. More than that, he saw it as the responsibility of architects to negotiate that relationship to serve the needs of society. As he said in a lecture: "The new architecture on its highest plane will be called upon to remove the old conflict between organic and artificial, between open and closed, between country and city… art and architecture which fail to serve for the betterment of our environment are socially destructive, aggravating instead the ills of an inequitable social system."[12] Through attention to the biological, Moholy-Nagy believed, architecture would overcome the burdens of its binary relationships: contemporary architecture that transcended the boundaries of the open and closed would also break down the antagonism of the organic and the artificial. The foregone conclusion was that interconnectivity of urban concentration with the diffuse density of the hinterland equaled social betterment. The question that remained to be theorized was how the biological would be architecturally materialized.

An effort at providing a structural response to this question was attempted during the CIAM deliberations regarding habitat. Peter and Alison Smithson, for example, would respond by arguing for the connection of things from the regional to the global.[13] For modernism to remain relevant, the Smithsons argued, its universal premises would have to become accountable to local difference. Following Patrick Geddes, they took the position that urban form, from the crofter's cottage to the town, was the outcome of human adaptation to the conditions of specific regions. Because the Smithsons argued in the manner of evolutionary biologists that the domestic scale was the basic unit of both social structure and urban form, the arrangements of the house became those of the neighborhood, district, and city. Further, the regional contingency of kinship structure provided a methodological tool directed at accommodating the unknowns that would emerge as a result of what they called the hierarchies of voluntary and involuntary human associations in different societies as one moves through scales of urban density. An architecture with a valid, associative notion of habitat would be thoroughly bound to the connections forged between people and their surroundings. Thus the community had to be considered as a totality unique to its environment in which the individual domicile that housed the primary natural unit of society was never separated from any other part of the life of the greater community.

The Smithsons' proposal relied on continuous forms that supported the associational imperative between interdependent ecological populations. In doing so, it expanded their interpretation of habitat to the entirety of the urban encounter. Because they determined that the dense configuration of the housing block was the most significant architectural challenge of their geographic location in the United Kingdom, this type of familial arrangement would be at the heart of their scheme for generating urban form. The Smithsons demonstrated how their particular form of the housing block emanated first from the multiplication of domestic units, and then showed how those aggregates would replicate to form a continuous web of similar units that would spread across the territory. They named the arrangement the "cluster," which they defined as "a close-knit, complicated, often moving aggregation, but an aggregation with a distinct structure."[14] As a result of

Figure 03.   Archigram, Instant City: the Network Takes Over, 1968.

the reproduction of homes and neighborhoods, the city was constituted as an open-ended pattern for a multicentered metropolis. They firmly connected the resultant "aesthetic of change" to the social ethics of the agenda. As they put it: "We have to create an architecture and a town planning which, through built form, can make meaningful the change, the growth, the flow, the vitality of the community."[15] If correctly configured, architecture would provide an ecosystem to cultivate the social well-being of a society.

Although the next generation of neo-avant-garde practitioners would reject the goal of social responsibility as the objective of community arrangement, the aim of a multiplicity of urban foci would not only endure but be developed into a broader discourse of environmental connectivity. With the shift from the 1950s to the 1960s, the cluster configuration of habitat expanded to embrace the complexity of an environmental network. In such a system, the focus on the familial unit was displaced by information as the basic condition of both biology and culture, the

continuity between which was reinforced by the appropriation of metaphors originating in information science and cybernetics into the discourse of life sciences.[16] The result was an increased emphasis on systems of encryption and decryption (coding), in which any complex system, from DNA to weather patterns and the dynamics of human populations, was transcribed into the language of information to be analyzed. This process of transcription into the lingua franca of data implied a greater contingency of organic and technological categories than the link of occupation to place on the Geddes spectrum. It also placed the dichotomy between building and the environment under active scrutiny.

In the work of the Archigram group, for example, the sustained emphasis on environmental networks would take on Moholy-Nagy's biological challenge to resolve the conflicts "between organic and artificial, between open and closed, between country and city" overtly. Network arrays minimalized the difference between architectural interventions and the environment: as

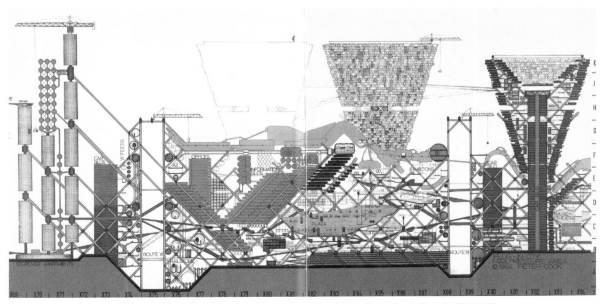

Figure 04.   Peter Cook, Plug-In City, 1964.

Hadas A. Steiner

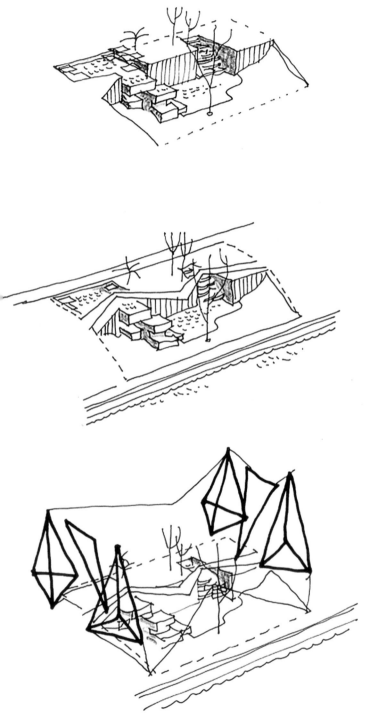

Figure 05. Cedric Price, axonometric of the layers of habitat for the Northern Aviary in the London Zoo, 1962.

Archigram famously reiterated, architecture was no more important than the weather in determining the use of space. Moreover, the integration of what had been considered the natural world with the built one undermined the classic distinctions between porous and hermetic systems, while deemphasizing the traditional distinction of the city as a field of engagement over the hinterland.

The fifth issue of Archigram magazine was dedicated to this integrative configuration of the "Metropolis" and featured urban projects that illustrated the diffuse concept of a multiplicity of centers implied by the web. The open-ended cities were also categorized in the geological terms of eruptions of crust and other emissions of the ground plane.[17] Lack of a unified core, or even a pivotal axis around which the city could arrange itself, was an important corollary of the continuous cluster, making decentralization the significant component of the urban question. As Peter Cook would claim about his project Plug-In City (1964) in Archigram 5, "The Centre is Everywhere and All the City is the Centre." Decentralization in these metropolitan iterations was not, as for the Smithsons and their like-minded colleagues, about the unfurling of an aesthetic, but about linking urban form to its extended territory. And in the manner of information, the trajectory of urban development did not flow along a single course, from city to suburb and beyond, but along the proliferation of nodes that formed the greater network. The collective Archigram project of Instant City (1968–70), for instance, delivered a bundle of cultural activities packaged as information outside of the traditional hubs of major cities. But more than that, it relayed information gathered from those locales to the areas normally thought of as the focal points of urban culture. The introduction of multidirectional feedback as an element that informed the aggregation of the built milieu was key in thinking about the environment along the lines of an ecosystem of networks.

Postwar cybernetics, an interdisciplinary field that explored how systems organized themselves and how information was exchanged, fed the conceptualization of architecture as an adaptive network.[18] Cybernetics as a discipline was concerned from the outset with the steering of information in biological, social, and mechanical systems. Gordon Pask, the cybernetician who collaborated with the architect Cedric Price, described cybernetics as a communications-focused discipline that cut "across the entrenched departments of natural science; the sky, the earth, the animals and the plants."[19] Within this encompassing view, Pask was

Figure 06. Cedric Price, Northern Aviary, 1961-65. Exterior view.

explicit in defining the architect as a mediator of systems. One of the hallmarks of the work of Pask was that he sought to define information not as a quantifiable entity but as a kind of energy whose perturbations qualitatively registered in a subject.[20] If earlier cyberneticists emphasized the production and observation of adaptive simulacra as a means for understanding systems, for those who became known as cyberneticists of the second order the observer was also considered a system, whose interactions with cybernetic objects was itself subject to investigation. In other words, systems observed systems. There were no observer-to-object relationships, only system-to-system ones.

Few projects explored this interpretation of reflexive systems as an environmental exercise more directly than Price's Northern Aviary at the London Zoo, an amalgam of biological and architectural experiments in the construction of habitat. Like most of Price's projects, the aviary was a thoroughly dynamic construction—whether expressed through the triangulation of its structure, the zigzag of its cantilevered bridge, or the diversity of its avian population. Its form is thus the momentary result of the network of environmental (natural and social) stresses to which it adapts, much as Waddington had described organic form as "something which is produced by the interaction of numerous forces which are balanced against one another in near-equilibrium."[21]

The cage, itself a system of structural equilibrium, produced an ecological system within a larger system of controlled environments—the London Zoo—itself a part of a larger urban organism. In this sense, the aviary was a system through which the many independent systems, including architectural technology, biological function, ecological milieu, and zoological criteria, were unified. The aviary was the machine by which all these systems were able to come together, not as an envelope but as an environment that aspired to change with and foster engagement. Architecture played the role of a series of influences rather than objects, even as it reflected these forces through its formal articulation.

Ecologies, though, are the products of duration; zoological pavilions do not have that luxury. Instead of time, they have architecture as Price defined it: "that which, through natural distortion of time, place and interval, creates beneficial social conditions

Hadas A. Steiner

Figures 07. Cedric Price, Northern Aviary, 1962. Interior views.

Figures 08. Cedric Price, Northern Aviary, 1962. Exterior views.

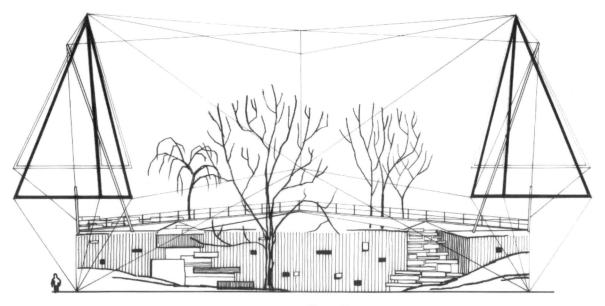

Figure 09. Cedric Price, Northern Aviary, 1962. Elevation of the cliff face.

NG06—Grounding Metabolism

that hitherto were considered impossible."[22] Thus architecture was an environmental intervention that allowed for the self-organizing system of the constructed habitat to adapt with the architect as orchestrator of the fields of information that must be synthesized. For Price this role included the cultivation of all levels of information. Systems, if truly self-organizing and able to accommodate complexity, always expand unexpectedly beyond their initial frames of reference. In the methodology of Price, observers always provide the "noisy data," over which the system has no predictive powers. Indeterminacy and enabling, two terms associated in the architectural literature with Price, are also tied to second-order cybernetic theory in which underspecified systems require the engagement of observers to complete them.

As Price said when remarking on the aviary in a lecture entitled "Technology Is the Answer, but What Is the Question": "Increasingly architecture must be concerned with mixing unknown emotions and responses, or at least enabling such unknowns to work together happily. It is beyond the art of the behavioural scientist to predict all the reactions of the users, whether they be human or animal, within any particular structure. Therefore architecture must be sufficiently accurate to enable this element of doubt and change to be contained."[23] Habitat for Price was not a replica of place but a site that harbored the interactions of all shades of participant, not just the human patterns of association championed by the Smithsons. By extending his design imperative to include natural, technological, and interspecies interactions, Price acknowledged the ecological nature of urban milieus, even as he shifted focus away from the bounded thresholds of regional habitats to the open-ended indeterminacy of cybernetic environments.

As environment, the aviary lacks the kind of aesthetic cohesiveness of the Smithsons' proposals. In Waddington's terms, it has "the character not of a precisely definable pattern but rather of a slightly fluid one, a rhythm," predicated on the ecological variables that affect its formation.[24] The formational aspect of Price's design is reinforced by its interpretational open-endedness as it is continually constructed through the varied perceptions of those who engage it. The work was left open to be completed by its users. Thus the abstraction of the "natural" features of the habitat was not a formalist gesture but part of a framework that allows interaction to happen. A cage represented no particular known or imagined habitat but a habitat waiting to be.

Notes

01. Julian Huxley, Evolution: A Modern Synthesis (Cambridge, MA: MIT Press, 2010), 228–229.
02. Conrad Waddington, The Nature of Life: The Main Problems and Trends of Thought in Modern Biology (New York: Harper & Row, 1961), 88–89.
03. Conrad Waddington, "Biology and the Human Environment," in, Human Identity in the Urban Environment, ed. Jaqueline Tyrwhitt and Gwen Bell (Baltimore: Penguin Books, 1972), 59–68.
04. The shifts in the presentation format of the CIAM grid are summarized in Annie Pedret, "Dismantling the CIAM Grid: New Values for Modern Architecture," in Team 10: 1953–81: In Search of a Utopia of the Present, ed. Max Risselada and Dirk van den Heuvel (Rotterdam: NAi, 2006), 252–257.
05. Volker Welter, "In Between Space and Society: On Some British Roots of Team 10's Urban Thought in the 1950s," in Team 10: 1953–81, Risselada and van den Heuvel, 258.
06. See Eric Mumford, The CIAM Discourse of Urbanism: 1928–1960 (Cambridge, MA: MIT Press, 2000), 218.
07. Mumford recounts the meetings at Sigtuna. The CIAM Discourse of Urbanism, 220–225.
08. Ibid., 242.
09. Alison Smithson, ed., Team 10 Meetings: 1953–1984 (New York: Rizzoli, 1991), 19.
10. Mumford, The CIAM Discourse of Urbanism, 237.
11. Peder Anker, From Bauhaus to Ecohouse: A History of Ecological Design (Baton Rouge: University of Louisiana Press, 2010), 9–36.
12. Quoted in Anker, From Bauhaus to Ecohouse, 16.
13. For an elaboration on the participation of Peter and Alison Smithson in the debate over habitat, see Hadas A. Steiner, "At the Threshold," October 136 (Spring 2011): 133–155.
14. Alison and Peter Smithson, Ordinariness and Light: Urban Theories 1952–1960 and their Application in a Building Project 1963–1970 (Cambridge, MA: MIT Press, 1970), 131.
15. Ibid., 130.
16. See Lily Kay, Who Wrote the Book of Life: A History of the Genetic Code (Stanford: Stanford University Press, 2000).
17. For an extended discussion, see Hadas A. Steiner, Beyond Archigram: The Structure of Circulation (London: Routledge, 2009), 182–217.
18. For further elaboration, see Bernard Scott, "Second-Order Cybernetics: An Historical Introduction," Kybernetes 33, no. 9/10 (2004): 1365–1378.
19. Gordon Pask, An Approach to Cybernetics (London: Hutchinson, 1961), 11.
20. Scott, "Second-Order Cybernetics," 1365–1378.
21. Conrad Waddington, "The Character of Biological Form," in Aspects of Form, 3rd ed., ed. Lancelot Law Whyte (Bloomington: Indiana University Press, 1961), 47.
22. Cedric Price, "Technology Is the Answer, but What Is the Question," Pidgeon Audio Visual (London: World Microfilms, 1979).
23. Ibid.
24. Waddington, "The Character of Biological Form," 47.

Image Credits
Figure 01: Courtesy of Het Nieuwe Instituut Collection.

Figure 02: The Alison and Peter Smithson Archive. Courtesy of Frances Loeb Library, Harvard University Graduate School of Design.

Figures 03–04: Courtesy of Archigram Archives.

Figures 05–09: Courtesy of Cedric Price Archive, Canadian Centre for Architecture.

Hadas A. Steiner

Ken Tadashi Oshima
in Conversation with
Daniel Ibañez and
Nikos Katsikis

On Metabolism and the Metabolists

A reexamination of important proposals of the Metabolist group with reference to contemporary conceptions of urban metabolism.

Ken Tadashi Oshima is Professor in the Department of Architecture at the University of Washington, where he teaches in the areas of transnational architectural history, theory, representation, and design. He has also been a visiting professor at the Harvard Graduate School of Design and taught at Columbia University and the University of British Columbia. Dr. Oshima's publications include GLOBAL ENDS: Towards the Beginning (Toto, 2012), International Architecture in Interwar Japan: Constructing Kokusai Kenchiku (University of Washington Press, 2009), and Arata Isozaki (Phaidon, 2009). He currently serves as First Vice President of the Society of Architectural Historians.

New Geographies: The concept of metabolism emerged in the nineteenth century as a metaphor for the exchange of matter between an organism and its environment. In biology, the term metabolism is mostly used to describe a process that occurs in individual cells and organisms that allows organisms to grow and reproduce and respond to their environments. In the social sciences, the concept was used by Marx to characterize the relationship between humans and nature, as derived from the work of the German soil chemist Justus von Liebig.[01] Today, the concept of urban metabolism is typically used to express a variety of exchanges between urban areas and their hinterlands, and the way in which social and ecological processes interact to produce urban environments. Two very different disciplines have influenced contemporary work employing the concept of urban metabolism: political economy and the biophysical sciences.[02]

To position and conceptually contextualize the work of the Japanese modernist movement, the Metabolist group, could you discuss how the group appropriated the term "metabolism"? What was their understanding of this metaphor and its etymological lineage?

Ken Tadashi Oshima: As you discuss, there are indeed many definitions and interpretations of "metabolism." In the context of Japan, metabolism can be understood by the term *shinchintaisha*, which literally translates as "renewal, replacement, metabolism." This term is often used within architecture in reference to reusing existing wood-frame structures, with rotten portions replaced as required. It also implies that a building is constantly evolving as a living entity. This term was appropriated by the Metabolist group, launched at the Tokyo World Design Conference in May 1960, which included journalist Noboru Kawazoe and architects Kiyonori Kikutake, Fumihiko Maki, Masato Ohtaka, and Noriaki (Kisho) Kurokawa. In their book Metabolism/1960 (with the subtitle "proposals for new urbanism"), they write:

> "Metabolism" is the name of the group, in which each member proposes future designs of our coming world through his concrete designs and illustrations. We regard human society as a vital process—a continuous development from atom to nebula. The reason why we use such a biological word, the metabolism, is that, we believe, design and technology should be a denotation of human vitality.

> We are not going to accept the metabolism as a natural historical process, but we are trying to encourage active metabolic development of our society through our proposals.[03]

In tracing the work of all of the members, you will see divergent interpretations of "metabolism." As Kikutake responded to Rem Koolhaas in his interview published in Project Japan (2011), he noted:

099

Figure 01. <u>Metabolism/1960</u>,
cover.

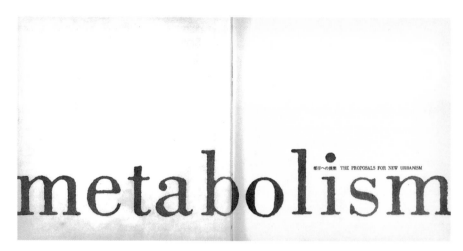

metabolism

都市への提案 THE PROPOSALS FOR NEW URBANISM

Well, we had each been doing our own thing before 1960, so we basically
collected our various viewpoints and works and made them into a book. It
was more of a give and take about methodology than a declaration of principle
or a manifesto… A hypothesis would emerge in our discussions, and from
there we'd have to consider whether or not we had the technical means
to prove it, and what kind of longevity it would have—it was in fact from
discussions like this that I came up with the concept of renewability—and
it was always the Kawazoes who acted as the leaders in this process.[04]

More recently, at the memorial service for Kikutake in April 2012, Maki described
the group much like a baseball team coming together for a common cause, to
address rapidly transforming postwar Japan through an organic architectural/
urban strategy.[05] Maki described Kawazoe as the coach, and Kikutake the
ace pitcher, with Kenzō Tange and Arata Isozaki behind the backstop.

The Metabolist group has gained widespread interest among younger architects
through <u>Project Japan</u> and the recent exhibition "Metabolism, the City of the Future"
at the Mori Art Museum in Tokyo. Yet among the general population in Japan, the
Metabolists are not well known and are often confused with the term "metabo"
that commonly refers to obese people suffering from "metabolic syndrome."

<u>NG</u>: The emergence of the Metabolist group is tied to a particular sociopolitical
context in Japan during and after World War II. The postwar, post-nuclear period
was also shaped by factors such as the scarcity of land due to population pressures
and the complex geography of Japan's archipelago; ecological fragility and the
constant risk presented by natural phenomena such as earthquakes, typhoons, and
tsunamis; and the development of modern technologies that gradually helped to
blur regional boundaries.[06] This context fostered the need for a plan to reconstruct
Japan. In addition, the unexpected economic consequences of the U.S.-led conflict
in Korea from 1950 to 1953 were fundamental to the visions of renewal and
transformation that could be found in the projects and ideas of the Metabolist group.
These elements suggest a particular set of material and territorial forces. What
was the response of the group to this context, and how do many of the principles
reflect and react to this context? As part of this reaction, what were the implications
of accepting Japan as a ground zero, denying time and place and forcing a
decontextualization of territory in order to develop projects, ideas, and visions?[07]

KO: In terms of "context," the Metabolism exhibition at the Mori Museum situated the Metabolist group's efforts before World War II, including plans for Manchuria (1933) and Datong (1938). With Japan's defeat and the loss of colonies for expansion, the postwar population boom prompted a need to expand within Japan that lay at the heart of the Metabolists' "proposals for new urbanism." While the abstract sketches and models of their proposals may appear decontextualized, many addressed specific problems such as the urban transformation around the west exit of Shinjuku Station in Tokyo, expansion into Tokyo Bay (especially in terms of Tange's 1960 Tokyo Bay Plan), and discussions of making the Tokyo-Osaka continuum a single massive city, leading to Prime Minister Kakuei Tanaka's Nippon Retto Kaizo Ron (Remodeling the Japanese Archipelago). The 1973 oil crisis and increasing environmental problems would dampen many of these efforts. Nonetheless, Kikutake would continue to explore his Marine City idea beyond Tokyo Bay, from Okinawa to Hawaii and beyond.

NG: Among the influences that shaped the group's approach to large-scale planning and territorial organization, two are of particular interest to New Geographies. The first is the influence of early twentieth-century Soviet planning, and in particular the so-called Disurbanists. Disurbanist theories and concepts of regional and national planning called for the combination of agriculture with manufacturing industries and the gradual abolition of the distinction between town and country, through a more homogeneous distribution of the population over the entire territory. The Disurbanist ideal of city design was characterized by a diluted mix of both linear city and garden city theories, extending the reach of planning to the regional scale.[08] How were these seminal models incorporated into the Metabolist group's thinking and expressed in their approaches to regional and territorial planning?

KO: There are clearly parallels between early twentieth-century Soviet planning and Japanese planning, both within Japan and in its colonies, especially Manchuria. These connections include the juxtaposition of town and country and the linking of cities through rail. Ebenezer Howard's Garden City ideal was influential in Japan throughout the twentieth century, particularly in suburban Tokyo with the construction of the garden city of Denenchofu and the Denentoshi (garden city) railway line.[09] Kikutake's "Ideas for the Reorganization of Tokyo City," which multiplied his own Sky House living unit to the urban scale of his "Marine City" and "Tower City," could be seen as extending the garden city ideal into the sea. He then revisited these ideas in his Pear City Project (1966), proposed as a "multi-nodal" urban development capable of inducing metabolic change in this area along the Denentoshi railway line. This scheme (which Toyo Ito worked on) connected small-unit communities with central civic facilities, including high-rise housing to cope with the expected population growth; it could be extended as a series of developments and thereby was scalable to a nationwide level.

NG: The second influence of relevance for us is the elaboration of alternatives to the Modernist principles stated in the Athens Charter, especially regarding the idea of scale. The divergence from Modernism by Team X was governed by the concept of scales of association that related patterns of social organization with particular environmental units and the assorted scales of complexity. Team X was concerned with the interrelated issues of density, scale, and identity. Indeed, they appropriated Geddes' Valley Section diagram to visualize the structures of human agglomeration and scales of association with different densities and in different settings.[10] In the case of the Metabolists, the importance of scale was based on the notion of scalability, where the formal principles of a structure should be independent from

Ken Tadashi Oshima, Daniel Ibañez and Nikos Katsikis

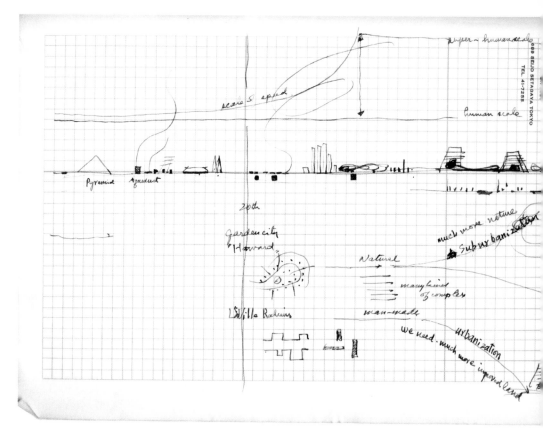

Figures 02. Kenzō Tange's notes from his notebook while a professor at MIT.

the scale and nature of its subject. In particular, Kenzō Tange was in search of a general system that would consistently govern urban constructions at all scales.[11] Could you build upon these notions of scalar association and scalability and the correlation with projects and conceptualizations? For the purposes of visualizing and contextualizing this question, we would like to bring up two images from the Tange archive that we hope could inform the response: one from Tange's notebook, where his conceptualizations on scale are very explicit, and another also from his time as a professor at MIT, which tries to position the Metabolists' urban and planning approach as part of an evolutionary lineage starting with the Egyptian pyramids and passing through the Ville Radieuse of Le Corbusier or the Garden City of Howard.

KTO: As I mentioned in regard to Kikutake's urban proposals, these ideas were indeed scalable to both the regional and national level. In exploring the connection with Team X, it's interesting to note that Tange presented Kikutake's "Ideas for the Reorganization of Tokyo City" at CIAM '59 in Otterlo for participants including Alison and Peter Smithson and Louis Kahn.[12] It is interesting to note that while Tange had led his 1959 MIT studio to design a "New Community on the Sea: 25,000 Inhabitants on the Boston Bay," he did not present his urban schemes at Otterlo, but rather his architectural designs for the Tokyo City Hall and Kagawa Prefectural Office. Following Kikutake's lead, Tange scaled up the Boston Bay plan to span all of Tokyo Bay in his 1960 plan. Tange explained:

> Living together are structures of two different scales: first, the human scale, and second, the extremely large scale made possible by technology which we might call super-human scale. But between the two, there is no harmony and no unity, either in the functional sense or in the visual sense. In connection with the problem of scale, I have for a long time been thinking of what I call "mass human scale." This differs from the individual scale and is a scale needed when men act as a mass…

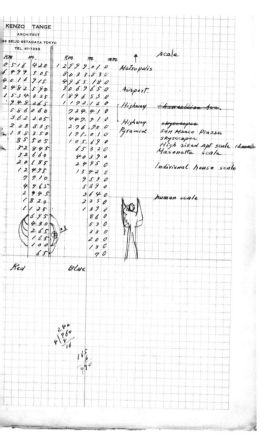

I think that we must necessarily think of an order of sequences of the human scale, the mass human scale, and the super-human scale mentioned above.[13]

He elaborated about this project:

> It happened to be designed on the ocean at Boston, but its location is not of primary importance; as it bears within itself more fundamental problems...I would like to consider several orders according to which this super-human scale can be led into the level of human scale. I thought that it would be necessary to think in terms of a kind of space organization which would give a well-ordered order of space from the super-human scale which is expanded more and more by the new technology from the scale of nature itself, to what I call in my own words the mass human scale, and finally down to the level of the individual human scale where the individual life takes place. What I called a moment ago the "mass human scale" is the scale which historically appears in places such as the square in large cities.[14]

Following this logic, Tange could be seen to be discussing dispersed "architectural elements (as) the basic structure of the city" beyond the megastructural "vertebrae" that would be the linear spine for the 1960 Tokyo Plan that extended into Tokyo Bay to address the problems of a burgeoning population.[15]

In regard to the evolutionary lineage from the Egyptian pyramids, Le Corbusier, Howard, etc., I think it's interesting to see how both Kenzō Tange and Rem Koolhaas could be seen to be within this trajectory, with similar urban utopian aspirations. Tange's notes from his time at MIT appear to span the scales of S/M/L/XL, with the addition of "scale of speed." While Tange's sketches seem to link speed to "urbanization" in a general sense, it was particularly relevant in Japan during this time of skyrocketing growth.

Ken Tadashi Oshima, Daniel Ibañez and Nikos Katsikis

NG: The consequences of the war were many and at multiple levels. On the one hand there was scarcity of available land and food in conjunction with rising population. On the other there were issues of risk associated primarily with natural disasters. These consequences led members of the Metabolist group to consider a different and more flexible way of life that simultaneously, nurtured a change in the urbanization goals. The group searched for solutions in every direction—on the land, on the sea, in the air—to escape from society in the form of geographic isolation, originating several hinterland utopias on territories typically left apart and unexplored.[16] The "Agricultural City" and the "Ocean City" are well-known examples of these projects. In your opinion, which were the most important factors leading to these "getaway" approaches promoting the urbanization of the hinterland, and what were the goals and consequences of the colonization of the productive landscapes? And also, were these projects prototypes of an urban form to be eventually implemented along the archipelago in multiple locations?

Figure 03. Kisho Kurokawa, Agricultural City, 1960. Plan and Section.

KTO: I wouldn't necessarily term these "getaway" approaches, but rather see them as an opportunity to realize large-scale urban plans that the existing Japanese urban fabric did not afford. For Kikutake, the ocean offered such infinitely expandable possibilities. In his Unabara plan sketches for an Ocean City (1960), he explicitly articulates his urban vision expanding organically through notions of cell division. In this case, I think they formed an expandable framework and conceptual model for urban expansion. In the end, Kikutake realized these ideas on the architectural scale of projects such as the Pacific Hotel Chigasaki (1966) or the Aquapolis Pavilion for the 1975 Okinawa Ocean Expo rather than as a "system of settlements."

NG: In the particular case of the Agricultural City, it is easy to draw some intellectual connections with the decentralization strategies of the Disurbanists and also with Wright's Broadacre City. The latter proposed an alternative to large agglomerations, emphasizing the utilization of productive land and agriculture as the city's economic base, in close accord with Kurokawa's City proposal.[17] However, apart from the contextual factors, it would be important to evaluate the design principles embedded in this proposal. The "structural approach" of the Metabolists, in general, had the quality of being implemented on various configurations of terrain, from an infrastructural landscape to megastructures isolated in the landscape, to big shed architecture in the suburbs.[18] In relation to the Agricultural City, could you develop the way in which (mega)structures were thought to organize the territory, but also how they get structured (adapt, grow, hover...) to the diverse set of social and ecological flows?

KTO: With regard to Kurokawa's Metabolist strategies, I think it's important to note this as an early work of his; he was the young, upstart member of the group, some six years younger than Kikutake and twenty-one years younger than Tange. The model and sketches for the Agricultural City project remain abstract and diagrammatic and raise questions of how effective they would have been. Nonetheless, Kikutake's inspiration for the scheme came from seeing the devastation to his hometown of Kanie (Aichi Prefecture), leading him to create a multilevel agricultural production center. The additive grid of Kurokawa's scheme indeed evokes the conceptual framework of Wright's Broadacre City, but at a much smaller scale. In the Japanese context, the square pattern could be seen as much more analogous to the layout of rice paddies. This is perhaps interesting in that the *kanji* character for town (*machi* 町) is composed of the pictograph of such a rice paddy, implying the inherent connection between agricultural production and the town. Also, Kurokawa's additive scheme could be seen to follow the system of wood-frame residential construction in Japan, thereby underscoring its scalability.

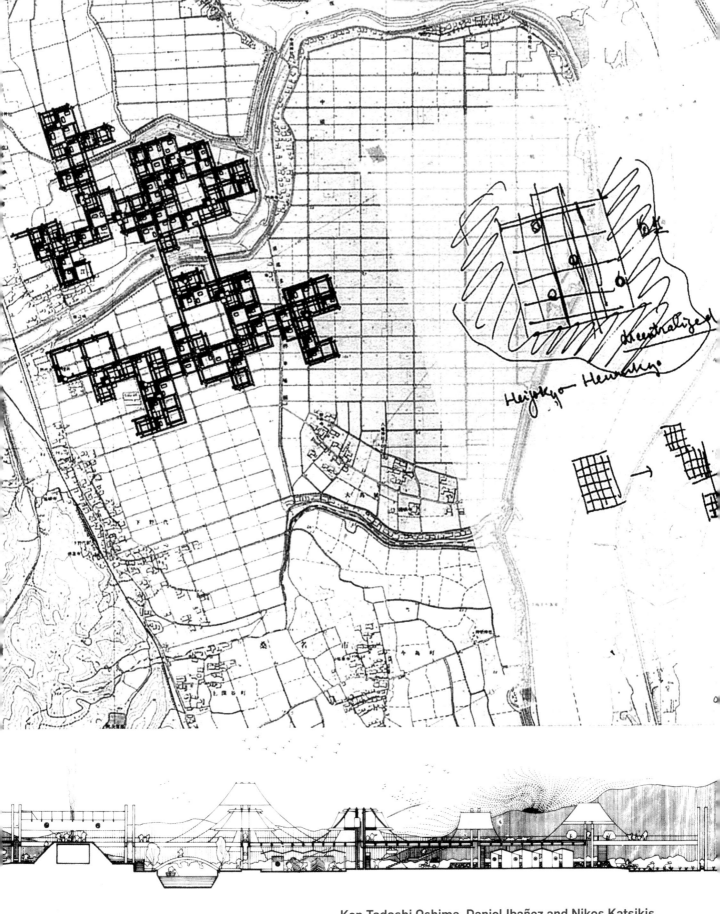

Ken Tadashi Oshima, Daniel Ibañez and Nikos Katsikis

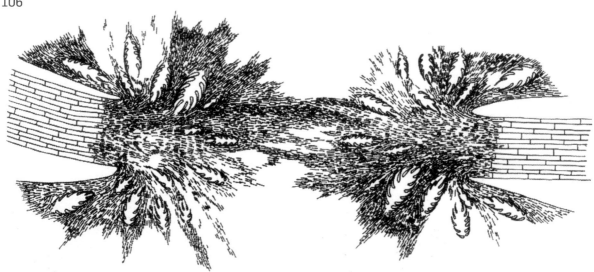

NG: It has been argued that the Metabolists' projects were dominated by a utopian desire to blur the geographical binary of city–hinterland. They explored the scale of utopia by expanding the domain of planning to the whole country with extensive linear cities. In addition, the group was dominated by a technocratic organizational ambition— that is, to control the development of the entire nation by means of modern technology, management, and planning.[19] However, it is the concept of circulation that remains constant across scales, aiming to interconnect and allow linkage and exchange along the archipelago, from a single house to the entire territory. This notion is explicitly visualized and articulated in the project by Kisho Kurokawa, Metamorphosis, and in some of the projects by Kiyoshi Awazu. Probably influenced by the diagrams of proposed traffic patterns for Philadelphia, by Louis I. Kahn, this approach brings to the forefront fluidity, movement, and exchange in the interconnection of spatial structures across scales. However, we wonder, was the idea of circulation put in place to act as connector between fractal surfaces, nested one into another, across scales?[20] Could you elaborate on these notions such as circulation, nested scales, and linear cities?

Figure 04. Kisho Kurokawa, Linear City Metamorphosis '65.

Figure 05. Kisho Kurokawa, Linear City Metamorphosis '65. Sketches of regional structure.

Figure 06. Kisho Kurokawa, Linear City Metamorphosis '65. General development plan for the Japanese archipelago.

KTO: There is indeed a fundamental, integral relationship between the Metabolists' urban schemes and transportation. Many of the layered schemes can be seen to build on the fluidity of Le Corbusier's 1932 Plan Obus for Algiers that integrates an elevated highway with housing along the waterfront. In the context of the increasingly congested capital of Tokyo from the 1950s to the 1960s, such a strategy to facilitate ease of movement becomes essential. The modern metropolis of Tokyo was built on the medieval defensive moat structure of Edo. Therefore Tange's linear extension of Tokyo into the bay in his 1960 Plan was designed in counterpoint to the spiraling structure of Edo and sought to provide fast, free urban access. This was also proposed in tandem with the urban infrastructure being built in preparation for the 1964 Tokyo Olympics, which included elevated highways above the feudal moats, and the elevated tracks for the Shinkansen Bullet Train. It is in this context that Louis Kahn's 1953 assertion that "expressways are like rivers" would take on profound meaning.

Although Metabolism/1960: The Proposals for New Urbanism does not explicitly articulate transportation designs or dynamics of flows, one perhaps could interpret such flows of transport as the necessary circulatory systems to maintain "human vitality" — like blood vessels in the human body.

In the case of Kikutake's "vision of Japan in a linear urban network," one could interpret Ocean City Unabara as connected to the expanding transportation network. In Kikutake's later years, he would in fact design for this transportation infrastructure through the design of highway rest-stop facilities in 1973, adjacent to the Kanmon Strait between the islands of Honshū and Kyūshū, and the Ebina Tōmei Highway Service Area Rest Facilities in 1991. Thus rather than interpreting Ocean City Unabara simply as paper architecture, one can see at least Kikutake's approach as designing actual buildings connected to the realized transportation networks across scales.

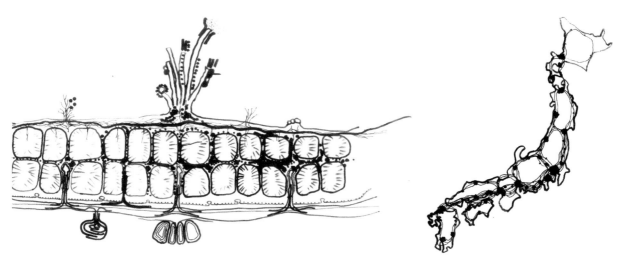

Notes

01. John Bellamy Foster, "Marx's Theory of Metabolic Rift: Classical Foundations for Environmental Sociology," American Journal of Sociology, 105, no. 2 (1999), 366–405.
02. Matthew Gandy, "Rethinking Urban Metabolism: Water, Space, and the Modern City," City 8, no. 3 (2004), 363–379.
03. Kawazoe Noboru, ed. Metabolism/1960 (Tokyo: Bijutsu shuppansha, 1960), 5.
04. Rem Koolhaas and Hans-Ulrich Obrist, Project Japan: Metabolism Talks (London: Taschen, 2011).
05. Fumihiko Maki, remarks at Kikutake Kiyonori memorial service, 13 Apr 2012.
06. Koolhaas and Obrist, Project Japan.
07. According to Cherie Wendelken, "The Metabolists proposed the acceptance of Japan as ground zero." She argues that "it is the very denial of time and place that gives Metabolism its meaning in postwar Japan." Cherie Wendelken, "Putting Metabolism Back in Place: The Making of a Radically Decontextualized Architecture in Japan," in Anxious Modernisms: Experimentation in Postwar Architectural Culture, ed. Sarah William Goldhagen and Rejean Legault (Cambridge, MA: MIT Press, 2000) 279–299.
08. Zhongjie Lin, Kenzō Tange and the Metabolist Movement: Urban Utopias of Modern Japan (New York: Routledge, 2010).
09. Ken Tadashi Oshima, "Denenchōfu: Building the Garden City in Japan," Journal of the Society of Architectural Historians (Jun 1996): 140–151.
10. Ibid.
11. Ibid.
12. Oscar Newman, CIAM '59 in Otterlo (Stuttgart: Karl Krämer, 1961), 184–185.
13. Amamiya Ryohei et al., World Design Conference 1960 in Tokyo (Tokyo: Bijutsu shuppansha, 1960), 181.
14. Ibid., 182.
15. Ibid., 222.
16. Koolhaas and Obrist, Project Japan.
17. Lin, Kenzō Tange and the Metabolist Movement.
18. Ian Abley, "Beyond Little Britain," Architectural Design 76 (2006): 16.
19. Lin, Kenzō Tange and the Metabolist Movement.
20. See the website of Kisho Kurokawa: http://www.kisho.co.jp/

Image Credits

Figure 01: Courtesy of Frances Loeb Library, Harvard University Graduate School of Design.

Figure 02: The Kenzō Tange Archive. The Gift of Mrs. Takako Tange, 2011. Courtesy of Frances Loeb Library, Harvard University Graduate School of Design.

Figures 03–06: Courtesy of Kisho Kurokawa.

Ken Tadashi Oshima, Daniel Ibañez and Nikos Katsikis

Douglas Spencer

Nature Is the Dummy

Circulations of the Metabolic

A critical investigation of contemporary design approaches, projects, and preoccupations under the metabolic paradigm.

Douglas Spencer currently teaches histories and theories of architecture, urbanism, and landscape within the graduate school of the Architectural Association, London. He is also a PhD supervisor at the AA, and at the Royal College of Art and the University of East London. His research and writing on urbanism, architecture, film, and critical theory has been published in journals including Radical Philosophy, The Journal of Architecture, Fulcrum, and AA Files. He has also contributed chapters to a number of collections on urban design, utopian literature, and contemporary architecture. His book, The Architecture of Neoliberalism, is due to be published by Bloomsbury in 2016.

To talk of meaning in design today seems tragically anachronistic. We have, after all, cast off our late-twentieth-century fascination with reflecting upon language, signs, and their interpretation. We are all good Deleuzians now. We don't ask "What does it mean?"; we ask "How does it work?."[01] Arch-architectural Deleuzian Jeffrey Kipnis has told us that now is the "time of matter," not of ideas, a claim rooted in the originary materialism of the universe: "There were no signs, no ideas, no concepts, no meanings, no disembodied spirits, no dematerialized abstractions whatsoever around during the first couple of seconds after the Big Bang, nor during the first million or billion years, or, for that matter, even these days."[02] Lars Spuybroek has proclaimed "meaning" a "horrible word that lets us believe that the mind can trade aesthetics for textual interpretation."[03]

Where continental theory had once drawn architecture into its world of free-floating signifiers, by the early 1990s the discipline had set about establishing its theory and practice on firmer ground. As well as turning to Deleuze and Guattari, with their apparent affirmation of production over meaning, it also took up the solid realities of matter and life, systems theory, and the science of complexity. "Material organizations," "emergence," "self-organization," and "morphogenesis" have since then become the keywords through which matter and life are figured as essentially organizational, processual, and productive phenomena. These capacities have been repeatedly represented within design discourse as the materialist and ontological grounds from which architecture, as well as landscape architecture and urban design, should derive their own operational paradigms to perform effectively, efficiently, and ecologically. Central to all of this has been the figure of "metabolism," a kind of catch-all term employed to describe the productive transformation of matter through its circulation, at all scales, within material, biological, social, and technical systems. Even where this tendency has not been so much a turn to a so-called new materialism as a return to a critically oriented *historical*

materialism, as in the case of urban political ecology, the ontological essence of metabolic processes have been foregrounded as central to its concerns and methods.

If it could be said by Roland Barthes, in 1973, that in matters of textual interpretation "everything signifies ceaselessly and several times"[04], today's organizational agendas demand instead that everything *circulates* ceaselessly and productively. What typically remains unreflected upon, however, are the ways in which the metabolic, and its kindred keywords and concepts, are themselves circulated—discursively, textually, and institutionally, in countless essays, books, course titles, and symposia—and the consequences of all of this in terms of what design does *and* what it means.

Metabolic Imperatives

One consequence of the discursive circulation of the metabolic, and related organizational tropes, has been to dislocate the designer from a position of creative or critical agency. Rather than having the architect as their author, design principles and practices are now authorized and underwritten by the laws of nature themselves. Proponent of "biourbanism" Stefano Serafini, for example, on being asked what distinguishes his teaching from that of conventional architectural schools, replies, "The fundamental difference is: 'The design is out there already.' Follow the force of gravity. Follow people's needs. Creativity is not about a 'genius' who finds great ideas in his head or in books and then fights to impose them on reality. On the contrary, creativity means flowing smoothly with the very structure of what exists… Reality is smarter than you are."[05]

In the essay "Metabolism and Morphology", architect and educator Mike Weinstock laments the fact that metabolism has never been properly integral to the concerns of architectural and urban form-making.[06] He argues, however, that "[i]n the natural world form and metabolism have a very different relationship. There is an intricate choreography of energy and *material* that determines the morphology of living forms, their relations

109

to each other, and which drives the self-organisation of populations and ecological systems".[07] This self-organized and self-organizing relationship between matter and energy to be found in nature should now, Weinstock states, "provide a set of models for what will become the new 'metabolic morphologies' of future buildings, and ultimately of cities".[08] What Weinstock refers to as "the metabolic imperative" is, he writes, "identical in plants and buildings,"[09] and it is through the recognition of such correspondences and their implementation within design, he argues, that the design of architecture and cities will be able to respond effectively to the crisis of global climate change.

In the articulation of positions such as this, the thought and practice of design is subsumed by the overriding logic of metabolic and ecological principles. Architecture and design, overdetermined by both the metabolic imperative and the urgencies of environmental crisis, are relieved of their hubristic dispositions and required to identify with the laws of nature to which their practice must now be equal. In effect, if not intention, such arguments assume an ideological character precisely because they are made to appear grounded in apparently incontestable ontological truths. Such misgivings might appear merely contrarian (particularly in light of the environmental conditions that form the motivational context for research such as Weinstock's), were the apparent nature of material organizations made prescriptive only for the *material* performance of architecture or urban systems. The logics, laws, and lessons to be drawn from metabolism, self-organization, and similar ecological principles have, though, typically been validated as positively applicable to the ways in which design is implicated in matters of the social, cultural, economic, and political.

Soft Futures and Weak Urbanisms

In his conclusion to "Metabolism and Morphology," for instance, Weinstock writes:

> The ecological opportunity that has arisen is part of the growing cultural fascination with fluidity and dynamics, with networks and new topologies, and with soft boundaries between private and public domains, and between interior and exterior space. The experience of being in spaces that flow one into one another, where differentiation between spaces is achieved less by rigid walls than by extended thresholds of graduated topographical and phenomenological character, and in which connectivity and integration are enhanced, is central to contemporary existence.[10]

Here the fluid, interconnective, and boundary-dissolving qualities attributed to metabolic morphologies are positively appraised in terms of their social and experiential performance. Far from unique to Weinstock, there is in fact a widespread tendency, within certain currents of design theory, to ascribe a progressive character to such morphological qualities. These qualities have been held to place architecture and urban design in touch with the realities of a zeitgeist of flexibility, adaptability, and opportunism, or to liberate the social subject from the strictures of spatial categorization and containment, or to answer to both aspirations at the same time, and through the same means.

Zaha Hadid Architects, in projects such as the Kartal Pendik masterplan for Istanbul (2006) and Galaxy Soho complex in Beijing (2009–2012), and with publication titles such as Total Fluidity: Studio Zaha Hadid Projects 2000–2010[11] and Zaha Hadid: Form in Motion[12] have, for example, contrived a virtual fetish of fluid dynamics. Hadid has written of her desire in her work to "organize and express dynamic processes within a spatial and tectonic construct",[13] and that her morphologies "operate via gradients rather than hard edge delineation. They proliferate infinite variations … They are indeterminate and leave room for active interpretation on the part of the inhabitants".[14] Thomas Mical, another advocate of biourbanism, has written of the need for "soft" urban infrastructures derived from a "biological imperative" and capable of "delivering responsive immediacy and re-structuring future malleability" within urban systems.[15] With their advantageous "flexibility and impermanence and mutability" these soft infrastructures will, he adds, operate "as organic generators of organic creative futures."[16] Mical proposes that architecture and urbanism are subsumed, within this schema, to "components of soft naturalizing systems" forming an "infrastructure-territory".[17] It is crucial, he continues, gesturing toward the social and economic valences of his proposal, that "the flexibility of soft infrastructures as organic design principles be conceptually grounded in a culture of innovation-risk".[18]

Similar calls for the adoption of the networked, the flexible, and the fluid have been central to landscape urbanism, both at its inception and in its subsequent development. Indeed the idea that the urban has in recent years been transformed, from a form composed of static architectural objects into a "field" of processes, networks, mobility, and infrastructural connectivity constitutes something like a founding myth for landscape urbanism. In his essay "Field Conditions,"[19] Stan Allen—a figure significant to the development of landscape urbanism before subsequently distancing himself—located the emergence of what he identified as a generalized shift from "object to field" in the postwar period. Allen defined this "field condition" as one of "loosely bound aggregates characterized by porosity and local interconnectivity...bottom-up phenomena, defined not by overarching geometrical schemas but by intricate local connections."[20] The use of these concepts in design, which Allen recommended, would place it, he argued, "in contact with the real."[21] Alex Wall, in an essay equally significant to the theoretical development of landscape urbanism, "Programming the Urban Surface,"[22] wrote that with contemporary urbanization, "infrastructures and flows of material have become more significant than static political and spatial boundaries...The emphasis shifts here from *forms* of urban space to *processes* of urbanization."[23] Consequently, he continues, we are now experiencing "a fundamental paradigm shift from viewing cities in formal terms to looking at them in dynamic ways. Hence, familiar urban typologies of *square, park, district*, and so on are of less use or significance than are the infrastructures, network flows, ambiguous spaces, and other polymorphous conditions that constitute the contemporary metropolis."[24] "The function of design," he continued, pursuing this line of argument to its seemingly logical conclusion, "is not only to make cities attractive, but also to make them more adaptive, more fluid, more capable of accommodating changing demands and unforeseen circumstances."[25]

The paradigms of fluidity, interconnectivity, and process promoted by figures such as Allen and Wall are echoed within the model of "weak urbanism" formulated by Andrea Branzi.[26] Describing "weakness" (derived from the thought of the philosopher Gianni Vattimo), he writes that "it does not imply ... any negative value of inefficiency or inability; this indicates rather a particular process of modification and cognition that follows natural logic, not geometrical logic diffuse, diluted processes, reversible and self-stabilizing strategies."[27] The ductile, reversible, and fluid qualities of "weak urbanism" are further elaborated through his adoption of the sociologist Zygmunt Bauman's concept of a "Liquid Modernity" that, for Branzi, indicates "the idea of a state of material that does not possess its own form ... and tends to follow a temporal flow of transformations."[28] In an essay titled "Fuzzy Thinking," he has also argued that the complexity of nature revealed by recent developments in mathematics presents an "evolved model to imitate in the process of building the new," and that this will constitute a "new naturalism."[29] Branzi's prescriptions for the future

of design are akin to those of the other figures considered here (themselves representative of a far more widespread tendency in design thinking): architecture and urban design will become progressive, or at least adequate to contemporary social realities, by turning to the principles of metabolism, complexity, self-organization, and emergence imputed to the realities of nature. The turn to these principles, furthermore, also happily coincides with the demand that design respond to conditions of environmental crisis.

Forced Exposure

What remains obscure, even obscured, in all of this is the question of how and under what conditions this seemingly fortuitous coincidence of natural and social paradigms has been produced, or even that this coincidence has been *produced*, rather than having spontaneously emerged in the natural course of things. In lieu of anything approaching a comprehensive response to such concerns, it will have to suffice here to gesture to the importance of formations and intersections of scientific knowledge, ecological thought, cybernetics, and neoliberal economics in the mid-twentieth century, and to the existing analyses of certain elements of these phenomena.[30]

Operaist and *Post-Operaist* currents of radical Italian thought provide ample analysis of how, in what interests, and with what effects social imperatives toward flexibility, networking, and adaptability operate. For thinkers in this tradition, such as Maurizio Lazzarato, Paulo Virno, and Antonio Negri, these conditions characterize life within post-Fordism. Under the new modes of labor and production in which post-Fordism is invested, communication assumes ever-greater significance as a source of value to capital. Communication becomes central to the production, organization, development, and delivery of the products of the service, leisure, and creative industries, as well as providing the means to integrate the intellectual and affective competences of the worker within the new managerial practices of more traditional industries.[31] What this development has suggested to the thinkers of Post-Operaism is that rather than seeking to discipline and confine subjects within specific roles and places, capital now aims to mobilize and connect them. Within this new organizational paradigm subjects are compelled to acquire competences in communicational and affective performance, networking abilities, and a disposition toward flexibility and adaptability in respect of when, where, and how they work. These traits constitute the requisite survival skills with which subjects must be equipped, and are to be exercised at any and every opportunity throughout the social "field."

Douglas Spencer

Architects and designers are implicated in these pro-cesses where they provide the spatial complement of an organizational model where divisions between, work, leisure, domesticity, and education are to be productively blurred as a means to economically valorize the communicational capacities of the subject.[32] Exemplified in the now ubiquitous "hubs" of universities, the "break-out" spaces of the office, or the new "malls without walls," the creation of spaces in which one is simultaneously at work and at play, where one is all at once networking, learning, and consuming, and the absence of the physical demarcations through which these activities were once separated serves to mobilize subjects as flexible, adaptable, and opportunistically motivated. This has been presented as a progressive and liberatory development within architecture, and effectively advertised as such through the elegantly organic, porous, and smoothly transitioning morphologies it has adopted. This can be seen, for instance, in SANAA's EPFL Rolex Learning Center in Lausanne, in Reiser + Umemoto's competition entry for the Kaohsiung Port Terminal in Taiwan, or in Zaha Hadid's Galaxy Soho complex in Beijing. These new spatial formulations of experience, however, render the subject immediately exposed to the demands and motivations of continuous conditions of contact, mobility, and performance as the more or less inescapable terms under which everyday life must now be lived. When the boundaries between private and public, and between interior and exterior, are softened and blurred in this way, the possibility of experiencing privacy and interiority, of a time and space apart from the labor of working upon oneself as an entrepreneurial project, becomes scarce.

So long as all of this is naturalized, however—whether implicitly, through morphological means, or explicitly, as in the case, for instance, of the green cloaking device deployed by AZPML in their envelope design for a power plant in Wedel, Germany, or the clichéd camouflage of the green roof—it remains difficult to contest. Combined with the circulation of a discourse in which the metabolic, the emergent, and the self-organizing are presented as the natural grounds authorizing and directing the practice of design, it would seem even irresponsibly unnatural to do so. It appears that nature—its laws, its organizational processes, and its productive efficiencies—is simply spoken through the medium of designers and their work. It is in fact, though, nature that is the dummy in this ventriloquist act. It is nature that is made to speak of efficiency, productivity, and organization, and in the service of other agents, interests, and agendas.

The Work of the Concept

Only by recognizing the human actants for what they are in this performance are we in any position to reflect on the kind of ideological work being done when nature is made to speak in this way. Only by raising the metabolic, and its cognate organizational paradigms, to the level of the concept can these emerge from their materialist underpinnings as subject to critical reflection, as *ideas* as well as a "material organizations," as forms through which *meaning*, as well as matter, are processed. It is not at all a question of denying or opposing the metabolic, but of engaging it in something like the "labor of the concept" and the "labor of conceptualization," the "*arbeit des begriffs*" to which Theodor Adorno and Max Horkheimer called attention in their <u>Dialectic of Enlightenment</u>.[33] As Steven Helmling has written, Adorno and Horkheimer's term—a "Hegelian chestnut"—"suggests both the work that concepts do, and the labor that making ourselves conscious of the problematics of the concept … imposes upon us."[34] In the thought of Adorno, continues Helmling, "the concept evokes (à la Hegel) the mind's engagement at once with the world *and* with its own self-consciousness in this engagement; for Adorno this self-consciousness of thought, this 'labor of the concept', is an imperative from first to last."[35]

This kind of critical self-consciousness regarding the work of concepts in design is rare, but not without precedent. Eva Castro and Alfredo Ramirez, of the practice Groundlab, for example, write in their essay "Thickening the Ground"[36] that the "'new' urban discourse advocating extreme connectivity, flexibility and adaptability, and capable of catering to the indeterminacy of programmes" is one "that happily complies with the overall uncertainties of the free market."[37] Statements such as this suggest a refusal on the part of the designer to identify absolutely with current organizational paradigms, and, in the process, the capacity to exercise their own discursive and political agency rather than concealing this within the "laws of nature."

A recent essay by Jane Hutton represents a significant attempt to understand the circulation of matter in the construction of landscapes in social, political, and ecological terms.[38] "Designers participate," she argues, "in [a] monumental shifting, reorganization and recycling of materials around the globe, the great majority of which is bound as urban parks, buildings and highways. These accumulated urban stocks produce at once ecological (the material exchanges produced through construction), economic (the trade made possible through infrastructural networks) and social (the discourse enabled through the public commons) conditions in situ".[39] "This reality," she continues, "is abstracted and concealed through the commodity form and is an overlooked, yet critical consideration for the discipline of landscape architecture today."[40] It might be added that this reality is also often concealed through the very morphologies through which designers imbue constructed landscapes with the appearance of organic and biomorphic elegance. The key point here, though, is that Hutton is working on the concepts of circulation and metabolic exchange to elucidate a critical position, as opposed to identifying these concepts as natural laws that legislate for practices built in their image.

Aside from a few, rather isolated examples of such perspectives as these, design thinking has not been greatly interested in the kind of work that metabolism, or indeed flexibility, interconnectivity, or fluidity, does as a *concept*. If metabolic and circulatory processes are presented as ontologically grounded in a reality that comes *before* thought, and to which we have immediate access, then the ways in which the concept of metabolism mediates between thought and material existence will tend to pass unnoticed. The work of the concept, in other words, will tend to happen behind our backs. In the process the agency of the designer will remain captured by metabolic and other organizational, processual, and productive imperatives.

Notes

01. Gilles Deleuze and Felix Guattari, <u>Anti-Oedipus: Capitalism and Schizophrenia</u>, trans. Robert Hurley, Mark Seem and Helen R. Lane (Minneapolis: University of Minnesota Press, 1983), 109.
02. Jeffrey Kipnis, "On the Wild Side," in <u>Phylogenesis: FOA's Ark</u>, ed. Farshid Moussavi, Alejandro Zaera-Polo, and Sanford Kwinter (Barcelona: Actar, 2004) 571.
03. Lars Spuybroek, <u>The Sympathy of Things: Ruskin and the Ecology of Design</u> (Rotterdam: V2_Publishing, 2004), 264.
04. Roland Barthes, <u>S/Z</u>, trans. R. Miller (Oxford: Blackwell, 1990), 12.
05. Stefano Serafini interviewed by Nicola Linza and Cristoffer Neljesjö, <u>Manner of Man Magazine</u> (2012), accessed 12 February 2014, http://mannerofman.blogspot.co.uk/2012/11/mm-interview-with-stefano-serafini.html.
06. Michael Weinstock, "Metabolism and Morphology," in "Versatility and Vicissitude," special issue, <u>Architectural Design</u> 78 (Mar/Apr 2008): 26–33.
07. Ibid., 27.
08. Ibid.
09. Ibid., 30.
10. Ibid., 32-33.
11. Patrik Schumacher and Zaha Hadid, <u>Total Fluidity: Studio Zaha Hadid Projects 2000–2010</u> (Berlin: Springer-Verlag, 2011).
12. Patrik Schumacher and Kathryn B. Hiesinger, <u>Zaha Hadid: Form in Motion</u> (New Haven: Yale University Press, 2012).
13. Zaha Hadid, Pritzker Acceptance Speech (2004), accessed 22 April 2009, http://www.pritzkerprize.com/laureates/2004/_downloads/2004_Acceptance_Speech.pdf.
14. Patrik Schumacher, <u>Digital Hadid: Landscapes in Motion</u> (Basel: Birkhäuser, 2003), 28.
15. Thomas Mical, "Soft Infrastructures for a Neo-Metabolism," <u>Journal of Biourbanism</u> 2 (2012): 64.
16. Ibid.
17. Ibid., 63.
18. Ibid., 65.
19. Stan Allen, "Field Conditions," in <u>Points + Lines</u> (New York: Princeton Architectural Press, 1999).
20. Ibid., 92.
21. Ibid.
22. Alex Wall, "Programming the Urban Surface," in <u>Recovering Landscape: Essays in Contemporary Landscape Architecture</u>, ed. James Corner (New York: Princeton Architectural Press, 1999).
23. Ibid., 234.
24. Ibid.
25. Ibid., 246.
26. Andrea Branzi, <u>Weak and Diffuse Modernity: The World of Projects at the Beginning of the Twenty-first Century</u>, (Milan: Skira, 2006).
27. Ibid., 14.
28. Ibid., 20.
29. Ibid., 29.
30. Philip Mirowski, <u>Machine Dreams: Economics Becomes a Cyborg Science</u> (Cambridge: Cambridge University Press, 2002); Philip Mirowski, <u>Never Let a Serious Crisis Go to Waste: How Neoliberalism Survived the Financial Meltdown</u> (London: Verso, 2013); Isabelle Stengers, <u>Power and Invention: Situating Science</u>, trans. Paul Bains (Minneapolis: University of Minnesota Press, 1997); Katherine N. Hayles, <u>How We Became Posthuman: Virtual Bodies in Cybernetics, Literature, and Informatics</u> (Chicago: University of Chicago Press, 1999); Bruce Caldwell, <u>Hayek's Challenge: An Intellectual Biography of F.A. Hayek</u> (Chicago: University of Chicago Press, 2004).
31. Douglas Spencer, "Replicant Urbanism: The Architecture of Hadid's Central Building at BMW, Leipzig," <u>Journal of Architecture</u> 15, no. 2, (2010): 181–207.
32. Ibid. and Douglas Spencer, "Architectural Deleuzism: Neoliberal Space, Control, and the 'Univer-City,'" <u>Radical Philosophy</u> 168, (Jul/Aug 2011): 9–21.
33. Max Horkheimer and Theodor Adorno, <u>Dialectic of Enlightenment</u>, trans. John Cumming (London: Verso, 1979), xiv.
34. Steven Helmling, <u>Adorno's Poetics of Critique</u> (London: Continuum, 2009), 19.
35. Ibid.
36. Eva Castro and Alfredo Ramirez, "Thickening the Ground," in <u>Design Innovation for the Built Environment: Research by Design and the Renovation of Practices</u>, ed. Michael Hensel (London: Routledge, 2011).
37. Ibid., 208–209.
38. Jane Hutton, "Reciprocal Landscapes: Material Portraits in New York City and Elsewhere," <u>Journal of Landscape Architecture</u> 8, no. 1 (2013): 40–47.
39. Ibid., 40.
40. Ibid.

Douglas Spencer

Felipe Correa and Tomás Folch

Resource Extraction Urbanism

and the Post-Oil Landscape of Venezuela

Felipe Correa is a New York-based architect and urbanist. He is Associate Professor and Director of the Urban Design Degree Program at the Harvard University Graduate School of Design. At Harvard he also directs the South America Project, a transcontinental applied research network that endorses the role of design within rapidly transforming geographies. Correa edited the book A Line in the Andes (ARD, 2013), which explores the transformative role of the first metro line currently being built in Quito, Ecuador. He is currently working on a second book titled Beyond the City: Resource Extraction Urbanism in South America (ARD Press, forthcoming 2014). Correa is also the cofounder of Somatic Collaborative, an award-winning research-based design practice.

Foregrounding challenges for design in the restructuring of crucial but often neglected territorial links in the greater hinterlands of metabolic processes.

Tomás Folch is a Chilean architect and landscape architect. He is a Professor at the Design Lab at the Universidad Adolfo Ibanez in Chile. Through his years of professional experience, his work has ranged through urban renovation, heritage, urban infrastructure, social housing, and landscape architecture. His studies and research focus on landscapes of extraction, going beyond reclamation to incorporate ecological processes and environmental externalities as values for the equation of production. His professional work has been recognized and presented in the Chilean Biennale of Architecture 2008, the Shanghai Exposition 2010, and the Venice Biennale 2010, among others.

The rapid urbanization of regions outside of consolidated metropolitan areas is a ubiquitous global condition. Within this context, the South American hinterland is experiencing processes of extreme rapid urbanization tied to the extraction of natural resources that are drastically altering the physical and experiential identity of traditionally remote locations. Although the scale and speed of this transformation is unprecedented, the relationship between urbanization and extraction has a long history that has positioned the city as a critical staging ground for a productive hinterland. From colonial Jesuit missions in present-day Paraguay to Belo Horizonte—a nineteenth-century planned city built as the new capital of gold and iron ore in the state of Minas Gerais in Brazil—to oil cities of the postwar era in Venezuela, the urban project has established crucial links between the city and the larger metabolic processes of resource extraction in open territories.

Of the many territorial inscriptions of resource extraction within twentieth-century South America, the effects of oil within the nation-state of Venezuela are among the most extreme. The discovery of large quantities of crude in the early 1920s, followed by its rapid global commercialization, gave way to the largest cultural, economic, social, and territorial reorganization in the country's history. Although oil exploitation by national enterprises dates back to the turn of the twentieth century, it is the discovery of the Barroso #2 Well in 1922, near Cabimas, that marks the beginning of this global export industry. Parallel to the discovery of the well, the Venezuelan government granted three large-scale international extraction contracts. Standard Oil, with its two subsidiaries Lago Oil and Creole Petroleum; Gulf Oil, with its subsidiary Mene Grande; and Royal Dutch Shell Oil Company became the three most influential private actors in the construction of Venezuela's oil landscape. The revenue from oil generated a new type of wealth, bringing vast structural changes. Traditional affluence, generally represented by large land holdings and artisanal agricultural production, was rapidly

superseded by new oil-driven investment centers, where land ownership was no longer the key to prosperity. These new hubs, which relied on international commercial networks, required basic urban services, promoting the rapid development of cities and prompting a radical shift from a predominantly rural society to an oil boom town. The story of two planned cities—Ciudad Guayana in the Venezuelan south and El Tablazo, proposed for the eastern edge of Lake Maracaibo— highlights the attempt of economic diversification through urbanization in Venezuela's immediate post-oil-boom landscape. The experience of these two cities underscores the critical agency of design in the context of new urbanization frontiers.

This drastic shift from agriculture to a newly emerging urban culture had three significant impacts on the territorial development of Venezuela. The first was the sweeping migration from the hinterlands to existing and newly formed cities, primarily along the northern half of the country. From 1920 to 1940, the urban population in Venezuela increased from 200,000 to more than 4 million. By the early 1960s, the country had a population of 8 million, of which more than 50 percent lived in cities—most with approximately 100,000 inhabitants.[01] The second impact was the vast disparity between rich and poor caused by the oil and hydrocarbon industry. Despite the vast public and private investment that resulted from the oil boom, crude proved to be a profitable business only to the foreign companies allowed to extract in the region and to the various governments that granted the concessions. Only a small percentage of the broader Venezuelan society benefited from this enterprise. Crude as an industry generated minimal increases in the overall labor force, helping accentuate an unfortunate layer of urban poverty in the very cities it helped to create. And third, the hydrocarbon industry created a deep socioeconomic divide between northern and southern Venezuela. By the 1950s, a territorial band that covered the western border of Colombia all the way to Barcelona and Puerto La Cruz was characterized as a national corridor with pockets of extreme wealth, where

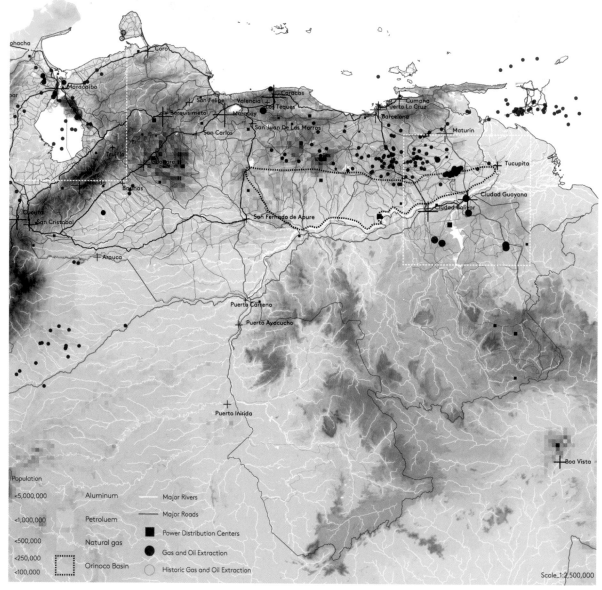

Figure 01. Map of Venezuela showing the country's oil landscapes, 2014.

Population

<5,000,000	Aluminum	Major Rivers
<1,000,000	Petroluem	Major Roads
<500,000	Natural gas	■ Power Distribution Centers
<250,000		● Gas and Oil Extraction
<100,000	Orinoco Basin	○ Historic Gas and Oil Extraction

Scale_1:2,500,000

newly finished highways tied Caracas, the nation's capital and its main economic hub, to the affluence of oil around Lake Maracaibo and the new manufacturing wealth emerging in the city of Valencia.[02]

These three conditions raised concern within the Venezuelan government, as the disparity between those affiliated with oil and those who were not reached an unprecedented peak. On one hand, oil corporations—following early twentieth-century paternalistic company-town models from North America and Europe—had created a significant number of company camps that provided a general image of progress, one that was experienced only by those on the companies' payrolls. On the other hand, the pull factor caused by the oil

industry had created secondary and informal economies that were rapidly metabolizing the mostly rural areas around oil fields and company camps. As a response to these pressing urbanization issues, in the late 1950s the government of Venezuela sponsored the conceptualization, design, and partial implementation of two key growth-pole projects. One was Ciudad Guayana, a major metallurgic industrial town at the confluence of the Orinoco and Caroní Rivers, intended to activate the mostly dormant economy of southern Venezuela. The second—smaller in size and ambition—was El Tablazo, revolved around a new large-scale petrochemical plant. Conceived as industrial cities that would expand national manufacturing, both plans proposed to diversify the oil-centric economy through the pairing of a physical and an economic plan.

The Guayana Region of Southern Venezuela and the Establishment of the Corporation

Guayana, the largest region in the country, accounted for less than 3 percent of its population in the early 1950s.[03] Located 500 miles south of Caracas, the region was known for its poor agricultural soil and had remained far off the radar of public and private investment. For centuries, the limited local population had survived through subsistence farming and cattle ranching, facing serious food shortages on a regular basis. Yet the fate of this remote region was soon to change when the national government saw in the south a plentiful supply of natural resources that could specifically help advance the national manufacturing agenda. Although not fertile, the landscape was extremely rich in mineral deposits. Iron ore, a key resource to advance Venezuela's emerging steel production, was abundant in the region. Gold, natural gas, and oil had also been found in smaller quantities. In addition, the strong water flow from the Orinoco and Caroní Rivers made the rivers ideal sites for hydroelectric infrastructure. Finally, the deep thalweg of the Orinoco required minimum dredging, making it ideal for fluvial access to the Atlantic Ocean. The confluence of the two rivers marked the center of a 200-mile radius that defined a new growth pole for Venezuela, and at the very center, Ciudad Guayana was to be established as a new industrial city that would serve as the staging ground for the exploitation of this mineral-rich territory.

The Corporación Venezolana de Guayana (CVG) was founded on December 29, 1960, as a decentralized, state-owned Venezuelan conglomerate under the direct supervision of President Rómulo Betancourt. The corporation was tasked with overseeing the comprehensive development of the Guayana Region. Heavily influenced by the American economist John Friedmann's concept of center versus periphery, Guayana was conceived as a new growth pole for the Venezuelan south. Under this mandate, the corporation established a new tripartite strategy. One critical component involved the advancement of the already present metallurgy industry in the region. Another key element was the development of hydroelectric energy along the Caroní River, exemplified by the Guri Dam, constructed starting in 1963 and expanded in the 1970s. Finally, the third aspect involved studies for the potential draining of, and flood prevention strategies along, the Amaruco Delta, to create new agricultural land. These three lines of action, paired with a strong governmental interest in advancing human capital in the region, would set

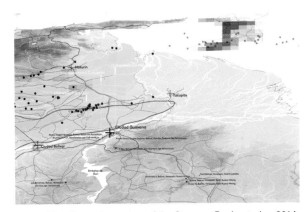

Figure 02. General overview of the Guayana Region today, 2014.

forth an unprecedented scale of development at the confluence of the two rivers and throughout the region The CVG's general scope and scale has been frequently compared to that of the Tennessee Valley Authority (TVA) and its economic development plan for its region—a signal reference in growth-pole experiments in the Americas—but the Guayana project differed t in multiple ways. The TVA focused on the reactivation of an economically depressed region planned mostly by local, state, and regional agencies, whereas the CVG initiative was conceived as a large-scale governmental project sited in Guayana yet designed in Caracas, and was seen as an enterprise of national magnitude. Furthermore, urbanization within the Tennessee Valley region was conceptualized as a more dispersed set of settlements that facilitated the gradual transformation of a productive landscape. Opposite this, Guayana proposed a much more centralized urban project, for it had to provide a range of basic services for the fast-paced migration that new productivity in the region was attracting. More important, it had to serve as a symbol of the arrival of modernity and progress south of the Orinoco.

The City as Center

The conception and establishment of the city played a central role within the larger Guayana project. Early in the project's timetable, the corporation, under the direction of General Rafael Alfonso Ravard, had designated 60,000 acres along the southern bank of the Orinoco for the construction of a new urban hub. Coincidentally, in 1959, while Ravard was still a colonel and before he officially became president of the CVG, he met Lloyd Rodwin, an urban planner and professor at the Massachusetts Institute of Technology (MIT), while Ravard was in Caracas on a consulting assignment with the Direccion de Urbanismo de Venezuela.[04] Following the initial

Felipe Correa and Tomás Folch

118

meeting, Rodwin conducted a reconnaissance trip to the Guayana Region, which led to a multiyear consulting agreement between the Joint Center for Urban Studies of MIT and Harvard University's Graduate School of Design, and the corporation. Rodwin, along with a select number of architects, economists, and urban planners—including Willo von Moltke, Rodwin's counterpart at Harvard, who would lead the urban design component—became the team that would give shape to Ciudad Guayana.

Departing from the mandate of its immediate predecessors, Brasilia and Chandigarh, India—two city-making projects of national magnitude, where the main motivation was to lay out the setting for future administrative bodies—the brief for Ciudad Guayana required a much more flexible and multifaceted approach. The city had to fulfill the desires of the corporation and become the new face of economic and social progress in southern Venezuela. The design

also had to adapt to the immediate demands of an industrial town that was attracting significantregional migration. The site was primarily defined by a plateau 300 feet above sea level that straddled both sides of the Coroní River, flanked by the already established industrial site on the western edge and the historic town of San Félix on the eastern bank. Prior to the CVG's involvement in the 1960s, the area already had multiple settlements that dotted the landscape, which were to be urbanized. These included the town of Puerto Ordaz, a government-sponsored steel mill, and the facilities of the Orinoco Mining Company already operating in the area.

Two chief design references drove the overall strategy for Ciudad Guayana. The first was the linear city that tied clearly zoned nodes through a continuous mobility infrastructure. The second was the development of discrete neighborhood units that would circumscribe the nodes to give them critical mass. The designers

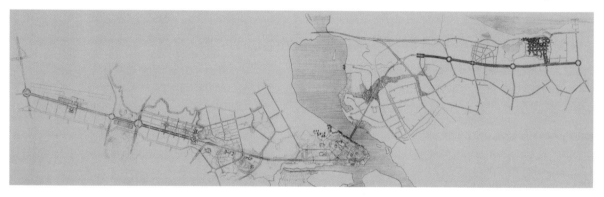

relied heavily, perhaps excessively, on the power of a linear form to give order by linking a series of existing and proposed centralities, which would make up the totality of the city. The spine was given physical dimension in the form of Avenida Guayana, which connected the steel mill on the western edge of the city with the old town of San Félix on the eastern edge, linking industry, the airport, the commercial center, the cultural center, the river, and the medical center as nodes along the way. As Willo von Moltke described, "a basic objective of the plan [was] to connect the city's three major visual units—San Félix, the central valley and the western plateau—along a central spine. The spine, Avenida Guayana, would join all major existing elements into a series of intervisible nodes providing continuity for all the activities and experiences along it."[05]

The relentlessness of the line, paired with the envisioned built mass of each node, aimed at guaranteeing the strong spatial and visual continuity aspired to in the original plan. This was particularly the case in the proposed commercial center, where the avenue transformed into a boulevard that traversed through a grid thickened by built fabric of a monumental scale, all equal in height and similar in massing. The conceptualization of neighborhood units, called *unidades vecinales* and abbreviated as UV in the plan, were also pivotal to the design of Ciudad Guayana. The UV's proposed a variety of housing types, which ranged from residences for the managerial class to self-built housing for workers. These residential units would then become the urban fabric that activated the linear form. The confluence of avenue, centrality, and neighborhood aspired to construct a collection of spreads and densities that would guarantee a vibrant urban environment and a city with a strong image.

From early critiques by Kevin Lynch,who visited the city in 1964including his claim that designers were applying standard planning techniques and extreme formal control in a context that begged for rapid on-the-ground action,—to Lisa Peattie's critique of the failures of the technocracies that planned Guayana, the discrepancies between the design aspirations and the realities encountered in the

Figure 03. General Plan of Ciudad Guayana by the Joint Center for Urban Studies and Wilo Von Moltke, 1964.

Figure 04. Detailed Drawing of Ciudad Guayana's Unidad Vecinal 4, Joint Center for Housing Studies and Wilo Von Moltke, 1964.

Figure 05. Aerial view of Guayana's Civic Center under construction. Corporación Venezolana de Guayana Annual Report, 1965.

implementation of the project have been extensively documented. Incongruent visions between the design team and the corporation, CVG's limited ability to implement and manage design guidelines, and the chasm between the urban aspirations formulated in Caracas and the actualities encountered on site paved the way for a host of critiques about the project throughout the 1960s, 1970s, and 1980s.

Fifty years after its conception, one can revisit the design project for Ciudad Guayana and assess how time has helped the city build on its original concepts and adapt them to the realities of its geography. The city evolved following the overall zoning scheme originally proposed by the Joint Center team. The general guidelines for the disposition of industrial land proved to be quite successful and have effectively accommodated more than 2,000 hectares.[06] Despite the fact that the linear city concept was not executed in its original image, the overscaled main avenue has served as an effective service corridor that anchors multiple urban fragments diverse in scale, quality, and speed of growth.

The Territorial Grid as Driver: El Tablazo in Lake Maracaibo
Throughout the 1960s, the Lake Maracaibo region and western Venezuela witnessed the enactment of new housing and urbanization policies. Two pressing issues guided the transformation. The first was the Venezuelan authorities' attempt to address the disparity in living standards inside and outside the company camps and,

Felipe Correa and Tomás Folch

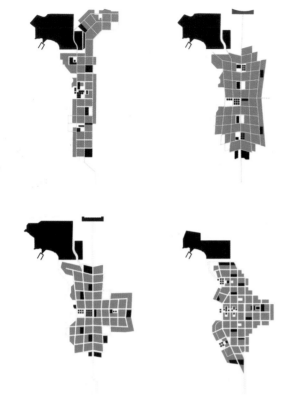

Figure 06. Proposed growth diagrams for El Tablazo. Redrawn from the original plan by Forestier-Walker and Bor.

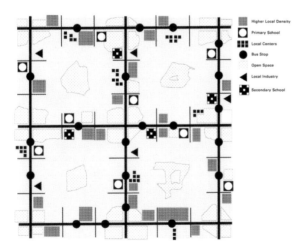

Figure 07. Prototypical block for El Tablazo. Redrawn from the original plan by Forestier-Walker and Bor.

in doing so, make up for the social disparity created by the oil industry. The government argued that the country not only had to improve the quality of the urban landscape outside the camps but it also had to diversify the economy of the region to improve the median income of those not directly affiliated with the oil industry.

In spring 1968, the Venezuelan Ministry of Public Works hired an interdisciplinary team composed of Forestier-Walker and Bor, architects and urban planners, and Nathaniel Lichfield and Associates, economic consultants, to plan a regional growth pole on the eastern edge of Lake Maracaibo, opposite Maracaibo City.[07] This new city, called El Tablazo, revolved around the construction of a petrochemical plant and was one of three new planned cities aimed at diversifying the oil-centric Venezuelan economy. The two other cities were Muy Tuy—a satellite city an hour away from Caracas, designed to alleviate migration from the countryside to Caracas—and Ciudad Guayana. The planning team was tasked with conceptualizing an urban structure that would effectively accommodate growth over time. The plan for El Tablazo had to account for the changing rates of migration to the region, the future performance of the oil industry in international markets, and the overall success of the petrochemical plant. The team was given an initial target population of 25,000 inhabitants— the base population that the petrochemical plant, as a sole industry, was expected to support. It was anticipated that the city would expand to accommodate a population of 350,000 by the end of the millennium.

Forestier-Walker and Bor, who later worked on a nonhierarchical supergrid for the new town of Milton Keynes in England, proposed a similar abstract grid concept for El Tablazo: a maxi-grid based on a 1-square-kilometer agro–urban unit that would accommodate approximately 10,000 people. The units would gradually expand over time, allowing for multiple degrees of design control. The prototypical superblock proposed a higher-density band adjacent to all primary roads. This band, where most of the design control would focus, would accommodate high-density housing and non-residential uses. The soft center of the cell was less planned and allowed for densification through self-built programs. Most urban activities would be placed along the periphery of the superblock, and these would align with the projected bus service along the 1-square-kilometer grid. The interior of the block, more residential and private, would accommodate open spaces for sports and recreation. Select portions of the grid were reserved for future industrial uses that would further diversify the petrochemical business. From a series of aggregation studies, three alternative configurations were drafted for the Ministry of Public works: a linear plan, a gridded plan, and a T-shaped plan. All three strategies connected the petrochemical plant on the northern edge of the city to the small town of Altagracia, about 15 kilometers south of the plant. Finally, the T-shaped plan was recommended as most effective in terms of growth flexibility and mobility efficiency. The selection made sense. This configuration allowed for a greater density along the water's edge, with a gradual decrease in urban growth as the city moved into the hinterland.

Construction on the new town of El Tablazo was expected to start simultaneously with the building of the petrochemical plant. The urban plan, developed in London and Caracas, took approximately ten months to complete. Upon delivery of the final report, the Ministry of Public Works opened a small office in Altagracia. This post was to oversee the development and implementation of the plan over five years. The absence of institutional mechanisms that would guarantee the implementation of the project, however, made its realization impossible from the start. The ministry, representing the national government, was too understaffed to advance a project of this scale. Meanwhile, agencies at a municipal and town level did not have the political clout or administrative know-how to execute the proposed plan. And although the private interests behind the construction of the petrochemical plant pulled enough weight to see the project through, the ambitious plans for the accompanying city slowly lost steam.

A comparative study of Cuidad Guayana and El Tablazo fifty years after their conception allows one to understand the value of the urbanistic project affiliated with resource extraction. In the case of Cuidad Guayana, the concept of the avenue lives up to von Moltke's vision as a spine that links and gives continuity to the loosely sprinkled settlements already present on the site. The project did not become an iconic linear city, but it does serve as a sound example of how a set of organizational principles can give structure to fast-growing, self-built settlements. Although not aesthetically regal, one of Ciudad Guayana's most significant contributions was its capacity to guide the construction of self-built neighborhoods. Conversely, in the case of El Tablazo, the projected 1-square-kilometer grid was replaced by entropic urbanisms that colonized abandoned oil-prospecting strips, creating a unique overlap between

city and extraction infrastructure, where subsurface operations led to urban development. Urban development, in turn, is left to deal with the devastating aftermath of oil extraction and its typical environmental effects, primarily water and soil pollution.

The comparison between these two case studies frames the current panorama of oil extraction in Venezuela and South America at large. The efforts made throughout the immediate postwar era to incorporate a larger territorial agenda in resource extraction vanished in the second half of the twentieth century. The private sector moved away from the company-camp model, and the public sector gave up in the face of implementation difficulties. Today, as large portions of the Brazilian, Ecuadorian, and Peruvian rainforest become the new frontier for oil extraction, it is essential to rethink the agency of design in these contexts—its ability to synthesize the diverse economic, ecological, and urban pressures shaping these terrains to draw together the various bureaucracies that oversee these sites. More than ever, there remains the need for a new resource extraction framework through which layering the delicate surface ecologies and vast subsurface black gold reserves produces a new territorial grammar, where urbanization can once again take center stage.

The material for this essay is based on research conducted by Felipe Correa for the forthcoming book, Beyond the City: Resource Extraction Urbanism in South America (Applied Research + Design, 2014).

Notes
01. John Friedmann, Economic Growth and Urban Structure in Venezuela (Cambridge, MA: Joint Center for Urban Studies, 1963).
02. Miguel Tinker Salas, The Enduring Legacy: Oil, Culture, and Society in Venezuela (Durham, N.C.: Duke University Press, 2009).
03. Anthony H. Penfold, "Ciudad Guayana: Planning a New City in Venezuela," Town Planning Review 36, no. 4 (1966): 225–248.
04. Lloyd Rodwin, Planning Urban Growth and Regional Development: the Experience of the Guayana Program of Venezuela (Cambridge, MA: MIT Press, 1969).
05. Willo von Moltke, "Visual Development of Ciudad Guayana," Connection (1965), 52–60.
06. Maritza Izaguirre, Ciudad Guayana y la estrategia del desarrollo polarizado (Buenos Aires, Argentina: Ediciones Siap-Planteos, 1977).
07. Alan Turner, and Jonathan Smulian, "New Cities in Venezuela," Town Planning Review 42, no. 1 (1971): 3–27.

Image Credits
Figures 01–02, 06–07: Drawings by Felipe Correa, John Frey.

Figures 03–04: Courtesy of the Willo von Moltke Collection, Harvard University.

Figure 05: Courtesy of Harvard University.

Felipe Correa and Tomás Folch

**Rahul Mehrotra and
Felipe Vera**

Ephemeral Urbanism

Learning from Pop-up Cities

Rahul Mehrotra is a practicing architect and educator. He works in Mumbai and teaches at the Graduate School of Design at Harvard University, where he is Professor of Urban Design and Planning, and Chair of the Department of Urban Planning and Design as well as a member of the steering committee of Harvard's South Asia Initiative. His practice, RMA Architects (RMAarchitects.com), founded in 1990, has executed a range of projects across India. Mehrotra has written and lectured extensively on architecture, conservation, and urban planning. He has written, co-authored, and edited a vast repertoire of books on Mumbai, its urban history, its historic buildings, public spaces, and planning processes.

Attempting a first classification of the material, spatial, and physical properties of temporal forms of urbanization and exploring the role of design in shaping ephemeral conditions of inhabitation.

Felipe Vera is a Chilean architect and urbanist. His research and design work focuses on advancing the understanding of urban ecologies and social patterns in emerging landscapes. Felipe is Instructor in Urban Planning and Design at the Harvard Graduate School of Design, and a Research Associate for the Sustainable Future for Exuma project. He is also Professor at the Design Lab of Universidad Adolfo Ibañez in Chile. He holds a Masters in Real Estate Development from Universidad de Chile and a Master in Design Studies with a concentration in Urbanism, Landscape, Ecology from the Harvard GSD. His awards include the Fulbright Fellowship, Becas Chile, ITEC Fellowship, and the Mario Recordón and Jaime Bendersky awards.

Cities with Dates of Expiration

The scale and pace of contemporary urbanization challenges the notion of permanence as a basic condition of cities. Ephemeral landscapes of pop-up settlements are constantly increasing in scale and confronting the notion of "The City" as a stable and permanent entity. In response to this condition, there are emerging discussions about how the discourse on urbanism would benefit by dissolving the binary division of ephemeral versus stable components in cities. For in reality, when cities are analyzed over large temporal spans, ephemerality emerges as an important condition in the life cycle of every built environment. Peter Bishop and Lesley Williams recently asked: Given overwhelming evidence that cities are a complex overlay of buildings and activities that are, in one way or another, temporary, why have urbanists been so focused on permanence?[01] Taking this argument further, other, more radical authors such as Giorgio Agamben argue that it is fundamental to "recognize the structure of the camp in all its metamorphoses,"[02] not only because of the need of a major emphasis on the temporal dimension of cities but actually because "today it is not the city but rather the camp" that is "the fundamental biopolitical paradigm of the west."[03] It is in this context that the exploration of temporal landscapes opens a potent avenue for research by questioning the illusion of permanence that surrounds cities and offering opportunities to extract lessons and trigger discussions about both apparently permanent and explicitly impermanent configurations within the urban condition.

The growing attention that environmental and ecological issues have garnered in urban discourses, articulated through the anxiety surrounding the recent emergence of landscape as a model for urbanism, are making evident that we need to evolve more nuanced discussions for the city—discussions that overcome the limited representation of it. As Richard Sennett's image of "the open city" suggests, cities should be seen as more than just the complex aggregation of discrete static objects. They are, among other things, the result of overlapping social and material flows that generate open metabolic processes, which operate and transform at different rates. In contemporary urbanism around the world, it is becoming clearer that for cities to be sustainable, they need to resemble and facilitate active fluxes in motion rather than static material configurations. To embrace this condition, we must shift our gaze from problems of space alone to those that factor in time, allowing more complex and nuanced readings to be deployed and new conditions to be included as part of the repertoire that surrounds discussions about urbanism more generally.

Consequently, thinking of a gradient from more permanent toward more ephemeral configurations, we focus on the impermanent end of the spectrum, bringing into the discussion cases of cities or urban conditions that are explicitly ephemeral, allowing us to observe extreme conditions of temporary space occupation grounded in the territory. In this context, however, the distinction between permanent and ephemeral is not a binary, referring to what remains versus what vanishes. Instead activates a broader concept of permanence in its meaning of what is more stable, static, and persistent in relation what is impermanent, but also of what is in the constant process of internal transformation, renewal, and reinvention, allowing for greater levels of instability. This approach then embraces a longer temporal scale from the effervescent forces of growth to tendencies of shrinkage, depopulation, and reabsorption.

Toward a Taxonomy of Ephemeral Cities

To expand the terrain of study and learn from temporary cities, the first challenge is how to organize an increasingly growing archipelago of heterogeneous cases. A useful organizing strategy could focus on the fact that temporary cities, unlike more permanent ones that have a range of elements that simultaneously support their continuity, are usually structured around

123

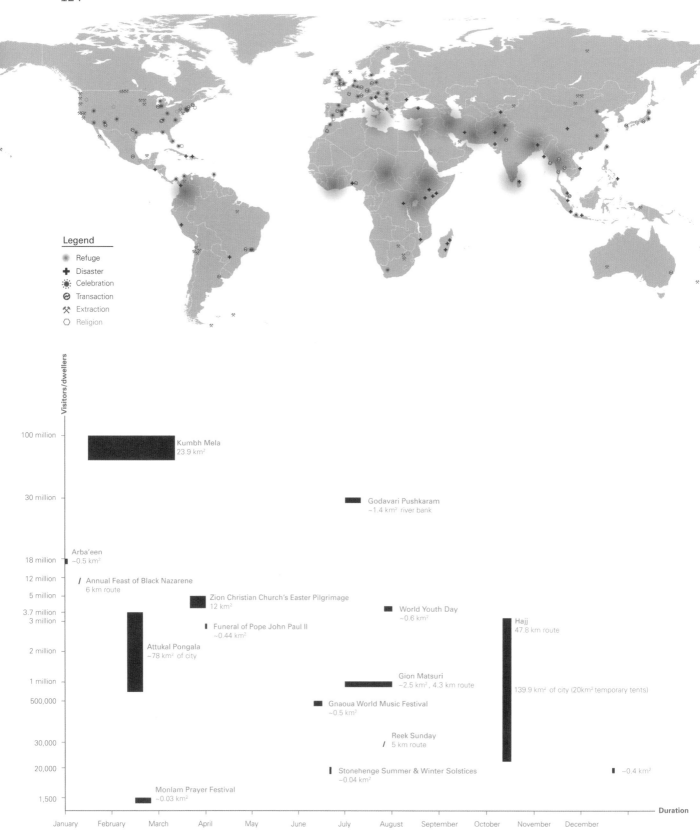

Legend

- Refuge
- Disaster
- Celebration
- Transaction
- Extraction
- Religion

Visitors/dwellers

100 million — Kumbh Mela
23.9 km²

30 million — Godavari Pushkaram
~1.4 km² river bank

18 million — Arba'een
~0.5 km²

12 million — Annual Feast of Black Nazarene
6 km route

5 million — Zion Christian Church's Easter Pilgrimage
12 km²

3.7 million — World Youth Day
~0.6 km²

3 million — Funeral of Pope John Paul II
~0.44 km²

Hajj
47.8 km route

2 million — Attukal Pongala
~78 km² of city

1 million — Gion Matsuri
~2.5 km², 4.3 km route

139.9 km² of city (20km² temporary tents)

500,000 — Gnaoua World Music Festival
~0.5 km²

30,000 — Reek Sunday
5 km route

20,000 — Stonehenge Summer & Winter Solstices
~0.04 km²
~0.4 km²

1,500 — Monlam Prayer Festival
~0.03 km²

Duration

January February March April May June July August September October November December one main purpose. This operates as a central force that not only defines their dimensions and complexity but also determines essential characteristics such as the life cycle of the settlement, its material composition, and the place it occupies in the cultural memory of the society in which it occurs. Following that argument, it is possible to categorize ephemeral cities in clusters of cases configured in diverse taxonomies fused by their commonality of temporality. Inside every group of cases we would find similarities such as time spans of deployment processes, supportive institutional structures, and morphological geometries, among several other possible shared attributes.

In recent years, for instance, there has been an extraordinary intensification of pilgrimage practices, which has translated into the need of larger and more frequently constructed structures for hosting massive gatherings.[04] Extreme examples of temporary religious cities are ephemeral constructions set up for the Hajj, as well as a series of temporary cities constructed in India for hosting celebrations such as the Durga Puja, Ganesh Chaturthi, and Kumbh Mela—the last a religious pilgrimage that, according to official figures, supports the congregation of more than 100 million people. These events are an expression of a range of ephemeral configurations deployed to accommodate gatherings that celebrate religious beliefs.

Natural disasters and changes in climatic conditions are increasingly making evident the importance of temporary shelters as holding strategies or short-term solutions, such as the recent cases of the Philippines, Haiti, Chile, and several others instances of temporary cities built in the context of disaster. Additionally, in many locations political tensions contribute to the displacement of people from their sites of origin, creating refugee camps around the globe. Extreme examples of humanitarian space for hosting the stateless and asylum seekers are the refugee camps located in the Cote d'Ivoire, which accommodate more then 900,000 refugees coming largely from Liberia but also from other adjacent locations. The most striking cases, however, are those of Dabaad in northeastern Kenya, which has been in existence for two decades and presently

Figure 01. Geographical distribution of ephemeral cities and their taxonomies.

Figure 02. Classification of ephemeral cities according to their demography and duration.

accommodates 500,000 people. The Breidjing camps in Chad, home to 200,000 people, as well as several camps in Sri Lanka that house 300,000 people displaced in the decade-long civil war, are further examples of this response. Surprisingly, these camps only hold a small fraction of the 45 million people that according to the United Nations High Commissioner for Refugees are currently displaced around the world and living in temporary accommodations.

Nonreligious cultural celebrations are also on the rise. Increasing in scale as well as frequency, they too cause the erection of temporary structures within and outside of urban areas. Extensive music festivals like Exit in Serbia, Coachella in California, and Sziget in Budapest also motivate the construction of extended ephemeral settlements that for short periods of time congregate large groups of people. They range from relatively small gatherings, like Burning Man in Nevada or Fuji Rock in Japan in which around 40,000 people congregate to enjoy music and celebratory events, to 350,000 people who gather for musical events such as Glastonbury in England, Roskilde Festival in Denmark, and Werchter in Belgium.

These examples could be expanded to include a range of cases such as temporal cities built for the exploitation of natural resources in mining, oil extraction, and forestry. The scope of extractive activities like the ones at play in the Yanacocha mine in Peru, with more than 10,000 temporal dwellers, the Maritsa Iztok Mines in Bulgaria, the Motru Coal Mine in Romania, and Chuquicamata, Salvador, and Pelambres sites in the north of Chile generate completely different sorts of temporary settlement, adding to the complexity of dealing with environmental consequences and incredibly large-scale operations that constantly modify the topography of a temporary landscape at a territorial scale. In these cases, the life cycle of temporary cities aligns with the duration of the extractive activity and the presence of the resource, so that most of these settlements have a known or predictable date of expiration.

These varied places add to a long list that enriches the diversity of taxonomies for temporary cities. The list could be further expanded to include, for instance, cities built for military or defense purposes in contested territories, pop-up cities that often are set up for transactions within and outside of city boundaries, temporary structures that support massive influxes

Rahul Mehrotra and Felipe Vera

NG06—Grounding Metabolism

of people around sporting events, or even the recent disruptive constructions inside formal settlements, such as the camps of the Occupy movement.

These varied taxonomies could be useful ways to organize cases that are differentiated through variables such as length, size, metabolism, level of risk they generate, patterns of spatial use, morphologies and complexity of their grids, technology, implementation logics, etc. They respond to particular conditions and contexts while sharing the certainty—or at least the promise—of a date of expiration. Thus they challenge us to develop tools for intervening and thinking about nonpermanent configurations as a legitimate and productive category within the discourse on urbanism. In fact, they represent an entire surrogate urban ecology that grows and disappears on an often extremely tight temporal scale. When temporal urban landscapes are seen as the expression of a distinctive form of urbanism, a potentially productive dialogue is established between ephemeral settlements as diverse as refugee camps and temporal urbanization that hosts massive celebrations.

The Case of the Kumbh Mela: Preliminary Observations

By analyzing some of these cases in depth, it is possible to extract useful lessons that are potentially transferable from one case to another. But more important, these lessons could expand the discussion about urbanism more generally. With this intention, the Harvard Urban India Project at the Harvard Graduate School of Design was structured as an interdisciplinary research project across five other schools at the University, under the umbrella of the South Asia Institute.[05] The project chose to focus on one extreme case of an ephemeral settlement that belongs to the category of the religious temporary city. The research, entitled Kumbh Mela: Mapping the Ephemeral City, challenged us to develop a methodology of analysis for discerning the patterns and logic that surround the making of these temporary settlements.

The Kumbh Mela is a Hindu religious festival held every twelve years at the conjunction of the rivers Ganges and Yamuna in the city of Allahabad, creating an extreme example of a religious congregation that

Figure 03.   One of the eighteen pontoon bridges that are deployed for the Kumbh Mela of 2013.

Rahul Mehrotra and Felipe Vera

128

generates a temporary settlement.. Approximately 5 million people gather for fifty-five days, and an additional flux of 10–20 million people who come for twenty-four-hour cycles on the six main bathing dates. The biggest public gathering in the world, it deploys a pop-up megacity of roads, bridges, shelter, as well as a plethora of social infrastructures such as temporary hospitals, markets, police stations, and social centers—all replicating the functions of a permanent city. Issues of social inclusion, urban diversity, and even expressions of democracy arise under the framework of neutralizing grids of roads that differ in structure, module, and geometry. The aggregation of units converge in an endless texture of textiles, plastic, plywood, and several other materials organized by a smart infrastructural grid that articulates roads, electricity, and waste. As a fecund example in elastic urban planning, it has much to teach us about planning and design, flow management, elements that support the accelerated urban metabolism, and deployment of infrastructure, but also about cultural identity, adjustment, and elasticity in temporary urban conditions.

One of the important aspects of this case is related to the flexibility of the institutional framework and the mechanisms of implementation that supports the Kumbh and the creation of the ephemeral megacity. Institutions that have agency for facilitating urban processes take time to form, and once they are created tend not to be malleable or flexible structures. In the case of the Kumbh, however, a temporary governance system plugs into a preexisting urban management system at the state level and draws its expertise from existing institutions—often pulling together, for just twelve months, the best administrators in the state. Over time the governance system gets more dynamic, reaching a climax when the Kumbh administration meets on the ground each evening during the festival in a framework that connects every level of the hierarchical administrative structure. This gives the administrator for the event the capacity to react to any unpredicted incident or requirement of the city quickly and effectively. In guiding a city that experiences enormous stress in receiving a vast population in increments over many short cycles of time, the administrators operate with the utmost elasticity in planning and management. Among strategies that the research has identified so far for handling such

fluctuating levels of intensity, some seem essential in providing the city with the required degree of robustness and avoiding univocal solutions.

One strategy for building resilience is a consistent tendency toward redundancy instead of optimization in making decisions about the quantity, dimensions, and organization of key infrastructural elements. Examples of this are the seventeen pontoon bridges that span the river, as artifacts that allow the grid to operate effectively under conditions of extreme flux. The distribution of risk among subcomponents of the infrastructural mesh is also found in the way in which spatial substructures are organized inside the settlement. Similar to how Le Corbusier's plan of Chandigarh organizes space in discrete subunits, the Kumbh Mela subdivides the space in basic operative areas defined by the grid. Complexities relative to the vast size are resolved by dividing the city, administratively and functionally, into self-organizing cells denominated as camps. These form a network that supports the functioning of the city in a way that avoids systemic collapse in situations of crisis.

How the floodplain is subdivided and the area of the river appropriated takes us to another important lesson. Unlike some of the other grids we see in temporary cities, which by the repetition of a constant module revoke singularity and identity, the basic grain of the Kumbh is not the repetition of a unique tent but the definition of a bigger open area, "the camp," which is given to religious communities without preconceived internal regulation. This grant's authority to each community for organizing the space in the form that most accurately expresses their internal structure and identity advocates for the emergence of spatial singularity. Walking within the settlement, one can see various spatial organizations: ones that are more spontaneously and incrementally arranged while others are more systematically structured, following more rigid grids. This is how the grid's neutralizing potential to facilitate democratic self-expression is employed in the planning strategies deployed at the Kumbh.

Figure 04. Plan of the city constructed in the floodplain of the Ganges of and the Yamuna for hosting the Kumbh Mela of 2013.

NG06—Grounding Metabolism

The grid not only organizes the residential space but also structures diverse layers of infrastructure such as water, electricity, sewerage, and infrastructure for mobility such as roads and bridges, which are articulated more as relational fluxes than as collections of superimposed elements. While usually the word infrastructure bring to mind heavy constructions that can support the continuity of processes that happen over time, at the Kumbh smart processes of incremental aggregation reach the scale of the interventions by presenting very soft infrastructure. The roads, for instance, instead of being paved are constructed from steel plates that can be carried by local people without heavy machinery. The unspecific and adjustable technology used for connecting pieces of infrastructure grants them the possibility of being reintroduced in the regional economies of construction once the festival is over. Given the ease with which this infrastructure can be dismantled, there is a prompt and effective recycling of the material used to construct the temporary city. Elements that are not reused are usually made of re-absorbable material such as thatch or bamboo, which get incorporated in the site or merged with the natural terrain through organic decomposition. This naturally allows the seamless reprogramming of the space into agricultural fields.

As an extreme case of ephemeral urbanism, the Kumbh demystifies and presents a distilled narrative surrounding the deployment of a city in time. Issues that are negotiated in this form of ephemeral urbanism are as diverse as memory, geography, infrastructure, sanitation, public health, governance, and ecology. These parameters unfold their projective potential, offering alternatives not only for rethinking cases within the boundaries of an ephemeral urbanism but also for embedding softer yet perhaps more robust systems in more permanent cities. This case exposes a sharp condition of how light, indeterminate, and unspecific instruments also empower agents and could be useful tools in the generation of robustness, allowing a highly complex process to flow easily.

Andrea Branzi advises us on how to think of cities of the future. He suggests that we need to learn to implement reversibility, avoiding rigid solutions and definitive decisions. He also suggested approaches that allow space to be adjusted and reprogrammed with new activities not foreseen and not necessarily planned. The idea of ephemeral urbanism acknowledges the need to reexamine permanent solutions as the only mode for the formulation of urban imaginaries. Instead, it posits new protocols that are constantly reformulated, readapted, and reprojected in an iterative search for a temporary equilibrium that reacts to a permanent state of crisis. These cases strongly inform this assertion of the simultaneous validity of both temporal and permanent urbanism in various dimensions, which questions permanence and stability as default conditions. But more important, these cases help us recognize the potential of these discussions to be productive in constructing a new imaginary for the creation of urban environments in the future.

Notes

01. Peter Bishop and Lesley Williams, The Temporary City (New York: Routledge, 2010), 10.
02. Giorgio Agamben, "The Camp as Nomos," in Homo Sacer: Sovereign Power and Bare Life, trans. Daniel Heller-Roazen (Stanford: Stanford University Press, 1998), 176.
03. Ibid., 181.
04. Diana Eck, India: A Sacred Geography (New York: Harmony, 2013).
05. People from the GSD who have contributed to the project: Oscar Malaspina, Vineet Dwardkar, Alykhan Mohamed, James Whitten, Felipe Vera, Aneesha Dharwadker, Alex Chen, Michael Lee, Johannes Staudt, Benjamin Scheerbarth, and Jose Mayoral.

Image Credits

Figure 01: Based on work by Chong Ying Pai, Jose Mayoral, Lucas Pauer, Aja Jeanty, Ana Victoria Chiari, Melanie Wanamunno, Qinqin Wu, Victor Rico Espinola, Martha Pym, Irene Figueroa Ortiz, Jaewoo Chon, Akhiro Moriya, Duncan Corrigal, and Carly Gertler (Harvard GSD) and Denise Cheng (MIT).

Figure 02: Based on work by Chong Ying Pai (Harvard GSD) and Denise Cheng (MIT).

Figures 03–05: Courtesy of Felipe Vera (Harvard GSD), Allahabad 2013.

Figure 05.   Constructions that accommodate different programs form the Kumbh. Residential tents, dining rooms, and gathering spaces of religious orders and others add a high level of formal diversity and programmatic specificity to the landscape of the Kumbh Mela.

Rahul Mehrotra and Felipe Vera

Paola Viganò

Territorialism I

Investigating the social and metabolic aspects of territoriality by revisiting seminal historical approaches and contemporary design research.

Paola Viganò is an architect and Professor in Urbanism at Università IUAV of Venice and at the EPFL (Lausanne). She is also a guest professor at several schools of architecture (including KU Leuven, Aarhus, and Harvard GSD. In 2013 she received the French Grand Prix de l'Urbanisme et de l'Art Urbain. In 1990 she founded Studio with Bernardo Secchi, realizing among other projects the Park Spoornoord and Theaterplein in Antwerp, the public spaces in Mechelen and in La Courrouze, Rennes, and the cemetery in Courtrai. In 2009 and 2012 Studio worked on the "Greater Paris" project and "New Moscow." In 2011–2012 Studio developed a vision for Brussels 2040. It is today part of the Atelier International du Grand Paris.

Territory, Territorialism:
Questions on Contemporary Urban Space

Territorialism is the appropriation of a certain territory by a species or group that defines its own territory and limits its movements within a precise area. Processes of inclusion and exclusion are connected to the idea of territorialism, as are boundaries and defensive strategies. Reflecting on territorialism for urban and landscape designers means considering the notion of territory at a high conceptual level and, in parallel, well grounded in a situated reality. What we perceive as a territory, or as our territory, is above all a mental construction inside which abstract and concrete appropriations meet the material nature of the site.

"Territorialism" is not an easy title for a design studio. My intention was to work on the megalopolis of the eastern part of the United States, in an effort to avoid the traditional opposition between metropolitanist and regionalist[01] that has strongly polarized the American debate since the 1920s. The term "region," with its need of homogeneity (natural, economical) is not attractive. Territory is a complex and polysemic term; different interpretations produce heterogeneous descriptions and representations that reveal diverse perspectives. Territorialism is a true act of biopolitics. As an investigative tool, it is a way to grasp the spatial dimensions of metabolic processes: through flows and energy cycles, it reveals and delimits space.

If the territory is an artifact, a principle of organization with social origins and characters, it is not a pure supporter of any given political and institutional forms. The relation between territory and power cannot be excessively simplified. The territory is a collection of particular places and positions; it is a resource, where goods, services, and values are produced.[02] The territory is a palimpsest,[03] not only a layered construction but a process of selective accumulation; it is a space of appropriation, an individual and collective construct and imagery.

In this short contribution I will use a series of situated design experiences within the frame of Territorialism I[04] to put forth general themes about the megalopolis and the contemporary urban condition. We have consciously left aside the more generic megalopolitan condition: the middle ground, a source of alternative values,[05] of "provincialism" and "counterrevolutionary ideology." The philosophy of the "middle state" between the savage and the refined[06] has asserted the idea that human intervention and the process of artificialization of the country have even ameliorated and reinforced natural processes. But the "middle ground" is a guest in this story, a shadow in the room. By observing the fractures and the voids opening up in the megalopolis, the insistence has been on the problems of residual areas, on the spatialization of social, ethnic, and racial differences. They have been an effort to understand the specific "spatial framework for unequal development"[07] rooted in neoclassical economics of growth, where inequality is more efficient than equality.

Two books have been fundamental in formulating the approach: The New Exploration and Megalopolis.[08] I will return to MacKaye and Gottmann, recontextualizing their work to utilize it as a research tool within the North American context. I will conclude with reference to territorialism and territoriality as design devices.

Concepts and Tools
Gazes

These studio reflections have been fostered by a strict and struggling examination of two books, The New Exploration and Megalopolis, whose gazes and positions have been assumed as inevitable references. Along with direct confrontation, the interpretations and scenarios produced comment on them, opening up a sedimentation process from which I would like to select some non-exhaustive but stirring points.

Gaze 1: The New Exploration

The context of The New Exploration is described by Lewis Mumford in his introduction to the 1962 edition. Perhaps even greater than the strong involvement of Benton MacKaye in the Regional Planning Association is the influence of some the authors and professors he encountered, such as William Morris Davis,[09] which I would like to emphasize. Davis developed the morphogenetic theory that introduced the study of the earth's landforms. It is thus important to understand MacKaye through the influence of geomorphology and Davis's theory of landform creation and erosion (the "geomorphic cycle"). This theory proposes the idea that mountains and landforms go through lifecycles, making Aldo Leopold's radical idea of "Thinking Like a Mountain" not so radical.[10]

Davis's amazing representations of the evolution of valleys, plains, and mountains through sections, bird's-eye views, and change over time, all represented in one drawing, connect three levels of reflection on a single surface—the comprehensive understanding of the bird's-eye view, the analytical cut of the section, and the evolution hypothesis in the representation of the process. Davis's images remain a fundamental lesson in environmental thinking.

Nathaniel Southgate Shaler, another influential geologist at Harvard, introduced the hypothesis that modern civilization depends not less but more on the environment: from the savage that had to learn to be a geologist to survive (think of Elysée Reclus, who referred to the farmer as a geologist, the "paysan géologue"),[11] right up to the "dependence of our Modern States upon the conditions of the earth."[12] Shaler also connects the dependence on geography and environment to the globalization of relations among different countries, leading to the dependence of the local on global environmental conditions. This hypothesis also clarifies why today environmental concerns are so central.

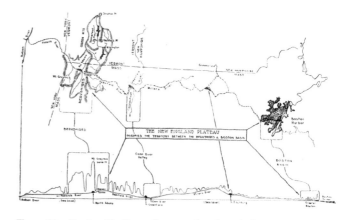

Figure 01. Benton MacKaye. Cross section through the Appalachians as part of the Atlantic Border Empire.

The beautiful dioramas that retrace the evolution of the landscape through three centuries at the Harvard Forest express the impressive transformation of a land, New England, from forest to agriculture, rapidly returning to forest when the frontier crossed over the Appalachian ridge.[13] As MacKaye comments, "Measured in terms of yearly growth, the most 'fertile' forest region in the temperate zones appears to be the Eastern United States, the nucleus of which consists of the Appalachian mountain area." Authors such as Thoreau ("living be thy sport") and Leopold are quoted in the book as defining MacKaye's philosophical and ethical line of thought.

Gaze 2: Megalopolis

While The New Exploration proposes an explicit design strategy, Megalopolis, a book by a geographer, is not offered as a project. My interpretation is that not only was Gottmann fascinated by the object of his study; he developed his research on the idea of megalopolis as an "implicit project"[14] also in terms of the reorganization of metabolic processes in a new spatial condition, inside of which different relations among resources and settlements were being defined.

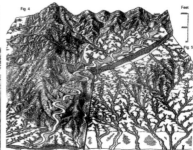

Figure 02. William Morris Davis, representations of landforms.

Gottmann refers to the inability of the flourishing studies on hierarchical systems to describe the formation of the megalopolis and its nebulous structure.[15] Since then the same misunderstanding has happened repeatedly, also in the interpretation of the European territory of dispersion. Apart from the classical image of the "main street of the nation," in Gottmann's words the megalopolis is "a cradle of a new order in the organization of inhabited space, a laboratory of urban growth,"[16] a space "at the threshold of a new way of life,"[17] "beyond urban and rural and a multipurpose concept of land use."[18] Gottmann clearly states the ambition of a re-foundation, both of the geographical gaze and of the idea of city: "Novus ordo seculorum?"

This question still engages many of us. In my personal research and design experience, the "horizontal metropolis" is a central concern. It is both an image and a concept to which I have devoted considerable thought during design work in Belgium and Flanders over the last twenty years.[19] It synthesizes an understanding and interpretation of that diffuse urban condition. It is also a project for a metropolis that establishes both nonhierarchical relationships between its different parts and osmotic relationships between built and open space, between mobility infrastructure and dwelling places. This is also the core of the "project of isotropy" research we are leading on the diffuse city of the Veneto region. In this type of urban space we have developed no-car scenarios and decentralized energy production, working with the fully inhabited and productive landscape.

The megalopolis anticipates many of these themes[20] and also the inherent threats, starting with the poor fertility of the soil of the megalopolis, as part of the urban resource mix, or with the insistence on the need to coordinate water resources: "Half a century ago we began to conserve our forests and other natural resources. It is high time that we begin to conserve our urban resources. They are not unlimited."[21]

Concepts
The idea of the city as a resource, like a mountain, river, or forest, is strongly embedded in American culture.[22] The perception of its limits is even stronger today than in Gottmann-Von Eckert's time. This suggests a new reflection on the lifecycle concept, on the embodied energy related to the process of accumulation and stratification typical of any urban environment, on the processes of inclusion and exclusion that traditionally follow or generate the beginning or end of

lifecycles. This is why "territorialism" is a concept that introduces in the field of urban and territorial design an alternative understanding of sociometabolic processes and investigates their spatial manifestation.

The shift I propose is "that the process of accumulation which is typical of urbanized territories (from overhead capital to social capital) can be 'renewable' under certain conditions and that this approach deserves specific investigation and design tools."[23] Recycling the spatial capital goes beyond brownfield recovery to all brown-, gray-, and greenfields. The redefinition of territories is by then an obvious consequence.

There are different ways to work on embodied energy. The first is to use the calculation of the (fossil) energy embodied in each material. A second way, more coherent to the urban field investigation, is to reconstruct the long history of territorial construction and its different rationalization processes, and evaluate the "immense deposit of labor" (per Carlo Cattaneo about the Po plain), considering not only the materials but also the human labor deposited there.

Figure 03. Jean Gottmann's illustration of the Megaloplitan water supply system. Map indicating various hydrological relations within the urbanized territory.

Paola Viganò

We have tried to read the main lifecycles (for example, the wood/agriculture/wood cycles in New England, with soil fertility as starting point); we have reconnected hydrology to water power, dams, canals, railways, and textile production, and reconsidered what is left over. We have questioned how each process has defined different social borders, for example, in the reading of the relations among geology, cranberry bogs, and new suburbs in the old south of Boston. The special tradition of renewal policies in North America, with a vast literature of both appreciation and harsh critique, makes this reflection particularly interesting here, as does the ongoing revision of the American renewal experience that authors such as Lizabeth Cohen are undertaking.[24]

Voids of the Megalopolis

Let us take a cross-section of New England from mountain crest to ocean port: from the Berkshires to Boston harbor, along the Hoosac Tunnel Route of the Boston and Maine Railroad.[25]

The research followed two east-west and north-south sections of the Boston metropolitan area, extending to the Berkshires. It focused on the disconnections and enclaves inside the homogeneous ground described by MacKaye in The New Exploration and by Gottmann in Megalopolis. Some of the important transformations affecting the social landscape, together with the economic and natural ones, sharply defined territories that have been highlighted and reimagined.

Places of Evil

Lawrence, Andover, and Methuen, with their common history of immigration, political contestation, and waterworks, and similar geological and geographical features, have made for rich battlegrounds. The theme of a concluded lifecycle, that of the mill town and the important remains thereof in terms of embodied energy and immigrant flows, has guided the interpretation.

Former nodes today constitute only weak satellites instead of being networked horizontally to their own territory. In this way the transformation of warehouses into middle-class "lofts," separated by the existing poorer housing stock, is part of a new suburbanization flow, but does not tangibly modify the situation.

The scenarios elaborated for this megalopolitan "void" broaches two important points. The first is the exceptional character of the former industrial city. The idea of making this exception the basis of future redevelopment relies on the autonomous architectural nature of the built structure. But it is ambiguous, because it reinforces the already strong isolation of the complex. At the same time it restores the mill town to the middle ground with the status of a campus: a well-defined territory and a classical figure of the American city.

The second scenario emphasizes the role of space in the representation of inherited memories and their reconstruction inside the idea of modest and incrementally assembled new commons. "Embracing new commons" means a new appropriation of natural and historical features, including the contemporary Latino culture that dominates Lawrence today. It touches a delicate topic: the relation between spatial interventions, collective memory, and territories.

Servant as Destiny: Future Environmental Stories and Present Spatial Injustice

The case of Chelsea is paradigmatic. It is Boston's polluted backyard. We are in the presence not of an empty node but of a hub of established spatial and environmental injustice that involves up to 42,000 inhabitants of the Boston area. The Mystic River and Chelsea Creek are the most polluted harbors in Massachusetts; diesel units are partly responsible for high nitrogen dioxide level; salt piles pollute the air; highly explosive materials including jet fuel are located close to living areas. Noise pollution, barriers of all types, waste and wasted spaces, immense impermeable surfaces, poor green areas, and weak public transport connections have been mapped through a patient exercise that has generated a representation of spatial and environmental injustice.

This terrifying map brings forth two contrasting scenarios. In the first, environmental history supports a radical shift in the urban and natural landscape in anticipation of the closing of the harbor in Chelsea due to climate change and rising sea level. It proposes the refoundation of its territorial qualities. The second imposes a "civic" perspective. The megalopolis, the giant machine that digests the flows arriving from inland and the sea, has produced several Chelseas, places that in the Benthamian perspective work for the greater good, even though they produce harm for the few people who live within their boundaries. There is something inevitable in the servant role and in the utilitarian justification of its existence. But the environmental, economic, and social/political cost of maintaining the situation rises with the sea level. In both scenarios edges and borders are the space inside which to mitigate and reformulate the conflicts, revealing the sublime side of Chelsea.

Liminal and Fringe Opportunities

The idea of nature has shaped the megalopolis more forcibly than any other megalopolitan context. The increasing fragmentation of open spaces, the conflicts about which strategies to adopt for better water management, the tensions between governmental and nongovernmental agencies, the construction of racial and social borders using natural features—all of this makes nature a non-simple investigation. The "streams and levees" idea of MacKaye for guiding Massachusetts's urban growth and sprawl has been rapidly dismantled and probably not entirely understood.

If we consider liminal and fringe conditions not only through topology but also as provisional and ever-shifting characters connected to economic, social, and natural dynamics, then the process of resource exploitation, degradation, reconstruction, or substitution can be investigated through the concept of lifecycle. In the cranberry bogs area in Boston's southern metropolitan region, the consumption of territorial conditions goes on behind the gentle and idyllic image of traditional agriculture. To valorize and engage self-management, a deep understanding of both site features and dynamics is required: of the subterranean hydrologic and sedimentary geologic infrastructure; of the sand and gravel extraction that modifies the topography of the region; of the population boom, mainly of elderly people. The agropolitan idea proposed by John Friedmann for the Asian context comes back as a resilient approach to development.

Voids of Megalopolis: Reversing the Gaze

If for MacKaye the crest line of the Appalachian system was the new frontier, the traditional marginality of places such as the Berkshires is still a fact. The first research question is the definition of the Berkshire territory itself: a result of plural imageries—local, metropolitan, megalopolitan—and of multiple physical layers. The matrix of the Berkshire landscape may evolve radically in the near future (see the emerald ash borer infestation), and this generates

the need to redefine this marginal region altogether. The ambiguity of landscape conservation is tackled in relation to its capacity to face dynamics and conflicts.

The scenarios make explicit the challenges of the actual environmental and economic transition: today it is still possible to evaluate the advantages of either remaining aside (valorizing the territorial asset, toward autosufficiency) or of a strong functional project that reconnects the Berkshires to the main flows in the megalopolis. In this second case an important investment in infrastructure is still necessary, and railway lines can be the main means of intervention. In both scenarios, strategic places emerge, along the rivers or on the crest line. Megalopolis is rich in marginal areas, which counter, by their very existence, orthodox territorial development theory.

Figure 04. Lawrence–Andover area of study. The map corresponds to an area of study of the Lawrence–Andover territory. The area selected in the drawing has the same measurements as the area that Frank Lloyd Wright used for studying Broadacre City in the model done in the 1930s. Two important things might be noted in the drawing: first, the division between Lawrence and the adjacent territory caused by I-495 (the white thick line); second, the difference in the tissues between the two areas. From the dense urban grid of Lawrence, this territory dissolves into a suburban landscape, formed by curved roads and cul-de-sacs, between forests and lakes. Both nature and urbanization serve to create a theatrical pastoral landscape, but also establish the limits and barriers of this territory as defined by private property.

Paola Viganò

138

Figure 05. Metabolic matrix: tooling thresholds.

NG06—Grounding Metabolism

Conclusions

Territorialism is a design tool with which to read situations where geographies of variable positions, individual and collective practices, and flows define territories. It aims to recognize the unique, the self, both in natural and social processes, as in Walt Whitman's Leaves of Grass. The lens of territorialism and territoriality highlights the formidable agents that constantly shape the environment in function of habits, social and cultural values, and ideals. Scenarios work along the same idea of revelation,[26] localizing this ambition in future time and space. What connects the two epistemologies is the concept of possibility, through which to integrate individual and social expectations: a lighter and deterministic-free idea that things might be different and that design imagination counts.

Notes

01. Robert Fishman, ed., The American Planning Tradition: Culture and Policy (Washington, D.C.: Woodrow Wilson Center Press, 2000).
02. Fred Hirsch, The Social Limits to Growth (London: Routledge & Kegan Paul, 1977).
03. André Corboz, "Le territoire comme palimpseste," in Diogène, no. 121 (1983).
04. Paola Viganò with Lauren Abrahams, option studio Territorialism, Harvard University Graduate School of Design, fall semester 2012.
05. John L. Thomas, "Holding the Middle Ground," in The American Planning Tradition, ed. Fishman, 38.
06. Thomas Bender, Toward an Urban Vision: Ideas and Institutions in Nineteenth Century America (Baltimore and London: John Hopkins University Press, 1982; first edition 1975, University Press of Kentucky). The author refers to the concept of "middle landscape," proposed by Leo Marx, which "was supposed to be the nursery of good citizens," 7.
07. John Friedmann and Clyde Weaver, Territory and Function: The Evolution of Regional Planning (London: Edward Arnold, 1979), 89.
08. Benton MacKaye, The New Exploration (Urbana: University of Illinois Press, 1962; original 1928); Joan Gottmann, Megalopolis (Twentieth Century Fund, 1961).
09. William Morris Davis' Geographical Essays (Boston: Ginn, 1902). Together with Nathaniel Southgate Shaler, Aspects of the Earth (1889) or George Perkins Marsh's Nature and Man (1864), these investigations are part of rising environmental concern.
10. Aldo Leopold, "Thinking Like a Mountain," in A Sand County Almanac 138 (1949).
11. Elysée Reclus in his essay "De l'action humaine sur la géographie physique. L'homme et la nature," in Du sentiment de la nature dans les sociétés modernes (Charenton: Editions Premières Pierres, 2002).
12. Nathaniel Southgate Shaler, Nature and Man in America (New York: Charles Scribner's Sons, 1891), 149.
13. See Philip Stott, ed., special issue, Journal of Biogeography 29 (Oct/Nov 2002).
14. Giuseppe De Matteis, Progetto implicito. Il contributo della geografia umana alle scienze del territorio (Milan: Franco Angeli Edizioni, 1995).
15. Gottmann, Megalopolis, 736. The reading of the polarized development and its failure is also in Friedmann and Weaver, Territory and Function.
16. Gottmann, Megalopolis, 9.
17. Ibid.,16.
18. Ibid., 250.
19. See Bernardo Secchi and Paola Viganò, "Bruxelles et ses territoires, Plan Régional de Développement Durable: Elaboration d'une vision territoriale métropolitaine à l'horizon 2040 pour Bruxelles, first report"; see also Paola Viganò, "The Horizontal Metropolis and Gloeden's Diagrams: Two Parallel Stories," OASE, no. 89 (2012).
20. Terry McGee includes in his famous 1991 essay "The Emergence of Desakota Regions in Asia: Expanding a Hypothesis" the words of Gottmann referring to the symbiosis of urban and rural in megalopolis—an aspect that, Gottmann writes, "will probably be repeated in slightly different but not too dissimilar versions in many other regions of the rapidly urbanizing world." Megalopolis, 257. Gottmann grew up in Europe and knew well its most diffused areas.
21. Wolf Von Eckerdt, The Challenge of Megalopolis: A Graphic Presentation of the Urbanized Northeastern Seaboard of the United States, A Twentieth Century Fund Report (1964), 63.
22. See Jennifer S. Light, The Nature of Cities (Baltimore: John Hopkins University Press, 2009).
23. Paola Viganò "Elements for a Theory of the City as Renewable Resource: Life Cycles, Embodied Energy, Inclusion. A Design and Research Program," in Recycling City, Lifecycles, Embodied Energy, Inclusion, ed. Lorenzo Fabian, Emanuel Giannotti and Paola Viganò (Pordenone: Giavedoni Editore, 2012).
24. Lizabeth Cohen, "Place, People, and Power: City Building in Postwar America" (inaugural lecture as Dean of the Radcliffe Institute for Advanced Study, Harvard University, Cambridge, MA, 15 Oct 2012) about her book project, Saving America's Cities: Ed Logue and the Struggle to Renew Urban America in the Suburban Age) revives the time of strong social ambitions, when "urban renewal" was not yet a disqualified expression.
25. Benton MacKaye, "The New Exploration: Charting the Industrial Wilderness," Survey Graphic 54 (1925).
26. MacKaye speaks of planning as revelation, emphasizing the role of the five senses. MacKaye, The New Exploration, 146–148. "The function of planning is to render actual and evident that which is potential and inevident," 148; see also 153.

Image Credits

Figure 01: B. MacKaye, "The New Exploration."

Figure 02: Davis, Geographical Essays.

Figure 03: Gottmann, Megalopolis.

Figure 04: Pedro Bermudez.

Figures 05: Alexander Arroyo and Michael Luegering.

Paola Viganò

Rania Ghosn and
El Hadi Jazairy

Hassi Messaoud Oil Urbanism

Rania Ghosn is an Assistant Professor of Architecture at Massachusetts Institute of Technology and partner of Design Earth. Her work critically frames the urban at the intersection of politics, aesthetics, and technological systems. She holds a Doctor of Design degree from Harvard University, a Masters in Geography from University College London, and a Bachelor of Architecture from American University of Beirut. She is a founding editor of New Geographies and editor-in-chief of NG2: Landscapes of Energy. Some of her recent work is published in Thresholds, Bracket, Perspecta, MONU, and JAE. Her current book project, Oil across the Middle East: The Trans-Arabian Pipeline, traces the system of a transnational oil infrastructure to document territorial transformations associated with the region's incorporation into a global fossil-fuel economy.

Uncovering the social and economic complexities and frictions associated with the territorial organization and (re)development of energy landscapes.

El Hadi Jazairy is a licensed architect and partner of Design Earth. He is currently Assistant Professor of Architecture at the University of Michigan. His research investigates spaces of exception as predominant forms of contemporary urbanization. He received a Diplôme d'Architecte from La Cambre, a Master of Architecture from Cornell, and a Doctorate of Design from Harvard. Prior to joining Michigan, he was Lecturer in Architecture at MIT and a Postdoctoral Fellow at Harvard. He is a founding editor of New Geographies and editor-in-chief of NG4: Scales of the Earth. Some of his recent work has been published in the Journal of Cultural Geography, MONU, and JAE.

Metabolism, or the Limits of
an Organicist Analogy

The modern transformation of the city, highly dependent on the mastery of territorial resources, was linked with the representation of cities as consisting of and functioning through complex networks of circulatory systems, the veins and arteries of which extended across the land and were to be freed from all possible sources of blockage.[01] Metabolic analogies have long been operative in conceptualizing the geographic footprint of urbanism. Prompted by discoveries on the vascular system, the "ideology of circulation" drew on physiological analogies, but also mirrored the accelerating mobility conditions of capital, people, resources, and information.[02] By the mid-nineteenth century, architects and planners began to speak of the city and of the territory using the scientific analogies of metabolism and circulation as key to spatial organization. Terms such as "hybrid natures" and "cyborg cities" have contributed to probing the legacies of modernist divisions between human and nonhuman, the social and the material, the city and nature. They convey the imperative for a simultaneous consideration of the production and reproduction of nature and power for "once we begin to speak of people mixing their labor with the earth, we are in a whole world of new relations between people and nature."[03]

Although significant, such concepts remain insufficient to theorize the political relations that underpin the harvesting of the earth's materials and the formation of urban settlements.[04] Donna Haraway reminds us that discourses of biology and organisms have "a plot with a structure and function...fashioned into factual truth, with intentionality in narration."[05] Biological metaphors instrumentalize the image of objectivity of science to ideologically explicit ends, in particular as they naturalize the politics of accumulation and circulation. They favor homeostasis, or a condition of balance of flows, to dismiss blockage, friction, and violence as the necessary corollaries of circulation. The image of objectivity that such scientific analogies perpetuate blurs the boundary between scientific rationalization and social control,[06] between the political economy of circulation and the emergent forms of territorialities. Rather than the annihilation of territory by circulatory networks, territorial organization is necessary to ensure the metabolism of resources.[07]

Resource Territories, Territorial Sovereignties

The exploitation of natural resources is grounded in forms of territories; it is enabled by a large infrastructural system to extract what is deemed "valuable matter" from the earth and by the sovereign's authority to legitimatize rights and demarcate zones of operation. Often operating in peripheral areas—regions that until the deployment of the industry were isolated from central power and unconnected to national and regional networks—the extractive logistics of resources "develop" the frontier by deploying roads, ancillary services, and security posts. Resources are not only spatially produced but also produce new spatial configurations. Resource outposts attract people with their opportunities for labor and other economic mobility; their associated structures of work, housing, and health and social services give a specific material shape to people's lives. The resource system fixates itself in space and, in the process, materializes a territory—simultaneously epistemological and geographical—that harnesses its own geography of places and relations. In this framework, the resource system is a "technical zone," a set of coordinated but widely dispersed regulations, calculative arrangements, infrastructures, and technical procedures that render certain objects or flows governable.[08]

Historically, the management of natural resources has been mediated and enabled through the consolidation of power over nature in the form of the concession, a right granted by a central political authority to extract value. In rentier economies, which derive all or a substantial portion of their national revenues from the rent of resources, the management of resource metabolism is entrusted to the sovereign. The notion of national sovereignty is thus intertwined with the state's control of economic resources embedded in its land, operationalized to govern population and settle and secure the national territory. This is particularly significant for a socialist rentier state where the government relies completely on its oil revenues to cover public expenditures, not least its investment in housing, education, and the military. Far from leading to consensus and cooperation, commodified nature becomes at times an item of contestation inserted into often deeply unequal and unsettled sets of social relations, in which the state holds the monopoly of both violence and resources. Rather than abolishing or transcending the violence necessary for extracting resources, the character of rentier economies thus bestows the role of landlord upon the state. Hence the contradiction between the territory of the resource and that of the sovereign is not abolished but is taken to a higher level as "capital now faces the territory of the nation-state as the external obstacle to be conquered and internalized."[09] The co-production of resources and the social order highlights resource geographies as sites where actors negotiate their political rationalities. From this perspective, territory is understood as a constitutive dimension of production, a tool for government, and a stake of contestation in itself, one that is being reordered by resource economies rather than eroded by metabolic flows. How does the state negotiate the circulators' imperatives of the "least possible friction in space" with the territorial imperatives or promises of resource systems to fix population and settlement in place?

Hassi Messaoud

The history of Hassi Messaoud could be read as a mediation of the relations of resources, population, and security in the sovereign's organization of territory, the contradictions of which are formalized on the extraction site. Hassi Messaoud refers to both Algeria's largest oil field and the township that developed in relation to the hydrocarbon industry in the Sahara desert. Since oil was first discovered in 1956, central authorities have changed the administrative status of Hassi Messaoud, with every generation of urbanism responding to a persisting territorial question: What is the appropriate form of settlement of an industrial site that plays a strategic importance to oil flows and ensures a large part of the national economy?[10] From its establishment by the French colonial administration through the two decades following independence in 1962, Hassi Messaoud was an industrial center managed by oil companies. Following the Algerian government's desire to settle a permanent population in the Sahara, the 1984 administrative zoning changed

the status of Hassi Messaoud from an industrial center to an incorporated town with an elected assembly. Over the following decades, it became the archetype of a dual-town with a series of corporate "*bases vie*" (worker compounds) walled off from other town sections, often literally with bricks and razor wire. In 2004, the town had grown into the perimeter of oil fields and infrastructures representing what the government perceived as a "zone of major risks." The town expansion as well as the desire of multinational corporations to secure their operations in the Sahara constituted the context for a 2004 government decree to relocate Hassi Messaoud away from the existing oil field-town grounds. The action plan froze the issuance of any building permit, public or private, for activities that were not necessary for oil operations. It launched as well the planning and relocation of the population to the New Town of Hassi Messaoud some 70 kilometers away from the existing town.

Although portrayed as a technological or engineering problem, the urban question of Hassi Messaoud is enmeshed in the state's territorial politics. Hassi Messaoud is a space in which resource metabolism and population settlement have come into play, and in doing so they become "contradictions of space."[11] On one hand, the space of resources favors metabolic analogies of circulation and energy flows. In this worldview, the territory is modeled as a network of industrial infrastructures—the oil field, pipeline, refinery—that extracts resources from the Earth, transforming them into commodities that support the national economy. On the other hand, population settlement requires fixity in space. It deploys buildings and land programs by which people attach themselves to the Earth's surface, come to occupy firmly or permanently one place, and establish themselves as residents with political representation. Both projects of state territory aim at reproducing social relations through space; as they project their contradictory interests in a place, however, they become contradictions of space. At moments when population growth is perceived to put the economy at risk of friction or clogs, their moment of density—the town in this case—is diagnosed as a pathological territorial organism that requires excision.

The case study of Hassi Messaoud's oil urbanism asserts territory as the inevitable couple of metabolism. Territory is the form of power over geography that interweaves political processes, material metabolism, and spatial form. The Oxford English Dictionary shows that in the late sixteenth and early seventeenth centuries, "population" referred to "a peopled or inhabited place."[12] The subsequent construction of population as an object of government dissociated population from place in favor of territory as a geographic appellation that ties the governor to the economy and security. It is "a rendering of space as a political category: owned, distributed, mapped, calculated, bordered, and controlled,"[13] and as such is re-formed with every claim over space. "The relation to the earth as property," as Marx claims in *Grundrisse*, is hence "always mediated through occupation of the land and soil, peacefully or violently."[14] In Terror and Territory, Stuart Elden draws on two etymologies of territory: *terra* "piece of earth," a terrain that sustains and nourishes the people, and *terrere,* "to frighten," a place from which people are warned off, closely associated with the maintenance and survival of the state. The linkage between "terror" and "territory," William Connolly insinuates, "is more than merely coincidental… To occupy territory is to receive sustenance and to exercise violence."[15] Territory becomes the object and site for the negotiation of the state's extractive capital and public expenditures.

I. Saharan Industrial Center, 1958–1984

The French conquest of the Sahara in the nineteenth century aimed to secure the empire's geostrategic interests in Africa and pacify internal revolts against colonial rule. The "poor" Sahara, or the Southern Territories, as the region was referred to in relation to the Algerian North, did not represent an economic interest in itself and continued to be portrayed as a "miserable" and "quasi-sterile" space for the first half of the twentieth century.[16] The value of the Sahara shifted radically in the mid-1950s with the beginning of the armed Algerian revolution and the discovery of oil. For French officials, the Sahara represented the utopian optimism for the economic development of the *Métropole* (referring both to the metropolis and the European territory of France). "For the majority of French people, the Sahara and its 4 million km2 represent the last chance for France to remain a major power," noted a French official. "It is the ultimate hope for the Franco-African whole, the panacea of all ills."[17]

The wealth of the hydrocarbon Sahara was predicated on the flow of material and labor into exploration fields and of the extracted resources out to markets. Hence, since the mid-twentieth century, the expansive hydrocarbon territory has been inscribed into circulatory networks. Prior to 1956 the Sahara had virtually no

tarmac roads.[18] So the first major work in 1956 was the construction of 2,000 kilometers of roads and 7,000 kilometers of tracks, funded by regional authorities and the oil companies. Exports soon began first via a combination of a short pipeline and railway to the Mediterranean port of Philippeville (Skikda), to be replaced in December 1959 by a more efficient 400-mile 25-inch pipeline to a new oil terminal at Bougie (Annaba). Oil-producing regions were also connected to the air network through a series of airports: Hassi Messaoud (1957), Ouargla (1960), In Amenas (1962), and Hassi R'Mel (1962).[19]

The revised administrative status of the Sahara established new logistical nodes. Long under military rule, the Southern Territories and its inhabitants were reformed in 1957 into a setup similar to that of the North or the Métropole. In December 1959 and July 1960, two ordinances instituted the "industrial centers" of In Amenas and Hassi Messaoud and assigned their management to the newly established Organisation Commune des Regions Sahariennes (OCRS), whose mission was the "development, economic growth and social advancement of the Saharan areas of the French Republic." Without being elected, the OCRS director held political and economic power over the organization of the territory.

The planning of the new centers posed a set of concerns. With the discovery of natural resources in its early days, the minister of the Sahara attested in 1958, "It is quite difficult to predict the future of these Saharian agglomerations. New explorations can still emerge in different places. The possibilities of expansion of a locality should not be followed up and the problem should be approached differently."[20] The planning studies were conducted to enable the centers to receive a threefold increase in population or operate should growth fall clearly below these numbers. "In other words," he concluded, "the planning projects in the Sahara should be conceived as living programs rather than fixed drawings, so as to anticipate new developments."[21] The corresponding spatial organization was the zoning of the center into sectors, programmatically assigned and with a set population density. The splitting of the oil field by the concession boundaries of the two operating French companies resulted in two camp settlements: the Maison Verte-CPFA in the north (currently known as Base February 24), and the Base Irara in the south. The industrial center had to compensate as well for the absence of agglomerations at short or medium distance and house the services and workers of the oil fields.

Rania Ghosn and El Hadi Jazairy

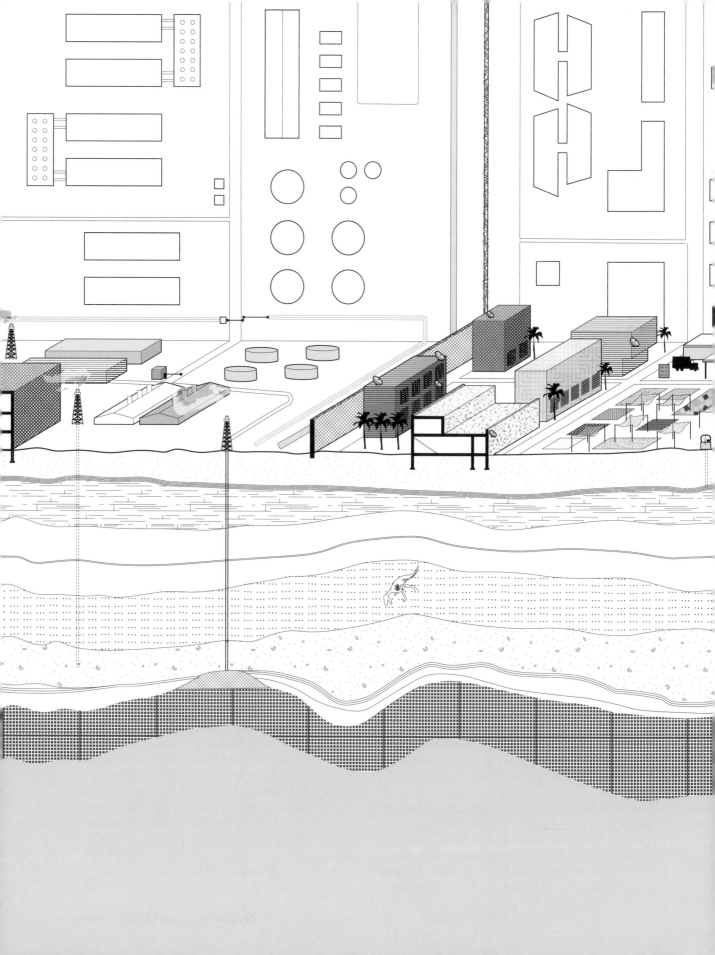

"The Miracle of the Sahara," <u>Time</u> Magazine had reported in 1957, promised to "cure France's chronic foreign-trade deficit."[22] Such a miracle, however, faced the reality check of the Algerian Independence war. Etienne Hirsch, head of the Fourth Republic's economic modernization program, warned that the war against Algerian independence had become a literal roadblock, with France's economic prosperity depending on Algerian roads and labor. "Moslem rebel gangs," <u>Time</u> reported, blocked vital routes to the Mediterranean, an implication that "without peace in Algeria, the Miracle of the Sahara could easily become a mirage."[23]

The long decolonization war led to Algeria gaining its independence from France in 1962. Shortly after that, Sonatrach was established as the national hydrocarbon company. The role of Sonatrach was initially limited to the construction of a third export pipeline, the first Algerian one, from Hassi Messaoud to the Arzew oil terminal on the Mediterranean, and progressively expanded to include all aspects of hydrocarbon exploitation—research, production, transformation, and commercialization—until the nationalization of the oil and gas sector in 1971. The nationalization of the hydrocarbon sector made the industry even more thoroughly bound up with national-level social and territorial agendas.[24] For the sovereign, the company and the hydrocarbon Sahara were the lynchpin of a self-contained heavily industrialized economy.

A series of administrative policies asserted the significance of the Sahara to the newly independent state. The Sahara was divided into nine *wilayas* (provinces), in relation to just two in 1962, and dotted with infrastructures such as hospitals, schools, universities, post offices, and banks. In 1965, The Algerian central authorities proclaimed Hassi Messaoud an "administrative center" to be governed by the central administration from the provincial capital in Ouargla, a status that Hassi Messaoud maintained after the nationalization of the industry.

II. Hassi Messaoud Commune 1984–2004

Owing to the tremendous growth of rents after the 1973 oil embargo, Algeria had ambitious plans to use its rising income from the hydrocarbon sector for the socialist modernization of its society and economy. The heroic model of industrial modernization was laid bare with the precipitous decline in oil prices and the intensification of socio-economic hardships in the 1980s. The

absolute power of the hydrocarbon sector was curtailed, with struggles among the state's power factions leading to the decentralization of Sonatrach and the subdivision of many of its responsibilities into separate enterprises. Like other oil-exporting economies that had engaged in heavy industrialization, Algeria faced problems with pronounced territorial distributional effects as well as an acute housing crisis and a fast pace of urbanization.[25] The new slogan *Pour Une Meilleure Vie* (For a Better Life) aspired to reduce dependence on the hydrocarbon sector and reorient development toward previously neglected sectors such as agriculture, consumer goods, and social infrastructure. In this respect, the government sponsored agrarian reform programs and investments in rural housing to improve the quality of farm life and the stability of rural population. Soon after, in the 1985 plan "The Sahara at Horizon 2000," the Ministry of Planning defined the fundamental objectives of relieving the acute pressure on urban housing and the Algerian coast and that by "redistributing population and activities" throughout the territory and making better use of the natural potential as well as the social advancement of the people and the country.

The potential economic opportunities of Hassi Messaoud incited the state to "develop" its productive hinterland and reinforce the presence of population over the diffuse territory. The limitations of the administrative center model had already been the subject of discussions in the 1970s. Hassi Messaoud was mostly tied to Algiers and the European capitals and did not offer a stable element for the future population. "The different nuclei are not the elements or a true urban ensemble," noted the geographers Marc Côte and Claude Castevert in 1970. "The urban fabric remains loose or even absent, not because of distances but because of the nature of the parts that forbids all centrality its raison d'être."[26] The Law of February 1984 on the territorial organization of national space lifted the exceptional status of Hassi Messaoud and zoned it as a municipality with an elected local assembly. The industrial oil zone was inscribed in national political representation. Following the change in its administrative status, Hassi Messaoud witnessed significant if unplanned growth. The political ascension of populist parties in the Sahara municipalities facilitated the acquisition of land at a nominal price and building permits in Hassi Messaoud. The town significantly grew in size and population during the 1990s, a decade when the highly secured city was one of the few secured sites in a country otherwise rocked by terrorism. Between 1987 and 1998, the population of Hassi Messaoud, not accounting for oil bases and informal settlements, grew thus from 11,428 to 40,368.

Figure 01. Hassi Messaoud core sample: a geological section through the town.

Rania Ghosn and El Hadi Jazairy

146

III. New Town of Hassi Messaoud, 2004–

Following the 1990s "Black Decade" of terrorism, the state embarked on the double task of liberalizing the economy and building "social peace" throughout its territory. In negotiation with the International Monetary Fund, the revised economic policies of the 1990s aimed to provide more competitive terms to attract foreign partners into oil and gas exploration in Algeria. The increased presence of multinational partnerships with the state oil company, as well as broader concerns of the settlement and security of the Sahara, brought forth the desire to dissociate the urban population of Hassi Messaoud from the industrial grounds. Hassi Messaoud's urbanization between 1984 and 2004 has mostly led to the uncontrolled growth onto the perimeter of the oil field, with some houses being built on pipelines and in proximity to oil infrastructures. In November 2004, Hassi Messaoud was proclaimed a "zone of major risks." Commissioned by the ministry of energy and Sonatrach, the experts' report defined risks of explosion, fire, contamination, and pollution that affect residents in areas adjacent to the petroleum installations. "These risks, should they advent, would cause the loss of human lives and the destruction of installations that have cost tens of millions of dollars." The minister of Energy and Mines, Chakib Khelil, emphasized how important it was that Hassi became again what it was originally, a zone of oil exploitation. "The logistics base should be separated from *la base de vie*."[27]

The latest iteration, the project of New Town of Hassi Messaoud, can be conceptualized at the intersection of two main lines for the state's policies in the 2000s: the security of its strategic hydrocarbon interests and the "Reconquest of the Sahara" within the national plan for the development of new towns. The desire to relocate the population joined the national desire to operationalize regional development as "peace balm." Although the incorporation of Hassi Messaoud ought to have brought it important industrial taxes from the oil operations, the town continued to be underinvested and presented little economic opportunities for its residents. Regional movements, such the Children of the South for Justice and the Movement of Citizens of Ouargla, protested against poverty, lack of provision of basic infrastructures, the nontransparent allocation of social housing, unemployment, and more broadly social exclusion from the state's territorial contract. State institutions painted a similar picture. The 2007 National Report on Human Development explicitly referred to

regional disparities and the unequal distribution of the "fruits of development." National planning schemes sought to balance the development of the Coast, High Plains, and the Sahara by establishing the new towns of Sidi Abdallah, Bouinan, and Boughezoul in the semi-arid areas south of the fertile coastal zone.

Born out of the concurrent desires for relocating Hassi Messaoud and establishing new towns, the Ville Nouvelle de Hassi Messaoud was promoted as a pole of innovation and productivity for renewable energy. The state has claimed a monopoly on the (violent) organization of space: the town was to be transferred out of the oil territory. The government declared Hassi Messaoud a matter of national interest, put in place a plan of action to secure the oil field of Hassi Messaoud, and froze all construction permits pertaining to activities that nonessential to the petroleum sector. A 2004 decree promulgated the delocalization of the population and the establishment of a new town, 80 kilometers from the existing Hassi Messaoud and equidistant to the other regional cities of Touggourt and Ouargla. The new city is projected to house around 80,000 inhabitants and occupy an area of 4,483 hectares, divided into an urban perimeter and a logistics activities zone. The regional governor in Ouargla was instructed to carry out the destruction of slums and illegal buildings erected in the oil zone and in the town of Hassi Messaoud. The compensation and relocation of the residents of Hassi Messaoud remains, however, a pending matter.

Conclusion

"Closely following the oil," as Timothy Mitchell suggests, means "tracing the connections that were made between pipelines and pumping stations, refineries and shipping routes, road systems and automobile cultures, dollar flows and economic knowledge, weapons experts and militarism"—all of which, as Mitchell says, do not respect the boundaries between the material and the ideal, the political and the cultural, the natural and the social.[28] For the modern Algerian state, closely following the oil takes you to Hassi Messaoud. The genealogy of Hassi Messaoud's statuses embodies the different territorial agendas in which resource metabolism was enmeshed in the state's projects of population, economy, and security. The sociopolitical contradictions between the reproduction of resources (metabolism) and the reproduction of the population and workers (settlement) become negotiated in the space of resource urbanism. In the early years of oil development, the state favored a strategy of

Figure 02. Spatial genealogy of Hassi Messaoud: from industrial center to town, and project for new town.

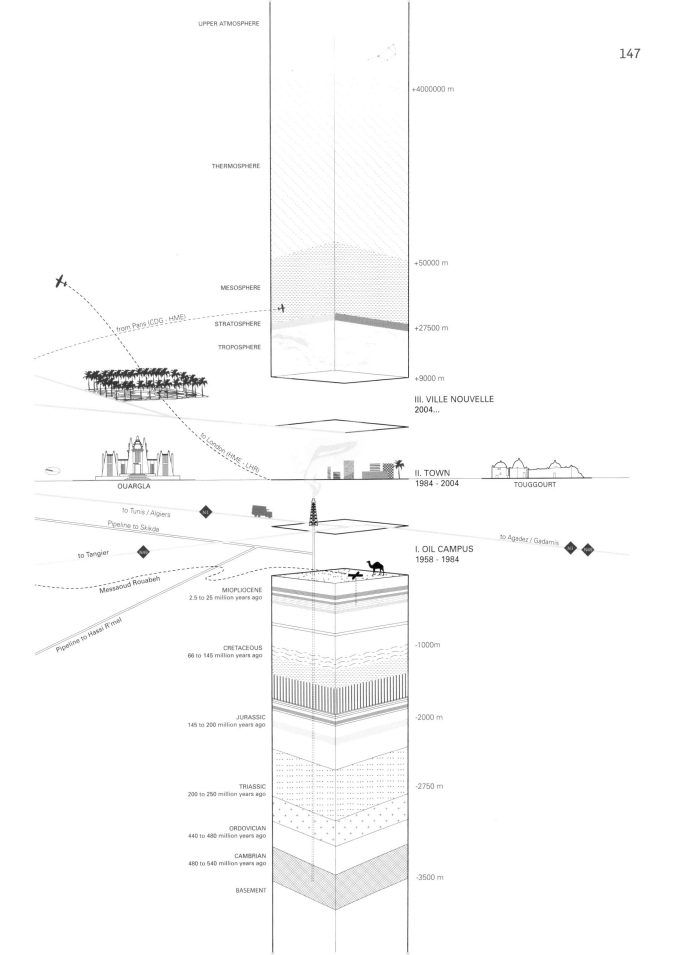

UPPER ATMOSPHERE

+4000000 m

THERMOSPHERE

+50000 m

MESOSPHERE

STRATOSPHERE   +27500 m

TROPOSPHERE

+9000 m

from Paris (CDG - HME)

to London (HME - LHR)

III. VILLE NOUVELLE
2004...

OUARGLA

II. TOWN
1984 - 2004

TOUGGOURT

to Tunis / Algiers   N3

Pipeline to Skikda

to Tangier   N49

Messaoud Rouabeh

Pipeline to Hassi R'mel

to Agadez / Gadamis   N3   N49

I. OIL CAMPUS
1958 - 1984

MIOPLIOCENE
2.5 to 25 million years ago

CRETACEOUS
66 to 145 million years ago   -1000m

JURASSIC
145 to 200 million years ago   -2000 m

TRIASSIC
200 to 250 million years ago   -2750 m

ORDOVICIAN
440 to 480 million years ago

CAMBRIAN
480 to 540 million years ago   -3500 m

BASEMENT

territorial exceptionalism to control the implementation of an idealized industrial site. From a deterritorialized site, Hassi Messaoud was gradually grounded in territorial population dynamics. Politically represented, the residents of the town of Hassi Messaoud could conceivably claim a larger share of the resource pie and become a nuisance in a region of high productive value for the state. The project for the New Town of Hassi Messaoud is a displacement of the contradictions at stake on the ground by displacing the population, the dissociated attribute from the territory, as defined above.

Through the case study of Hassi Messaoud, we interrogate whether it is possible to conceptualize the landscape of resources (or *paysage*) by recentralizing the country (*pays*) and the worker of the land (*paysan*) in the organization of nature's metabolism. Could we conceive of a Hassi Messaoud that negotiates the triad of *pays-paysan-paysage*? Otherwise the cities of Hassi Messaoud might be continuously fleeting the shadows of productive Hassi Messaoud. From this perspective, Hassi Messaoud becomes the ground zero of the metabolic conceptualization of the city-territory, in which urbanization is a process of contiguous deterritorialization and reterritorialization through metabolic circulatory flows.[29] The forms of territorial ordering associated with industrial bases, so vividly embodied by Hassi Messaoud, appear less as a spatial exception and more as an integral dimension of urbanism, in the sense that the securitization of industrial ecologies, the containment of risks and clogs, and the externalization of undesired costs have been the cornerstones of the urban condition.

Acknowledgments

The authors would like to thank the following individuals for their valuable contributions to the Hassi Messaoud visit: Ali Bouguerra, Mourad Zeriati, Salah Mekmouche, Yacine Laroui, Ouahiba Atoui, Hammoudi Moussa. We also thank Alexandra Chen for her graphic collaboration on this essay.

Notes

01. Erik Swyngedouw, "Circulations and Metabolisms: (Hybrid) Natures and (Cyborg) Cities," <u>Science as Culture</u> 15, no. 2 (2006):105–121; Erik Swyngedouw and Maria Kaika, "Fetishizing the Modern City," <u>International Journal of Urban and Regional Research</u> 24, no. 2 (2000): 120–138.
02. Richard Sennett, <u>Flesh and Stone: The Body and the City in Western Civilization</u> (New York: W.W. Norton, 1994).
03. Raymond Williams, "Ideas of Nature," <u>Culture and Materialism: Selected Essays</u> (London: Verso, 1980), 76.

Figure 03. Landscapes of Hassi Messaoud: base-vie and torchers.

04. Erik Swyngedouw, "The City as a Hybrid: On Nature, Society, and Cyborg Urbanization," Capitalism, Nature, Socialism 7 (1997): 65–80; Swyngedouw, "Circulations and Metabolisms," 105–121; Matthew Gandy, "Rethinking Urban Metabolism: Water, Space, and the Modern City," City 8, no. 3 (2004): 363–379.

05. Donna Haraway, Primate Visions (New York: Routledge, 1989), 4.

06. Matthew Gandy, "Introduction," Concrete & Clay: Reworking Nature in New York City (Cambridge, MA: MIT Press, 2002).

07. David Harvey, Spaces of Capital: Towards a Critical Geography (Edinburgh: Edinburgh University Press, 2001), 328.

08. Andrew Barry, "Technological Zones," European Journal of Social Theory 9, no. 2 (2006): 23–53. Gavin Bridge "Global Production Networks and the Extractive Sector: Governing Resource-Based Development," Journal of Economic Geography (2008), 389–419.

09. Mazen Labban, Space, Oil, and Capital (London: Routledge, 2008), 53.

10. Hydrocarbons play a crucial role in Algeria's economy, accounting for roughly 60 percent of budget revenues and over 98 percentof export earnings. See John Entelis, "Sonatrach: The Political Economy of an Algerian State Institution," Middle East Journal 53, no. 1 (1999): 9–27.

11. Henri Lefebvre, The Production of Space (Oxford: Blackwell, 1991), 365.

12. Stephen Legg, "Foucault's Population Geographies: Classifications, Biopolitics, and Governmental Spaces," Population Space Place 11 (2005): 137–156.

13. Stuart Elden, "Governmentality, Calculation, Territory," Environment and Planning D: Society and Space 25, no. 3 (2007): 562–580.

14. Karl Marx, Grundrisse: Foundations of the Critique of Political Economy (New York: Vintage Books, 1973), 485.

15. Stuart Elden, Terror and Territory: The Spatial Extent of Sovereignty (Minneapolis: University of Minnesota Press, 2009), xxviii–xxix.

16. For a history of the Algerian South, 1830–1980, see Taoufik Souami, Aménageurs de Villes et Territoires d'Habitants; Un Siècle dans le Sud Algérien (Paris: L'Harmattan, 2003).

17. Daniel Strasser, Le Sahara Francais en 1958, quoted in Souami, Aménageurs de Villes et Territoires d'Habitants, 289.

18. Louis Blin, L'Algérie du Sahara au Sahel (Paris: L'Harmattan, 1990).

19. Hassi Messaoud is currently the busiest Saharan airport in terms of passengers—590,000 in 2002—and the fourth Algerian airport with international direct connections.

20. Souami, Aménageurs de Villes et Territoires d'Habitants, 369.

21. Ibid.

22. "Algeria: Miracle of the Sahara," Time, 5 Aug 1957.

23. Ibid.

24. Konrad Schliephake, Oil and Regional Development: Examples from Algeria and Tunisia (New York: Praeger, 1977), 97.

25. Miriam Lowi, Oil Wealth and the Poverty of Politics: Algeria Compared (Cambridge: Cambridge University Press, 2009), 92.

26. Marc Côte and Claude Castevert, "Hassi Messaoud," Annales Algériennes de Géographie 9 (1970): 107–116.

27. "Pour Raison de Sécurité, Hassi Messaoud déménage," Le Quotidien d'Oran, 10 Jan 2005.

28. Timothy Mitchell, "Carbon Democracy," Economy and Society 38, no. 3 (2009): 399–432, 422.

29. Swyngedouw, "Circulations and Metabolisms," 22.

Image Credits

All images courtesy of the authors.

Rania Ghosn and El Hadi Jazairy

Reinier de Graaf / OMA

Moscow after Moscow

Questioning how design can respond to the challenges posed by the need to plan for the expanding scale of social and metabolic processes around post-metropolitan forms of urbanization.

Reinier de Graaf is a partner of OMA. He directs the work of AMO, the research and design studio established as a counterpart to OMA's architectural practice. Over the last several years, he has worked extensively in Moscow, overseeing OMA's work on the masterplan for the Skolkovo Centre for Innovation, or "Russian Silicon Valley." In 2012, AMO led a consortium that proposed a development concept for the Moscow Agglomeration: an urban plan for Greater Moscow. Since 2010, De Graaf has also been involved in the founding and curriculum development of the Strelka Institute for Media, Architecture and Design, and continues to teach as part of its postgraduate educational program.

In the context of a discussion about urban metabolism, Moscow is impossible to ignore. When it comes to ideas on how a city should function, Moscow not only represents the manifestation of two opposing ideological propositions but (perhaps more important) also the difficulties that arise when attempting a transition between them. After the dissolution of the Soviet Union in December 1991, Russia joined a global process of economic liberalization. From a former communist stronghold, Russia became the world's next "laissez-faire playground" almost overnight. While this shift clearly affected Russia as a whole, the effect is most palpable in its capital city. Moscow, in many ways the showcase of a supreme belief in central planning, had to adapt to the whims of the free market. Suddenly the formerly controllable territorial entity had turned into an organism, subject to its own seemingly autonomous processes, irrespective of— and often at odds with—the ideas of those supposedly in control. In the 1990s, "governance" became a matter of "watching events as they unfolded" and trying to derive maximum economic gain in the meantime.

Despite (or maybe because) of this relatively recent history, Moscow's current state is both impressive and daunting. The city's population is around 11.5 million (illegal migrants not included). Its size suffices to denote Moscow as Europe's only megacity (i.e., one with more than 10 million inhabitants). Unlike most megacities, Moscow's numbers are not a reflection of the general population trend of the nation in which it is located. Instead Moscow's growth presents a contrast to Russia's prevailing demographic picture: during the last twenty years Moscow's population has grown by 24 percent, while the Russian population as a whole shrank by 3.6 percent.

With large parts of Russia dwindling, Moscow continues to thrive. It is a strange paradox that the capital of the largest country in the world is increasingly exhibiting the character of a small

sovereign territory. In the same way that Switzerland represents an exception in the context of the EU (in the middle, but not a member), Moscow represents an exceptional condition within Russia: it occupies 0.05 percent of Russia's territory, while it contains 8 percent of its population. In other areas the asymmetry is even more dramatic: Moscow accounts for 10 percent of Russia's employment, 22 percent of its GDP, and 65 percent of all foreign investment in the country

These statistics reveal a strange paradox: the more important Moscow becomes for Russia, the less it becomes like Russia. Moscow has come to constitute a kind of universe on its own: a state within the state. Muscovites enjoy a range of special conditions and privileges that, although originally devised to help them withstand the first shocks of a capitalist system, have created a strange divide within the city. On the one hand is the official Moscow, as reflected in censuses and municipal data, while on the other hand is the unofficial—or rather, real—Moscow with a large number of nonregistered (illegal) residents, creating an economy unrecognized by official statistics. There is Moscow and there is Moscow. An ever larger bureaucracy has to go to ever greater lengths to administer an ever more schizophrenic reality.

The transition to a market economy has brought a sharp reduction of the city's public sector. Successive, often rushed privatizations have created a situation of disarray in the absence of adequate means to manage it. As a result, Moscow today suffers from a number of predictable problems, many related to a growing level of inequality among its citizens. Even though Moscow boasts the largest number of billionaires of any city in the world, for most of its citizens the past twenty years have meant an escalation in the cost of living without a comparable rise in income. A booming property market has driven up the price of homes, particularly in the center; increased commuter

151

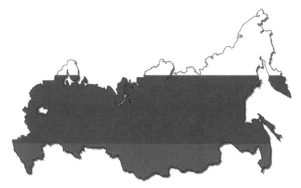

Figure 01. Moscow

Figure 02. Population Growth in Russia and Moscow.

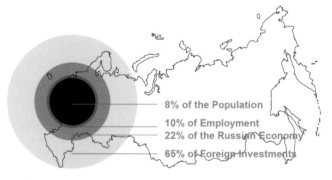

8% of the Population
10% of Employment
22% of the Russian Economy
65% of Foreign Investments

Figure 03. Moscow's Russian holdings.

traffic has brought Moscow's transport system to the brink of exhaustion; and illegal migration has created an ever-larger shadow economy.

It remains questionable whether Moscow's current status can be maintained in the long run. Moscow's wealth is largely generated by Russia's natural resources, which, although mostly managed from Moscow, are certainly not extracted from Moscow's soil. In many ways Moscow is exemplary of the ambiguous position of many cities in today's urbanized world: their seeming independence and political autonomy does little to conceal their ultimate dependence on resources from elsewhere: the more prominently cities claim a position on the global economic stage, the more they find themselves entrapped in a web of mutual dependence with the territories left behind in the wake of their expansion.

Although it is predicted that Russia will experience economic growth of 3.1 percent over the coming year, any positive outlook is tempered by the fact that the country's economic outlook depends on the continued level of world demand for oil and natural gas.[01] As more countries shift toward renewable energy sources and sustainable technology, the demand for Russia's supply will inevitably diminish. (By 2050, oil will comprise only 20 percent of the total consumption of primary energy resources in the world).[02] If Moscow's economic future depends solely on being the administrator of the oil wealth of its hinterland, that future will increasingly look bleak.

With Moscow's position as the cosmopolitan storefront of Russia as a whole no longer guaranteed, there are ample reasons for Moscow to revisit its relationship with its immediate surroundings. Over the last twenty years, the Moscow Oblast (the region around Moscow) has provided refuge for those who cannot afford to live in the expensive city center. For years, through a bizarre inverse relationship of land value and land availability, building activity (mainly of residential developments) in the oblast has been outstripping that of Moscow, exacerbating urban flight. The transformation of former dacha settlements into forms of permanent habitation (and even commercial ventures) has done the rest.

In the context of decreasing oil and gas revenues, there is a compelling case to be made for more intimate ties between Moscow and the Moscow Oblast. Moscow's economy is already highly dependent on resources from the Moscow Oblast. A combination of Moscow and the oblast can be self-sufficient when it comes to energy provision.[03] Approximately 16 million cubic meters of solid minerals are extracted from the fertile soil in the Moscow region annually, by more than 6,000 mining companies.[04] In a bid to become less dependent on China, Russia will invest a further $1 billion in rare earth elements production by 2018: the majority of this production will take place in the Moscow Oblast.[05] With more than 7,000 produce, agriculture, and meat- or dairy-producing farms, Moscow Oblast is one of the leaders in the production of agricultural products within the Russian Federation.[06] The majority of Russia's agricultural subsidies—aimed at promoting self-sufficiency and reducing Russia's need for agriculture imports—are granted to the Moscow Oblast.

But by far the most important resource of the Moscow Oblast is its people. Urban flight, generated by high property prices within Moscow's municipal borders, has given Moscow Oblast an economically active population of more than 4 million people (more than 60 percent of the oblast's total residents), many of whom travel into Moscow for work or other social and economic benefits.[07] In coming years the dependence of Moscow on the labor force commuting from Moscow Oblast is only likely to increase. At the same time, Moscow Oblast has become an economic powerhouse of its own. Between 1991 and 2006, the number of companies and corporations there increased from 8,000 to more than 207,000.[08] When added to the number of companies and corporations within the official Moscow city limits, the Moscow region accounts for more than 45 percent of the employment of the entire Russian Federation.[09]

Moscow may have to make some serious changes. The cultivation (and at times opportunistic exploitation) of the differences between Moscow and the oblast, coupled with the conservative positions that have ensued, have created an increasingly problematic gridlock, with both sides eager to claim the other's advantages without a real willingness to renegotiate their own. Meanwhile many of Moscow agglomeration's real problems (traffic congestion, unequal distribution of employment) have remained unresolved. So far, the city has tried to fix its problems in its own right, within the borders of its administrative jurisdiction. It is clear that a reorientation in the context of a combined effort with Moscow region could offer an entirely new perspective to the benefit of both.

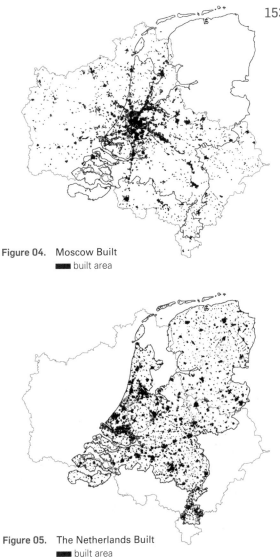

Figure 04. Moscow Built
▬ built area

Figure 05. The Netherlands Built
▬ built area

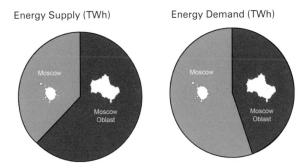

Figure 06. **Moscow's self-sufficiency.** Moscow's demand for Energy is higher than its current supply; however, if Moscow would integrate with the Moscow Oblast, the joint territory would be self-sufficient in terms of energy.

Reinier de Graaf

The International Competition:
A Concept for "Big Moscow"

In July 2012, through presidential decree, Moscow's borders were changed to include large new territories to the southwest, meaning that the city suddenly grew to 2.5 times its previous size. In the context of this decree, an international competition was launched to "draft an Urban Development Concept for the expansion of Moscow into the newly appropriated territory." OMA participated in this competition, along with nine other teams.

OMA's proposal aims to drastically transform the way the city functions—its metabolism—without necessarily having to change the physical substance of the city itself. Through a series of interventions in the city's regulatory framework, the proposal intends to influence the essential processes that shape the city. The proposal also hopes to correct a number of the city's most persistent systemic deficiencies.

OMA's proposal is based on the implementation of five principles over time:

01. In matters relating to territorial planning, far-reaching integration between the administrative systems of Moscow and the Moscow Oblast.

02. The abolition of inflexible zoning laws that limit the process of urban transformation and an equal distribution of jobs.

03. The introduction of new satellites in the Moscow oblast—so-called New Magnets—to relieve the dependence of the agglomeration's residents on the city center.

04. The introduction of sustainable and energy-efficient infrastructure to serve the New Magnets.

05. Forced regeneration of the city center through the introduction of penalties for underutilization of valuable inner-city lands.

Figure 07. Invisible transformation of existing structures under land-use re-categorization.

01. Integration between Moscow and Moscow Oblast

Moscow's new borders bring up the long-standing issue of the relation between the city and the region. It is difficult to conceive of a change in territorial relationship between the two without also revisiting their administrative structure. Given its strong role in Russia's economy, Moscow already occupies a pivotal position inside the Russian political system. A new administrative merger with the oblast—a joining of forces, with greater integration and coordination—would present the opportunity to create a larger entity with considerably greater leverage within the administrative system of the Russian Federation.

02. Abolition of Inflexible Zoning Laws

In Moscow, land currently belongs to one of twenty-four allowed land-use categories. Regulations prevent land owners from transferring their holdings from one use to another, so that land use changes unofficially, resulting in a poor cadastral evaluation and reduced tax revenue for the government. Perhaps more important, this also leads to a smaller number of "official" jobs, as it is difficult for land to be zoned in a category that would encourage employment. Thus the current land-use system is dysfunctional for all parties.

The revised proposal for land categorization and zoning would utilize existing and planned development more efficiently. The categories prime for development (and therefore for the creation of jobs) would merge into a single "urban" category. Under this system, all urban plots could transition from housing to business to production without the typical bureaucratic hurdles. This change in system would result in higher tax revenues for the government and more flexibility for small business owners. One of the most attractive aspects of this change, however, would be that the city's current periphery could drastically change use without changing its physical substance.

03. Introduction of "New Magnets"

To relieve the pressure on the Moscow city center, the development of the agglomeration would be reoriented toward four satellites or "New Magnets." Strategically placed near the airports, these magnets would take advantage of the services and provisions that the airports and their sites currently offer. They would be linked to the city and the oblast through high-speed rail, but integrate all forms of infrastructure: transport, broadband, industry, and energy.

Figure 08.   Proposed polycentric structure of Moscow.

Figure 09.   Each satellite will be a mixed-use development.

Figure 10.   The developments are realized through a combination of government and private financing.

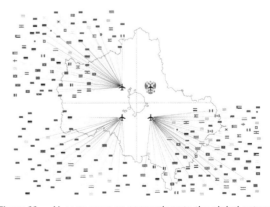

Figure 11.   Airports serve as connections to the global network.

Reinier de Graaf

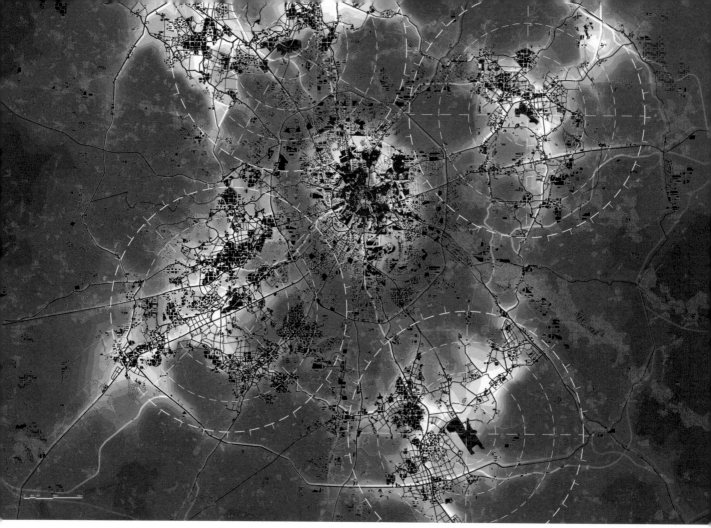

Figure 12.   Proposal for four satellites or "New Magnets."

Developments inside the catchment areas of each the four magnets would take advantage of the infrastructure and connections of the neighboring airports, but would also take into account the protected noise contours inside which certain developments are not possible. At the urban level, each magnet is typecasted according to a certain programmatic profile, based partially on existing conditions, partially on prevailing opportunities.

To encourage the participation of private companies, we propose to make the New Magnets subject to their own special economic and legal regime, where certain restrictions to (foreign) business laid down by Russian federal law will not apply. Such measures would significantly facilitate investment from Russia, Europe, and the rest of the world and would greatly reduce dependence on government funding.

04. Sustainable and Energy-Efficient Infrastructure
The four satellites and their related developments would be physically connected by a dual (electric)

infrastructure loop, primarily built on existing and proposed rail- and roadways, allowing for immediate implementation without the necessity for excessive pre-investment. One of the loops would be devoted to high-speed rail, and one to electric public transport. The proposed road loop could be connected using 88 percent of existing or proposed roads, while the rail ring uses 60 percent of existing or proposed rail lines.

Within the new development zones, a system of "electric enclaves" is introduced in which electric vehicles would be available and encouraged. This is accomplished through an electric vehicle-sharing program, which prevents gridlock and the pollution typical of carbon-based vehicles. Siemens has successfully implemented a similar system in Berlin, allowing residents to enjoy carbon-free vehicular movement.

05. Forced Regeneration of the City Center
In addition to an effort to decentralize Moscow's urban agglomeration and "emancipate" the periphery,

Figure 13. Transportation proposal for "Big Moscow."

the proposal also offers a future scenario for the inner city itself. The fast deindustrialization after the 1990s generated a number of leftover and derelict tracts of land scattered within the city limits. Privatization of assets through lottery allowed "insiders" to acquire many of these lands without putting them to new use. OMA's proposal prioritizes the reuse of former industrial areas and the regeneration of green and public space. A new set of policies, including penalties for leaving land within the city underutilized, would promote the proper redevelopment of land plots. The subsequent increase in economic activity would prompt economic development at a local and regional scale and truly promote Moscow as a new global model of an authentic urban economy.

Conclusion

Notwithstanding any possible ulterior motives behind the decree to expand Moscow's borders and the decision of the Moscow authorities to launch this competition, the effort could constitute an interesting

new beginning: the first in a series of moves to eventually put the whole Moscow metropolitan region under a single administrative system. Moscow could become the first megacity with administrative borders large enough to manage its entire agglomeration and therefore—at least in theory—have the mandate to deal with its problems in an integral way.

Moscow's new administrative borders are more than just a matter of expanding the city or creating of a new district for the federal government; they also provide a serious impetus to rethink complex issues. The scale of Moscow's new territory, somewhere between a large city and a small country, presents an interesting challenge both to conventional methods of urban planning and to models of city governance. Perhaps the combination of an extensive history of state control and sudden exposure to the free market could unexpectedly help Moscow find a new balance between the public and the private, between planning and politics.

Reinier de Graaf

NG06—Grounding Metabolism

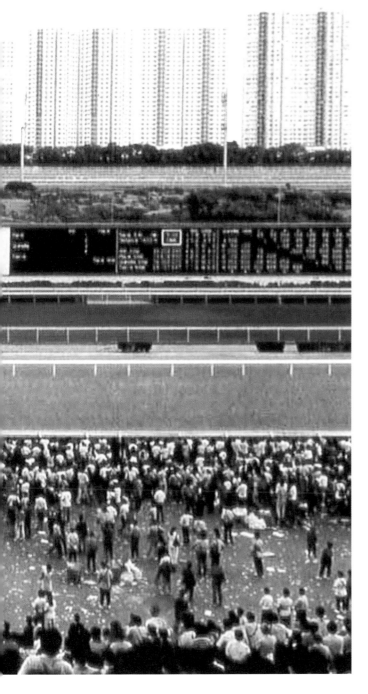

Notes

01. World Bank, <u>Working for a World Free of Poverty: Report on the Russian Federation</u> (2013).
02. Royal Dutch Shell, <u>Shell Energy Scenarios to 2050: An Era of Revolutionary Transitions</u> (The Hague: Shell International BV, 2008).
03. Moscow Municipal Services, "Moscow Is Successfully Implementing Its Programme, Energy Conservation 2012–2016 and on to 2020," press release, 13 Nov 2013.
04. Ministry of Foreign Affairs of the Russian Federation, Passport of Moscow Region, www.mid.ru.
05. Reuters, "Rostec Agrees $1Bln Rare Earth Deal in Bid for Self Sufficiency," <u>Moscow Times</u>, 11 Sept 2013.
06. Ministry of Foreign Affairs of the Russian Federation, Passport of Moscow Region, www.mid.ru.
07. Ibid.
08. Business Information Agency, <u>Business Profile of the Moscow Region of Russia</u> (2007).
09. Ibid.

Image Credits
All images courtesy of OMA.

Reinier de Graaf

Vicente Guallart

Barcelona 5.0

The Self-Sufficient City

Exploring how a city could attempt to maximize the internalization of regional and global material interdependencies.

Vicente Guallart is chief architect of Barcelona City Council with the responsibility of developing the strategic vision of the transformation of the city and its major development projects. It was also the first manager of Urban Habitat, a new department encompassing the areas of urban planning, housing, environment, infrastructures and information technologies. Previously he founded the Institute of Advanced Architecture of Catalonia (IAAC), where he led projects such as Media Houseproject (with MIT's CBA), HyperCatalunya, or the Fab Lab House. His professional office, Guallart Architects, has developed projects such as the ports of Fugee and Keelung in Taiwan, the Sociopolis neighborhood in Valencia or Gandia Sharing Blocks. He is the author of books such as Geologics and Self-Sufficient City. His work has been exhibited at the Venice Biennale, MOMA, and the AIA in Washington.

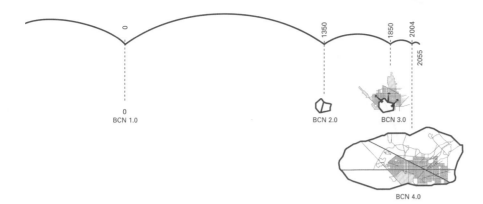

The anatomy of a city

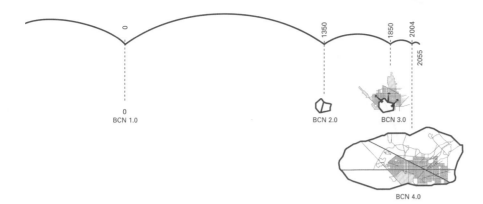

W hereas urban design in the nineteenth century added value to agricultural land though its development into urban land, the regeneration of the city that began in the twenty-first century aims at the amelioration of urban land by making it self-sufficient. Being self-sufficient makes sense because cities can be more resilient in the face of potential global conflicts, and local communities are empowered to decide their own future. Self-sufficiency for people and, as a direct result, for their communities, is based on their ability to produce food, energy, and goods on a local level. In the case of goods, digital manufacturing is the paradigm by which distributed production, in the context of cities, will be possible. Recycling materials should also form part of the new self-sufficient economy.

When it comes to energy, any place in the world can produce the energy necessary to continue functioning, using the appropriate technology and drawing on natural resources found in the immediate environment, including air, water, and land. When considering food, in the majority of cases cities have the water and nutrients necessary to cultivate the foodstuffs they need; they do, however, need physical space, in which to do so, which can normally be found nearby. Therefore a new metabolic layer needs to be added to the physical structures of cities as a way to internationalize the management cycles of a city's resources.

Telecommunications networks now allow us to access nearly any piece of information produced by other human beings, which, if the process is properly managed, can produce knowledge. The internet has changed our lives, but it hasn't yet changed our cities.

Figure 01. Major urban shifts in Barcelona. The acceleration of the transformation of cities: 1.0 Roman city, 2.0 Capital of state, 3.0 Industrial city, 4.0 Olympic city, 5.0 Self-sufficient city.

Figure 02. City protocol.
[over] The anatomy of a city: structure (environment, infrastructures, and built domain), information, and people.

How will cities and habitats be able to extract knowledge from the network and produce resources locally in the new society that is emerging within the information age? Cities and the human habitat are the reflection of the culture of each era. They use knowledge and technological advances to create the most effective living conditions from an economic, social, and environmental point of view, using the resources within their reach in a rational way. But now we live in a world of cities that in many cases are already built. How can we add value to our cities?

161

Rather than adding informational layers on top of an obsolete city, new ways of organizing urban space should be promoted, featuring functional hybridization and ways of dealing with mobility that make cities more efficient from a structural perspective. The internet should not replicate the life of cities as we know them now; it should allow for their reengineering. First, however, we should define the anatomy of cities as a shared, common foundation on which to operate.

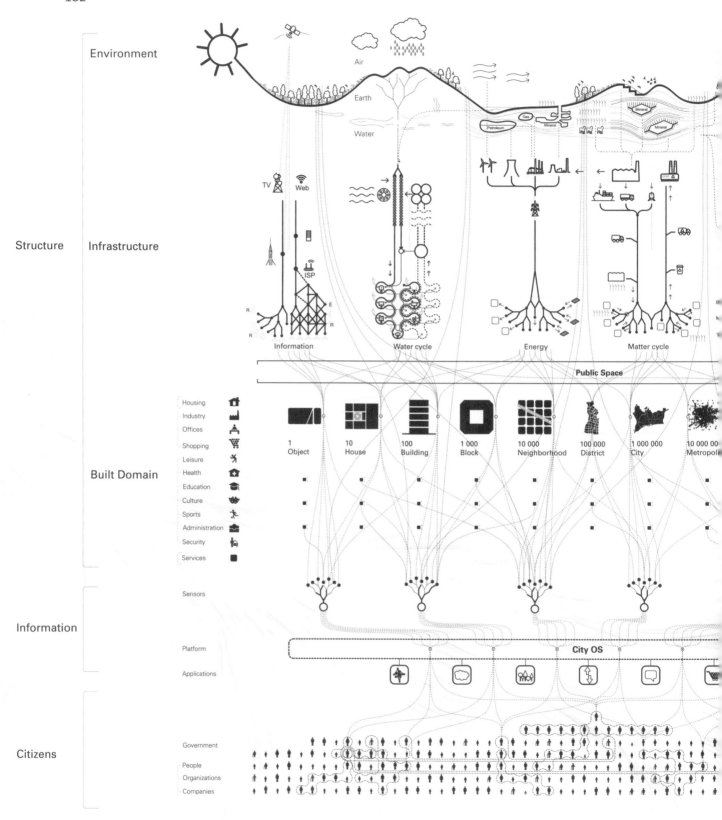

Environment

Air

Earth

Water

Structure

Infrastructure

TV
Web
ISP

R   E
R
R

Information

Water cycle

Energy

Matter cycle

Public Space

Built Domain

Housing	🏠
Industry	🏭
Offices	🏛
Shopping	🛒
Leisure	🤸
Health	🏥
Education	🎓
Culture	🎭
Sports	🏃
Administration	💼
Security	🚓
Services	◼

1
Object

10
House

100
Building

1 000
Block

10 000
Neighborhood

100 000
District

1 000 000
City

10 000 000
Metropoli

Information

Sensors

Platform

City OS

Applications

Citizens

Government

People

Organizations

Companies

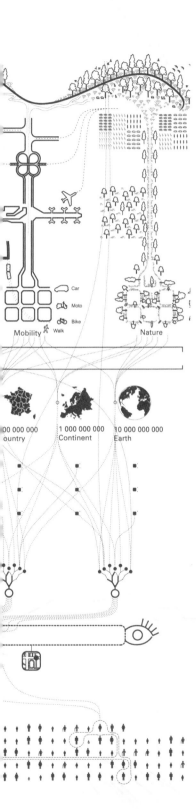

Mobility — Walk — Nature

Car
Moto
Bike

00 000 000 / ountry — 1 000 000 000 / Continent — 10 000 000 000 / Earth

Cities should not simply consume what industries offer them but should be able, as a collective, to produce the essential elements for global urban progress. Similarly, they should define new models for good governance that break away from the traditional siloed approach that has been used to govern cities until now. This new model will allow for the integration of the resources necessary for urban regeneration into a unified vision and into different projects. Cities are not merely a physical manifestation of the societies that inhabit them; in the face of deep changes in the economic structure of society, cities should be physically transformed, taking on new economic roles and new social relationships on which they are based.

Citizens cannot simply be spectators of their own lives but must be leaders of their future. To make great changes in cities, specific projects must be developed that initiate the transformation toward a new future and define plans that play themselves out in the coming years and allow for the global transformation of a city. Small-scale projects can give meaning to strategic plans. This is how we work in Barcelona, a place where we have defined a new mantra for the transformation of our city that speaks to the work that is being done to become a city made up of productive neighborhoods working at a human speed within a hyper-connected metropolis. A useful model incorporates the best aspects of life in small cities and the best aspects of urban density and the dynamism of big cities into an information society. This is also why we develop projects on all urban levels that allow for the transformation of the city on different scales and at different speeds.

The information society's economy is oriented toward the management of services more than the sale of goods. For this reason, projects such as the Sagrera high-speed train station have changed the traditional model of "issuing" zoning permits in certain areas, when public administrations need resources to fund themselves, to defining a project in which the activities are connected to the mobility of millions of passengers; the associated services can create a large part of the resources necessary for financing the project.

The Plaza de las Glorias, the central square designed by Ildefonso Cerda but never built, will become a new type of urban space where all of its parts, both mineral and vegetable, will be fused, which will guarantee the flow of urban mobility and the connectivity of the network of green spaces that can be found throughout the city, promoting the re-greening of the whole city, starting at its heart.

In Glorias, the urbanization process of the last large-scale square in the city will help to define a new model for urban spaces. And from this point on, the transformation of the circulatory system of the city—including a new orthogonal bus system and a "super city block" system that will set aside more public space for pedestrians in a structural and systematic way—will begin.

The city of the future will be a metropolis of neighborhoods rather than wealthy enclaves with immense peripheral areas that are built up independently. Or at least that is how it should be. And to achieve this, a system of public buildings, services, and spaces such as schools, libraries, and open markets must be defined and, in most cases, integrated into hybrid buildings that are constructed to provide a service as well as help give an identity to the local communities that make up the city.

Vicente Guallart

Nevertheless, it will be the city blocks, the buildings, and the architectural scale that will include the use of new materials and techniques in their designs and thereby contribute to the definition of the new scale of the city through the transformation of old buildings into productive structures that create exchange networks for energy, water, and the resources between them and the other buildings in the area.

Moreover, when a building cannot be built in an area, this space should be open to public access in collaboration with the city's town council and social organizations, much like what occurs in the "Pla BUITS" (plan to designate urban brown spaces for territorial or public use) in Barcelona.

In Barcelona, urban self-sufficiency is fueled by projects such as Fab Labs that bring about innovation and local production in the neighborhoods of the city that, along with large industries, will allow for the development of Fab Cities. Or by urban agriculture on the outskirts of the city, urban gardens, or rooftop gardens across the city that promote growing food for one's own consumption. Or even self-sufficient buildings and the centralized cooling and heating networks that will allow the majority of the energy that the city consumes to be produced locally in the decades to come.

All of these projects and scales come together on multiple transversal planes that can most clearly be seen in the interaction between information networks and the main urban service providers that are integrated along the concept of the "internet of everything" for public spaces in cities.

We live in a world of cities. Nowadays, beyond the necessity of having a physical plan that is based on a social project for cities, we must also create governmental structures that allow this to be possible. In Barcelona, we have created the Habitat Urbà (Urban Habitat) department as a way to integrate, under a unified project and management structure, the urban planning, housing, environmental, infrastructure, and information technology sectors. Scientific and technical knowledge must also be brought together to make this all possible. For this reason, the City Protocol Society, which is promoted by cities, universities, and businesses that follow the Internet Society model, works to recognize transformational projects and to define new standards based on a consensus among experts, so that the collective progress for cities around the world can be sped up.

Overall, cities need to have a long-term plan to know how to act in the short term. Transformative ideas need political leadership to become possible. The administrative machinery of the cities and states have been created, selected, and trained to manage but not to innovate. Today, however, within the last crisis period, changes in cities are imperative for them to survive. The twenty-first- century cities should be about transforming their current productive model, which only transforms goods into waste along a linear metabolism. And finally, and most important, all those transformations need to be done through plans and projects where design plays a principal role, for them to become part of our culture and transcend historically.

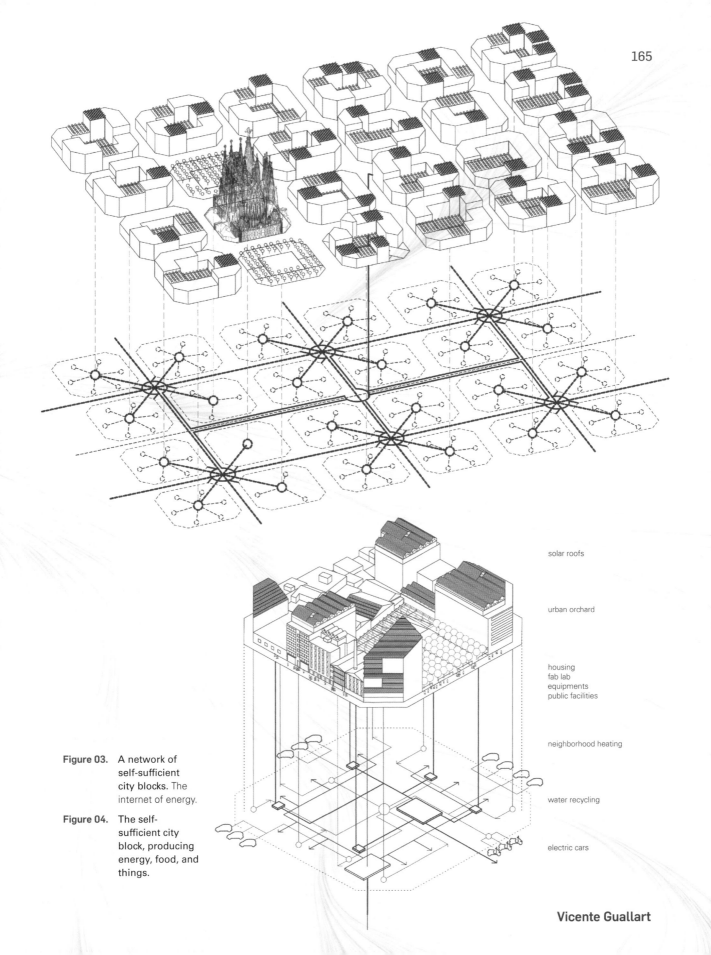

solar roofs

urban orchard

housing
fab lab
equipments
public facilities

neighborhood heating

water recycling

electric cars

Figure 03. A network of self-sufficient city blocks. The internet of energy.

Figure 04. The self-sufficient city block, producing energy, food, and things.

Vicente Guallart

Philippe Rahm

Toward a Thermodynamic Urban Design

Introducing projective approaches to design derived from a contemporary understanding of environmental specificities, climate, and thermodynamics.

Philippe Rahm is an architect and principal in the office of Philippe Rahm architectes, based in Paris, France. His work, which extends the field of architecture from the physiological to the meteorological, has received an international audience in the context of sustainability. His work has been featured at the Venice Biennale. From 2010 to 2012, he held the Jean Labatut Professorship in Princeton University. He will teach at the Harvard University GSD in Fall 2014. His recent work includes the first prize for the 70-hectare Taichung Gateway Park in Taiwan, currently under construction. Monographic books include Physiological Architecture in 2002, Distortions in 2005, Environ(ne)ment: Approaches for Tomorrow in 2006, and Architecture météorologique in 2009.

Over the last forty years, the history of urban and regional planning has been written from a macroscopic and aesthetic point of view, rather than a microscopic and physiological perspective. By reanalyzing this urban story through a microscopic prism, we discover other significant factors in the construction of cities and the composition of their forms. A reassessment allows us to offer an alternative to urban development now based on unbalanced economic globalization, which is inhuman and unfair. Our ambition is to look to a more sustainable, humanistic, just, and equitable global urbanization for all.

If we think of urban planning in terms of thermo-dynamics, we can start to imagine a new strategy of globalization: a global redeployment of industrial production based on energy and climate criteria rather than financial or economic imperatives. In the context of the current crisis of the European model of post-industrial society, France, for example, has decided to reindustrialize itself. This seems necessary to achieve balance in the coming years between the South and the North. If the North is to experience a reindustralization, the South will have to improve the social and health conditions of workers. If we are looking for a new equilibrium to achieve this new stage of globalization, we must know which criteria will become important when planning at global scale.

The division between design conception and industrial production that can be observed globally arises because industrial production is planned around countries where labor is cheaper and labor law least restrictive. The result is a continual shifting of the site of production, as industries search for the cheapest country, producing unacceptable social and ecological inequalities. We need to find a future with an overall balance between cost and working conditions.

To begin to define the concept of urban thermo-dynamics, we can draw on three examples that show how companies have, in a new and effective way, managed to exploit energy resources related to their unique geographical positions. The first example is the relocation of Facebook servers from California to Lulea, Sweden, in the Arctic Circle. Computers that hold huge amounts of digital information require a lot of energy to be kept cool. The average annual temperature of Lulea is 2 degrees Celsius, while in California's Mediterranean-like climate, the annual temperature is 19.5 degrees Celsius. It is easy to understand the decision to relocate the servers, a step that realizes huge energy savings for the American company, worth billions of dollars. The second example is found in the small village of Trient in Switzerland, nestled in the rugged mountains of Valais with a population of 150. In coming years, the village will receive several million Swiss francs in hydraulic royalties, thanks to its unique glacial dam whose water supplies electricity to the Swiss railway network. The third example is the German Desertec project, which proposes to cover a small part of the Sahara Desert to capture solar power to meet the electricity needs of North Africa and Europe [**Figures 01–03**].

These three examples reveal surprising geographical locations for new urban development: the far north, the vast desert, the remote mountainside. Thus the twenty-first century is going to see a radical change in the criteria of geographical value; we may witness a relocation of human population that will cause the creation of new cities and the decline of old. The climate can play a primary role in the future urbanization of the planet: global thermodynamic values related to parameters of geographical location, latitude, and altitude can be proposed as a guide for a globalization no longer based on wages or worker exploitation but on ecological and climatic factors, toward sustainable development for humanity. We could call this new type of urbanization "thermodynamic urban planning," or redistribution of the urbanization on the planet according to the locations of renewable energy resources.

At the scale of cities, climate could also play a major role in the design of urban morphology and the choice of its materiality. Two recent projects of our office are promoting climate as the major factor for urban design. The first is a study for the city of Copenhagen. The second is a new park under construction for Taichung in Taiwan. Copenhagen is situated in a cold and dry latitude, while Taichung has a warm, humid climate. For these two projects, we aim to produce high-quality public spaces. But we believe that the quality of public space is not only about the conviviality of the program and the size of the space; it also encompasses the notion of comfort in its fullest sense—thermal comfort, health comfort, sound comfort, etc. Designing public space with strong consideration given to the climate will offer sensorial qualities to the city while meeting the new target of energy saving and sustainability. In Copenhagen, we propose to define a new urban network that is no longer based on cars and visual representation but on sound quality, reduction of air pollutants, and a natural increase in outdoor heat. In Taiwan, we propose a park whose urban composition is based on a site analysis of temperature, humidity, and pollution.

Public Air-1, Copenhagen, Denmark, 2013–2014
Collaboration between Philippe Rahm architectes and Frans Drewniak. Supported by the Danish Arts Foundation and Dreyers Fond

The Public Air project for Copenhagen aims to rethink the formal and technological heritage of the twentieth century in favor of new physiological criteria, to mitigate the air and noise pollution brought on by automobiles and industrial processes [**Figure 04**]. Cycling has recently become very popular in Copenhagen, in spite of the city's vehicle-centric design and materials. Consequently, cyclists share the road with cars, a result of twentieth-century urban planning. The physical exertion of riding a bike causes bicyclists to breathe more deeply, inhaling the air pollution emitted by automobiles. Because it is both socially and politically impossible to ban the use of cars in the city, the city has recently proposed a "Green Bike Network" to be developed in the near future. This proposal comprises a network of paths reserved for bicycle and pedestrian traffic, parallel to roadways. The routes wind through parks and vacant spaces , thus avoiding both motor vehicles and their exhaust fumes. Rather than fighting against air pollution and the automotive-centric design of the twentieth century, this project proposes the creation of a new physiological vocabulary for the Green Bike Network. By analyzing and reconceptualizing each element of the inherited built environment that contributes to undesirable physiological consequences, we can return to the causal relationship between physiological necessity and the impulse to build. Based on a study of urban forms and materials, focusing on how they contribute to air pollution, noise pollution, and heat gain, each element of the built environment has been reconsidered in terms of its ability to negate undesirable physiological consequences. Soil, façade material, street furniture, street layout and orientation, air, light, sound, and smell are elements that can be manipulated to create improved city air quality, a lower noise threshold, and an elevated atmospheric temperature, even in the cold climate of Northern Europe.

Figure 01. Facebook data center in Luleå, Sweden.

Figure 02. Concentrating solar power plant in Abu Dhabi.
Similar to the proposal of the Desertec project that would cover a small part of the Sahara Desert.

Figure 03. Hydroelectric dam of Emosson, Valais, Switzerland.

Our goal is to provide a comfortable street network and atmosphere for cyclists that protects them from cold winds, utilizes light to simulate the warmth of the sun, and minimizes air and noise pollution. In a way, the new street, a public space, will have the comfort and quality of life—specifically, warmth, clean air, quiet—that are usually exclusive to private space in a house or the inside of a car. To optimize the comfort of pedestrians and cyclists, we are offering research and ideation toward conceiving a new street layout, construction, building orientation, and material usage. To do so, we have analyzed each physical component of the proposed Green Bike Network according to the following criteria:

Heat

To bring heat into the cold Northern European climate of Copenhagen, we propose to use low albedo (nonreflective) street materials to transform the visible and invisible rays of the sun into heat energy through contact with absorptive,

nonreflecting surfaces such as dark and porous asphalt. Within a short zone of influence, these materials will conduct and radiate heat to human bodies. We also propose the use of high albedo (reflective) façade and signage materials to reflect heat downward, toward the absorptive, low-albedo street materials. Further, reflective building and signage orientation should be angled to catch sunlight and reflect it downward. Materials will be placed to protect people from wind chill. The wind increases heat loss from the body because it convects and conducts heat energy away from the skin, which increases the feeling of cold. The street orientation and programmatic clustering that accommodates specific activities throughout the day is based on the sun's position in relation to the streets. For lunch breaks, streets used to travel to food outlets and restaurants will be oriented in a north-south direction to absorb maximal sunlight. For the commute to and from work, in the late afternoon and early morning, the streets used to go to work

Philippe Rahm

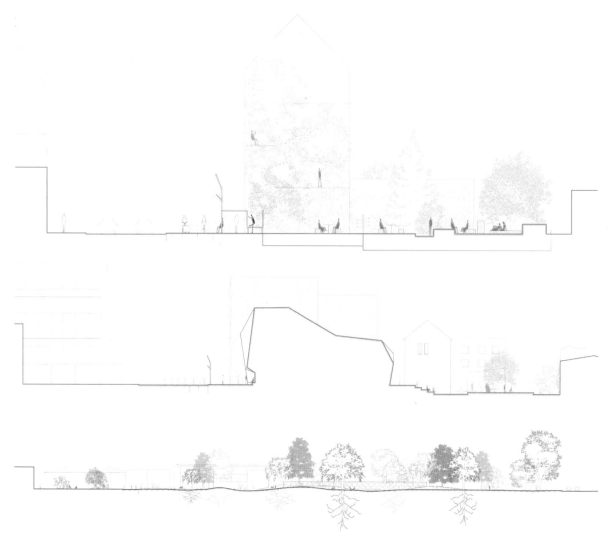

are oriented from east to west to absorb maximal sunlight. Geothermal heat pumps can be used to extract or dissipate heat from the ground to heat the air above. Street and façade materials made with a high thermal conductivity can rapidly absorb sunlight and transfer heat to bodies and the air during times of day and seasons with little or no sunlight. This will maximize the amount of heat that can be absorbed from whatever sunlight there is during the day.

Depollution

To create better air quality, we will use pollution-absorbing street and façade materials, especially in areas near major roads, industrial processes, and power plants. Recently developed street and façade materials formulated with titanium dioxide can be used to attract and decompose nitrogen oxide, a harmful pollutant put into the air by vehicles and industrial processes, into harmless nitrate. We will use only nontoxic street and façade materials that

will not add more pollutants, specifically aerosols, to the atmosphere. The absorption of dust can be achieved by planting trees with downy leaves, as well as with the use of certain materials.

Noise

To create more quiet public spaces in response to car noise, we propose to use soft, porous soil and vegetation as well as sound-absorbing façade materials to dissipate noise coming from the streets. We also propose to plan a drawing and cutting profile of the streets to optimize the sound quality in public spaces, such as theaters, using nonparallel storefronts.

Figure 04. No cold, no noise, and no pollution: Public Air, Copenhagen, Denmark. *Philippe Rahm, Frans Drewniak, and Louise Dedenroth Høj, 2013—2014.*

Figure 05. Jade Meteo Park, Taichung, Taiwan. *Philippe Rahm architectes, Mosbach paysagistes and Ricky Liu & Associates for the Government of Taichung city, Taiwan.*

Jade Meteo Park, Taichung, Taiwan, 2012–2015

A collaborative project by Philippe Rahm architectes, Mosbach paysagistes, and Ricky Liu and Associates for the Government of Taichung city, Taiwan

The ambition of our project is to give back the outdoors to residents and visitors by creating exterior spaces where the extremes of the climate of Taichung are lessened [**Figures 05–06**]. The exterior climate of the park is modulated to produce spaces that are cooler (by adding shade), less humid (by reducing humidity in the air), and less polluted (by adding filtered air); we also seek to make the park less noisy and freer of mosquitoes. The design composition principle of the Taichung Jade Meteo Park is based on climatic variations that we have mapped by computational fluid dynamics simulation: some areas of the park are naturally warmer, more humid, and more polluted, while others are naturally cooler (because they benefit from cold winds coming from the north), dryer (because they are protected from the southeast wind that brings humidity from the sea), and cleaner (because further from roads). We have augmented these variations in climate to create more comfortable spaces for park visitors.

Beginning with existing conditions, we defined three gradation climatic maps based on the results of three computational fluid dynamics simulations. Each map corresponds to a particular atmospheric parameter (heat, humidity, pollution) and its variation of intensity throughout the park. The maps will enable us to keep areas within the park from reaching extreme natural conditions as we reinforce coolness, dryness, and cleanness. The three maps intersect and overlap to create a diversity of microclimates and many varied sensory experiences in different areas of the park depending the hour of the day or month of the year. At a certain place, for example, the air will be less humid and less polluted but it will still be warm, while elsewhere in the park, the air will be cooler and dryer, but may remain polluted. The three climatic maps illustrate a gradation that ranges from a maximum degree of uncomfortable atmospheric levels that usually exist in the city to areas that are more comfortable where the heat, humidity, and pollution are lessened.

To materialize these climatic maps, we invented a catalogue of climatic devices (natural and artificial) that reinforce areas that are already more comfortable. Natural cooling devices are trees that have many leaves or big leaves that create heavy shadows, or white flowers and waxy leaves that reflect the sun's rays, or trees that produce a strong evaporation, cooling the surrounding air because of the physical change of phase from liquid to gas. Artificial cooling devices use meteorological phenomena such as convection, conduction, evaporation, and reflection to cool the air or the human body directly. The convective cooling devices, named "Anticyclone" and "Underground breeze," blow cool air chilled by underground heat exchange. The conductive cooling devices, named "Night light" and "Vertical night," expose black

Philippe Rahm

NG06—Grounding Metabolism

surfaces chilled by cold water, providing a cooling effect when touched by human skin. The evaporating cooling devices named, for example, "Stratus cloud" and "Blue sky drizzle," emit mist or rain, refreshing the surrounding air temperature by their change of phase from liquid to gas. The reflective cooling devices named "Moon light" and "Long waves filters" filter or reflect the sunlight.

Drying devices aim to protect the body from the rain and reduce the excess of humidity in the air that amplifies human discomfort by slowing the evaporation of perspiration. These objectives are reached by artificial shelters and trees with dense fronds that protect visitors from the rain, and by both natural drying devices that absorb humidity (e.g., via floating roots) and artificial drying devices that blow air dried by silicate gel exchangers, named "Dry cloud" and "Desert wind."

Devices to reduce atmospheric pollution, noise, and the presence of mosquitoes include trees that absorb oxides of nitrogen and other aerosols and make effective sound barriers. Artificial depolluting devices such as the "Ozone eclipse," for example, blow in filtered air free of polluting gases. The "Preindustrial draft" blows in air without the particulates produced by industry and cars. The ultrasound repellant device repels mosquitoes by emitting sound waves above the human auditory range and at the same frequency as the beat of a dragonfly's wings—combating mosquitoes using the sound of their predators.

According to the density and quantity of climatic devices deployed in a given area, we can create spaces that are more or less enjoyable, more or less comfortable. The climatic properties sometimes overlap, separate, regroup, densify, and dilute, generating a variety of atmospheres and experiences for visitors to choose as they see fit. With these two projects, we argue that climate could be the main element in the design of the city. We know that the global warming phenomenon creates anxiety about the future of the planet. We maintain that if climate is the problem, it could also be the tool for rethinking the urbanization of the planet and the city in a more ecological and sustainable way, providing a new quality of life that is more comfortable and more attuned to the senses.

Figure 06. Jade Meteo Park, Taichung, Taiwan. Real-Time mapping of climatic data regarding heat, humidity, and pollution. Philippe Rahm architectes, Mosbach paysagistes and Ricky Liu & Associates for the Government of Taichung city, Taiwan.

Image Credits
Figure 01: courtesy of Facebook.

Figure 02: courtesy of Masdar.

Figure 03: courtesy of Christophe Jacquet (Creative Commons BY-SA 2.5).

Figures 04–06: courtesy of the author.

Philippe Rahm

Kiel Moe

The Nonmodern Struggle for Maximum Entropy

Exploring the broader material geographies associated with the production of discrete architectural objects, viewed through the lens of energy.

Kiel Moe is a registered practicing architect and Associate Professor of Architecture & Energy in the Department of Architecture at Harvard University Graduate School of Design. He is a Co-Director of the MDesS program, coordinator of the Energy & Environments MDesS concentration, and Co-Director of the Energy, Environments, and Design research lab at the GSD. He is author of What Is Energy and How Else Might We Think about It? (2014, with Sanford Kwinter), Insulating Modernism: Isolated and Non-Isolated Thermodynamics in Architecture (2014), Convergence: an Architectural Agenda for Energy (2013), and Thermally Active Surfaces in Architecture (2010).

Without wastefulness or festive overspending there is only the vulgar economy.
–Peter Sloterdijk[01]

The concept of metabolism, which refers to the material and energy transformations that float the operations of any living system, is a subset of thermodynamics. Any thermodynamic system—such as a human body, an architectural typology, or an urban metabolism—emerges and exists to dissipate available energy gradients.[02] As a primary drive of metabolism, life produces ultimately yields a rich, myriad variety but it only emerges, survives, and, most importantly, thrives by dissipating available energy in the most powerful ways possible. How systems of matter and energy form, how they behave, as well as what they yield all depend on their dissipative structure design: their particular formation of energy dissipations and pathways for energy degradations.[03]

The thermodynamic constitution of non-isolated, non-linear systems—such as buildings, cities, ecosystems, and life itself—will tend to do three things: circulate and transform the most available energy, at the fastest rate possible, and with the most reinforcing feedbacks.[04] These three dynamics—the volume, velocity, and feedback of energetic quality flux—govern the power, behavior, and fate of any system. Given these dynamics, nonequilibrium systems will prevail that thus produce maximum entropy designs: having captured, trans-formed, and thus extracted maximal work from the most available energy, the designs thereby re-radiate the most unavailable energy at the lowest energy level possible.[05]

The universe, you see, abhors an available energy gradient and life is a most vital sport of dissipation for any gradient.[06] As Ludwig Boltzmann observed in 1886,

> The general struggle for existence of animate beings is therefore not a struggle for raw materials—these, for organism, are air, water, and soil, all abundantly available—not for energy, which exists in plenty in any body in the form of heat albeit unfortunately not transformable, but a struggle for entropy, which becomes available through the transition of energy from the hot sun to the cold earth.[07]

Without a grasp of these maximum entropy production dynamics, little of any ultimate purpose will be discerned, or designed, of urban metabolisms: the struggle for maximum entropy production in urbanization.

This struggle begins with the burden of an enormous available energy gradient: the incident solar gradient that supplies Earth with some ~160,000 terawatts of *exergy* annually.[08] (Humans, for scale, consume about 16 terawatts of exergy annually.) It is difficult to construe claims about energy shortages in this context; only questions about volume, velocity, feedback, and *design* are adequate to address this gradient. We can only work to discern and design ways to best degrade this insolating exergy in the most powerful, if not magnificent, way possible.

Much of this exergy is used to drive manifold terrestrial processes while other portions are stored in matter, for example in buildings and cities. How to best to modulate the relative velocity of exergy dissipation and degradation is thus a fundamental task for design. Rather than a question of managerial platitudes about efficiency or conservation, the excess of our solar gradient must be, as Georges Bataille in the Accursed Share notes, "always poised in terms of extravagance. The choice is limited to how the wealth is to be squandered."[09] Designers *completely* underestimate the magnificence of the necessary excess inherent in this necessary squander. Nonmodern architecture and cities were once powerful, if not magnificent, reinforcing thermodynamic agents and should be once again.

175

The pulsing of matter and energy cycles of the three-thousand year evolution of what is now Rome, for instance, help illustrate the fluctuating thermodynamics of an urban metabolism. The volume, velocity, and feedback of energetic quality flux of Roman metabolisms are interesting to consider. To build the Baths of Caracalla, for instance, four million pounds of materials were installed every day for six years.[10] For a single building, this represents a significant pulse of matter and energy, one designed for the purpose of thermodynamic and hygienic feedbacks among many other ennobling ends. As but one of endless massive constructions in Rome, the geologic scale of the Imperial Roman metabolism, and its persistence, offers one way to help envision the modulating velocities, storages, and sustained usage—the power—of the matter and energy of an urban metabolism design.

In a modern context, examples of powerful dissipations of this excess exergy abound as well in recent human metabolisms: consider the explosion of petroleum consumption, the expansion of Neoliberal modes of production, or the ever-escalating circulation of information. From a strict thermodynamic/evolutionary perspective, these metabolisms emerged and developed so as to increase the volume and rate of energy dissipation that make the human species more powerful agents in ecological systems. Each uptick in metabolism is an inevitable evolution of the universal tendency towards maximal available energy gradient dissipation [Figure 01].

In this regard, there is nothing inherently un-ecological or un-thermodynamic about such modalities: as thermodynamically obedient agents, humans have continuously sought increasingly powerful ways to dissipate available energy gradients at ever escalating volumes with ever escalating velocities. As applied physicist Andrian Bejan notes, "for a finite-size flow system to persist in time (to live) it must evolve such that it provides greater and greater access to the currents that flow through it."[11] Modern metabolisms undoubtedly grant increasing access to available energy gradients and, ultimately, this could be urbanization's greatest ecological asset, but only if the other terms of maximum powered are also designed with equal intensity.

The central ecological/thermodynamic problem constitutive of these modern metabolisms, though, is that the metabolisms of these dissipative structures have never been powerful enough. They at best only mind two-thirds of the thermodynamic purpose of energy dissipating structures: maximal intake and transformation, although the efficacy of

many transformations is open to question. Modern metabolisms, most importantly, habitually lack a full reckoning of the third critical component of any maximal power system: the requirement for feedback reinforcement. In modern metabolisms, feedback reinforcements include both the "goods" of modern metabolisms (liberating, powerful systems of knowledge, mobility, and industrial production) as well as the externalized "bads" of Modern metabolisms (counterproductive, ultimately power-draining systems of capital accumulation, chronic carbon cycles, resource degradation, amongst other externalized costs and system effects).[12]

The first and second contradictions of capitalism are prime fetters of this thermodynamic reality.[13] Questionable energy transformations when coupled with the lack of adequate feedback recognition and feedback design ultimately choke the modern metabolism and its dissipative flow structure design. In this regard, consider the effects of climate change in the coming century as a delayed, undesirable feedback of maximal power intake without adequate feedback design. Consequently, decreasing energy will eventually cycle through such a system and thus it will wane, even as living systems will constantly seek the most powerful designs from the available energy.[14] In short, modern metabolisms have not been as powerful as possible with their particular dissipations of massively available energy gradients.

This feedback rift constitutive of modern metabolisms is foremost characterized by what has been externalized in the paradigmatic processes of petro-technics, Neoliberalism, and, somewhat ironically, acutely escalating information exchange. The thermodynamic basis of this rift is not new, however, and it is no mere historical coincidence that Karl Marx based his critique of the emerging metabolic rifts of the nineteenth century industrial agriculture on the work of Justus von Liebig.[15]

Extending Liebig's work on chemical fertilizer inputs, Marx began to detect a woeful shift to increasingly unidirectional nutrients flows. Marx's primary example was the industrialized agriculture in late nineteenth century England wherein rural nutrients were shipped to urban centers at such a volume and velocity with little or no feedback—in terms of night soils as in the pre-industrialized mode—that the gap had to be filled by imported guano from Peru.[16]

177

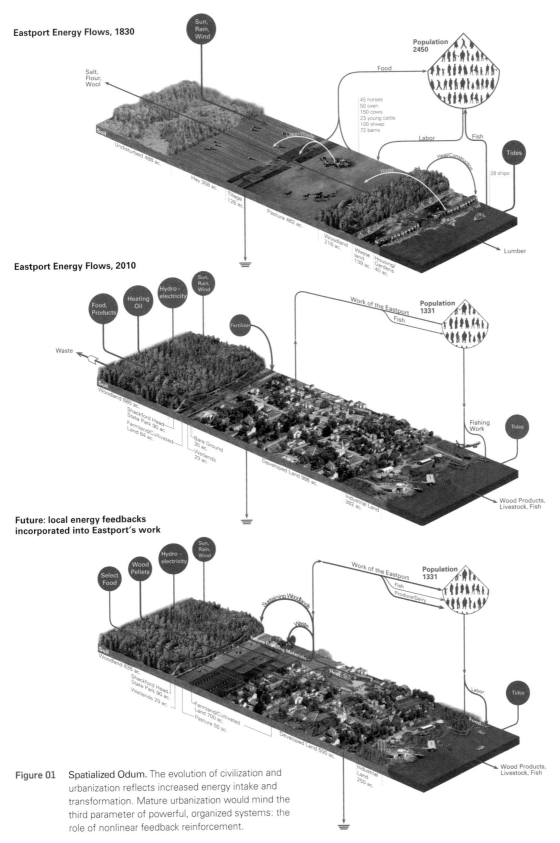

Eastport Energy Flows, 1830

Sun, Rain, Wind

Salt, Flour, Wool

Food

Population 2450

45 horses
50 oxen
150 cows
23 young cattle
100 sheep
72 barns

Labor

Fish

Labor/Waste

Tides

Waste

Heat/Construction

28 ships

Soil

Undisturbed 488 ac.

Hay 358 ac.

Tillage 126 ac.

Pasture 482 ac.

Woodland 218 ac.

Waste land 139 ac.

Housing/ Gardens 40 ac.

Lumber

Eastport Energy Flows, 2010

Food, Products

Heating Oil

Hydro - electricity

Sun, Rain, Wind

Fertilizer

Work of the Eastport

Population 1331

Fish

Waste

Fishing Work

Tides

Soil
Woodland 635 ac.

Shackford Head State Park 90 ac.
Farmland/Cultivated Land 84 ac.

Bare Ground 30 ac.

Wetlands 29 ac.

Developed Land 966 ac.

Industrial Land 382 ac.

Wood Products, Livestock, Fish

Future: local energy feedbacks incorporated into Eastport's work

Select Food

Wood Pellets

Hydro - electricity

Sun, Rain, Wind

Sustaining Woodlands

Work of the Eastport

Population 1331

Fish

Produce/Dairy

Waste

Entire Building Materials

Heat

Labor

Tides

Food

Soil
Woodland 635 ac.

Shackford Head State Park 90 ac.
Wetlands 29 ac.

Farmland/Cultivated Land 700 ac.

Pasture 50 ac.

Developed Land 500 ac.

Industrial Land 250 ac.

Wood Products, Livestock, Fish

Figure 01   Spatialized Odum. The evolution of civilization and urbanization reflects increased energy intake and transformation. Mature urbanization would mind the third parameter of powerful, organized systems: the role of nonlinear feedback reinforcement.

Kiel Moe

In that period, Liebig was known equally well for his thermodynamic postulation of the mechanical equivalent of heat as his work on the chemistry of soils. In this context, Marx thusly identified first and foremost a thermodynamic problem as he articulated a metabolic problematic. The thermodynamic basis, explanations, and designs of our metabolism—and the fetters of its rifts—are today absolutely central to more sane modes of design and urbanization in the future.

Metabolic Rift and Shift

To best address this thermodynamic rift, a radical shift in epistemology is required. Transcending the linear platitudes about energy efficiency and conservation with accurate and powerful praxis should be the dominant métier of design. Maximum power systems require the three principles articulated above: circulate and transform the most available energy, at the most designed velocity possible, and with the most reinforcing feedbacks.

Today, we circulate tremendous amounts of energy. How or why we transform this energy—to what end, to what quality of work—could be modified. The third, perhaps most consequential and yet most absent maximum power parameter—feedback—requires a praxis that is altogether distinct from the narrow thermodynamic system boundaries that constitutively yield the externalities of contemporary metabolisms: the object-constrained system boundaries that are the enabling fictions of our contemporary metabolic rifts.

When it comes to metabolism, modern designers— coddled on concepts such as autonomy on one hand and autarky on the other—offer little insight on the topics of feedback and cogent system boundaries for the non-isolated thermodynamics of buildings and urbanization. In the first case, the metabolically consequential topic of architectural formation was reduced in the twentieth century to diagrams of object shape which in turn, from a thermodynamic perspective, left architecture in abject shape. A cosmopolitan perspective on the role of architectural formation was sacrificed in the purifying pursuit for an isolating autonomy that the world never grants. In the latter case of autarky, a reductive, managerial posture of efficiency and optimization was coupled with Calvinist cultural concepts of frugality and calling.[17] This modernist discourse on energy in design had, and has, limited ultimate efficacy in the world: in technical terms it is only applicable to isolated thermodynamic systems. The metabolisms of buildings, cities, and landscapes, however, are absolutely non-isolated systems. As such, in formal and technical terms, designers today continue to suffer misguiding concepts of what constitutes architectural formation as well as the thermodynamic constitution of building and urbanization. In doing so, design makes the future a colony of the present. But no autonomy and no autarky will persist for long in the thermodynamic universe.

Metabolic design today demands a nonmodern agenda for the nonequilibrium thermodynamics that support fecund and vital forms of life. A nonmodern, nonequilibrium, nonlinear approach to the metabolisms of buildings and urbanization offers a more totalizing perspective on the actual energetics of the world and thus offers better indicators of how designers can best intervene so as to maximize the ecological *and* architectural power of design. This abrupt turn to the nonequilibrium thermodynamics of metabolisms is a necessary epistemological shift, a way around the corners and the failures of the Modern preoccupation with evasive isolation and externalities.

Since non-equilibrium thermodynamic systems exist to maximize entropy production, the implications for design are multiple and simultaneous. Two brief examples of ongoing design research on the topic begin to explicate maximum entropy production and maximal power in architectural and urban terms.

PLOT: Empire. State. Building.

Shockingly, architecture and landscape achitecture do not document or analyze the literal material and energy corpus of construction endeavors: the ecology of a city. Peering into the contingencies of individual plots of land in cities over time—in this case Central Park and the Empire State Building—illuminates much about that ecological and urban efficacy of two of the most iconic parcels of land in the world [**Figure 02**].

In an ongoing design research project, Jane Hutton and I have identified, modeled, quantified, and

Figure 02　The energetic block morphology of the Empire State Building site. "Morphology—the study of change shapes—is not only a study of material things and of the forms of material things, but has a dynamical aspect, under we which deal with the interpretation, in terms of force, of the operations of Energy." D'Arcy Thompson, On Growth and Form, 14.

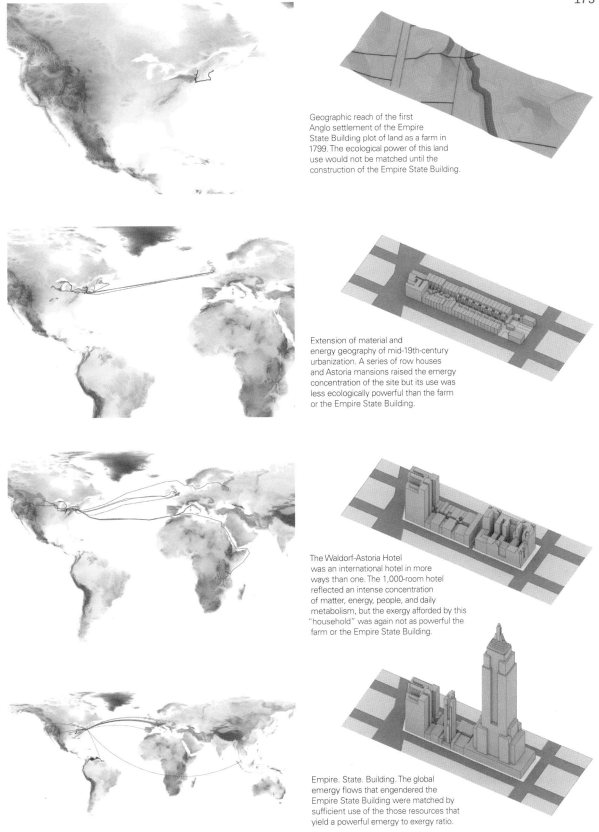

Geographic reach of the first
Anglo settlement of the Empire
State Building plot of land as a farm in
1799. The ecological power of this land
use would not be matched until the
construction of the Empire State Building.

Extension of material and
energy geography of mid-19th-century
urbanization. A series of row houses
and Astoria mansions raised the emergy
concentration of the site but its use was
less ecologically powerful than the farm
or the Empire State Building.

The Waldorf-Astoria Hotel
was an international hotel in more
ways than one. The 1,000-room hotel
reflected an intense concentration
of matter, energy, people, and daily
metabolism, but the exergy afforded by this
"household" was again not as powerful the
farm or the Empire State Building.

Empire. State. Building. The global
emergy flows that engendered the
Empire State Building were matched by
sufficient use of the those resources that
yield a powerful emergy to exergy ratio.

Kiel Moe

mapped all the materials and energies used on these respective plots over the past 200 years. This renders not only an account of the energetic and material inputs involved in each construction but maps their extended geographical relations by tracing material source, transportation, and labor dynamics: the literal becoming of the city's corpus. Habitually dismissed in design as externalities, in reality these extensive constructions are massive, intrinsic formations of matter and energy in their own right. In particular, this historical accounting of the material and energy flows of urban construction endeavors affords unique means to evaluate the relative ecological efficacy of different construction paradigms while simultaneously affording clear perspectives on the shifting geographies, cultural dynamics, and labor conditions constitutive of cities.

To articulate the latent ecological power of buildings and city parcels as open thermodynamic systems it is important to articulate them in ecologically exacting terms. If *emergy* records the present and past flux of energy on the parcel, then the ecological efficacy of that flux can only be known by placing it in context of the work done by that flux. It should be noted that emergy is used here as a form of scale analysis that helps determine the relative magnitude of various forms of energy, as opposed to an alternate accounting methodology. As such, emergy to exergy ratios, for instance, are used as thermodynamic indicators of relative ecological power of these respective urban metabolisms.[18] Some of the early outcomes of this research highlight the importance of

certain clear thermodynamic indicators and scaling laws that point towards metabolically ideal material and energy flux. Rather identifying which construction is more or less "efficient", the aim is to identify thermodynamic trends in the various phases of urbanization.

Stackhaus

The Stackhaus, designed with and for Ron Mason, is an ambitiously modest thermodynamic proposition that thinks bigger about small "things": small projects and practices, minute properties of wood, and nonmodern techniques for contemporary architecture [**Figures 03–05**]. The walls of this building are composed as a single stack of 6x8 spruce timbers. The preponderance of solid spruce timbers in this project—a thoroughly "inefficient" use of wood— actually affords a maximal use of the material as an exergy design proposition. It is maximal in that it uses a massive amount of material but, in this case, it also does a maximal amount of work in the building: it is the structure, enclosure, finish material, and insulation for the building and uses the unique thermal conductivity, diffusivity, and effusivity of spruce for the body-building feedbacks of its "heating and cooling system" (it has no energy input other than the sun and some wind in the summer). What Bataille would describe as the "Accursed Share" of this project is not directed towards non-architectural effects (transporting a materials extracted and processed elsewhere to Colorado, for instance) but rather accumulated in the building itself.

Figure 03. **Stack. House.** Construction sequence. A massively inefficient use of wood yields a maximum power building.

Figure 04. Stack. House.

Kiel Moe

The 6x8 timbers of spruce were grown, harvested from beetle-kill stands, and processed in an adjacent valley near the project site. This is a key part of its feedback design at this scale: the accumulation of wood in the building is likewise an accumulation of regional feedbacks. Further, wood is the only material that sequesters carbon. Here the massive use of this material sequesters nearly twice the carbon that is inherent in the construction. This is simply impossible with any other material and likewise would not be possible with a more "efficient" use of the same material.

The primary reason this building performs the way it does is that its formations of energy are not conceptualized in terms of scarcity, conservation, or isolation. *By no means is this project efficient.* This building that makes no effort to conserve energy or be efficient is the only building I am aware of to sequester twice its own carbon. Perhaps most importantly, the building is far

from autarkical in its ambitions. Rather it is a maximal use of wood that allows the building to sequester so much carbon and to consume no operational energy at all. This is the base of its ecological power.

Thus from small scale material and building considerations of a small wood building to the material and energetic becoming of the Empire State Building and Central Park plots, the nonlinear, nonequilibrium thermodynamics of any metabolism poses new questions for design today as well as for the future of buildings and urbanization. While the exact methods, systems boundaries, and design practices of maximum power and maximum entropy systems are not yet well established, the thermodynamic purpose of design is well established in this regard: dissipate available energy gradients in the most powerful and reinforcing way possible. This is the task, and potential magnificence, of metabolic design.

STACK

01. 1x6 SYP T&G Cladding
02. 6x8 Spruce Timbers
03. R19 Batt Insulation
04. 2x6 SPF Lumber Framing
05. 1/2" Plywood
06. 30lb. Building Paper
07. 2x4 Pressure Treated Nailers
08. 2x6 SYP Rainscreen Cladding

STICK

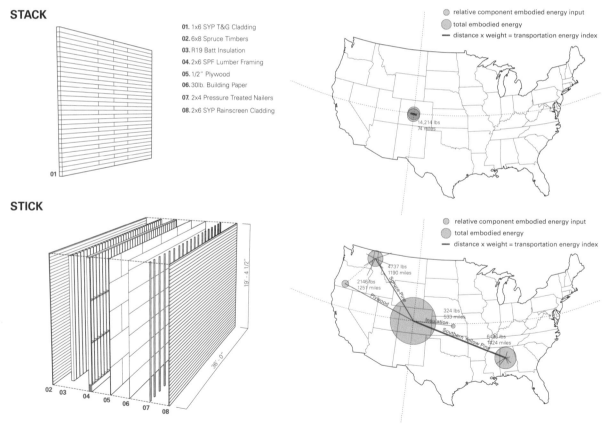

Figure 05. The absurdity of layered construction logics is exacerbated by their contingent geographies. For a building with no operational energy, maximizing the power of the construction ecology is the thermodynamic task. Otherwise routinely externalized by design, this design recursively oscillated between micro energy systems and territorial energy systems.

Glossary

Energy: the measure of the capacity of a system to do work on its surroundings.

Power: the rate at which work is done, the rate at which energy is consumed

Emergy: the available energy of one form that is used up in transformations directly and indirectly to make a product or service.

Exergy: the available energy in a system, a measure of the maximum work potential in a system before it reaches equilibrium

Unavailable energy: energy in a sytem that can no longer do work.

Energy gradient: a difference between maximal and minimal energy states.

Dissipative structure: a non-isolated, far from equilibrium thermodynamic system that yields quasi-steady state conditions through exchange of matter and energy with its surroundings

Maximum entropy production: the systems which prevail in a process of natural selection will be those designs that extract maximal power from an available energy gradient, and in so doing maximize the production of entropy, thus reradiating remaining energy at the lowest possible level.

Maximum power: during self-organization processes, systems develop and prevail that maximize power intake, the transformation of that energy, and that reinforce production through feedback.

Nonlinear, non-equilibrium thermodynamics: to be distinguished from classical, linear thermodynamics, the branch of thermodynamics focused on systems that persist far from equilibrium.

Non-isolated: thermodynamic systems are either isolated (no material or energy exchanges with its surroundings), closed (no material exchanges with its surroundings), or open (material and energy exchanges with surroundings are constitutive). Non-isolated refers to systems that exchanged at least energy, if not matter as well. Bodies, buildings, and cities are all non-isolated systems.

Notes

01. Peter Sloterdijk, Neither Sun nor Death (Cambridge, MA: Semiotext(e)/Foreign Agents, 2011), 331.

02. Axel Kleidon and Ralph D. Lorenz, Non-equilibrium Thermodynamics and the Production of Entropy: Life, Earth, and Beyond (Berlin: Springer, 2005).

03. Eric Schneider & James Kay, "Order from Disorder: The Thermodynamics of Complexity in Biology," Futures 26, no. 6 (1994): 626–647.

04. Howard T. Odum as quoted in David Rogers Tille, "Howard T. Odum's Contribution of the Laws of Energy," Ecological Modeling 178 (2004): 121–125.

05. R.E. Ulanowicz & B. M. Hannon, "Life and the Production of Entropy," Proceedings of the Royal Society, London Series B 232:181–192.

06. Eric Schneider and Dorion Sagan, Into the Cool: Energy Flow, Thermodynamics, and Life (Chicago, University Of Chicago Press, 2006).

07. Ludwig Boltzmann, "The Second Law of Thermodynamics," Populäre Schriften, Essay 3, address to a formal meeting of the Imperial Academy of Science, 29 May 1886, reprinted in Ludwig Boltzmann, Theoretical physics and philosophical problem, trans. S. G. Brush (Boston: Reidel, 1974), 24.

08. Weston A. Hermann, "Quantifying Global Exergy Resources," Energy 31, no. 12 (2006): 1685–1702

09. Georges Bataille, The Accursed Share: An Essay on General Economy, (New York: Zone Books, 1988).

10. Charles Walker, Wonders of the Ancient World (Gallery Books, 1980), 92–93. For a more explicit account of the construction of the Baths of Caracalla, see Janet DeLaine, "The Baths of Carcalla: A Study in the Design, Construction, and Economics of Large-scale Building projects in Imperial Rome," Journal of Roman Archaeology Supplementary Series, no. 25 (1997).

11. Andre Bejan, "Constructal-theory Network of Conducting Paths for Cooling a Heat Generating Volume," International Journal of Heat Mass Transfer, no. 40 (1996): 815.

12. Anthony Giddens, The Consequences of Modernity (Stanford: Stanford University Press, 1991); Ulrich Beck, World at Risk (London: Polity Press, 2010).

13. James O'Connor, Natural Causes: Essays in Ecological Marxism (New York: The Guilford Press, 1998): 158–177.

14. Howard T. Odum, A Prosperous Way Down (Boulder, CO: University Press of Colorado, 2008).

15. John Bellamy Foster, "Marx's Theory of Metabolic Rift: Classical Foundations for Environmental Sociology," American Journal of Sociology, 105, no. 2 (Sep 1999): 366–405; Jason W. Moore, "Transcending the metabolic rift: a theory of crises in the capitalist world-ecology," Journal of Peasant Studies 38, no. 1 (2011): 1–46.

16. Foster, "Marx's Theory of Metabolic Rift: Classical Foundations for Environmental Sociology."

17. For more on the concepts of frugality and calling inherent to modern energy managerialism, see Max Weber, The Protestant Ethic and the Spirit of Capitalism, trans. Stephen Kalberg (New York: Oxford University Press, 2010).

18. Simone Bastianoni and Nadia Marchettini, "Emergy/Exergy Ratio as a Measure of the Level of Organization of Systems," Ecological Modeling 99 (1997); M.T. Brown, S. Ulgiati, "Emergy-based Indices and Ratios to Evaluate Sustainability: Monitoring Economies and Technology toward Environmentally Sound Innovation," Ecological Engineering 9 (1997): 51–69.

Image Credits

All images courtesy of the author.

Figure 01: drawn by Alexia Friend.

Kiel Moe

Pierre Bélanger

Ecology 5.0

A radical framing of urbanization as a metabolic field of flows, speculating on the potential of design as agent in their (re)organization.

Pierre Bélanger is Associate Professor of Landscape Architecture at the Harvard Graduate School of Design, Co-Director of OPSYS, and Advisor to the US Army Corps of Engineers. As part of the Department of Landscape Architecture and the Advanced Studies Program, he teaches courses on the convergence of ecology, infrastructure, and urbanism in the interrelated fields of design, planning, and engineering. He is author of the forthcoming book, Landscape Infrastructure: Urbanism beyond Engineering (MIT Press, 2014), and editor of the Landscape Infrastructures DVD (2009). Recent publications include Urbanism beyond Engineering (Infrastructure Sustainability & Design, 2012), The Agronomic Landscape (2011), Regionalization (2010), Redefining Infrastructure (2010), and Landscape as Infrastructure (2009).

Imagine the planet as a big brownfield. Consider it less as a virgin resource (to protect) or a sensitive system (to shield), but rather as a big ball of oscillating waste (to keep moving): materials and fluids in different concentrations whose varying distributions are in constant motion brought upon existing earth processes, accelerated or arrested by emerging modes of production and evolving technological systems, thickened, adjusted, and layered by the human, animal, vegetal hand. We swim in our shit.

On this planetary surface, waste is the impetus for improved production, enhanced consumption, integrated exchange. As a commodity without a market, waste is simply a good without an acquired taste.

If "the shift from one mode [of production] to another," according to spatial theorist Henri Lefebvre in the last century, "must entail the production of a new space," then the transformation of industrial systems (closed, linear systems that produce commodities and wastes) toward urban economies (open, circular systems that cultivate commodities from wastes) should also produce new spaces, and open new geographies. If waste naturally and necessarily charts new scales of influence, how then do we design and direct our future?

The United Nations' 2008 Global Atlas of Excreta charts a path toward this banal utopia. More than simple upscaling of the Sanitary City, the Atlas marks a shift in planetary sanitation and defecation from cities into the open ocean. Reforming the downstream dead zones of coastal waters of the world, the concentrated sludge and shit of citizens is moving upland and upstream towards farms and factories as fodder, feedstock, and fertilizer. It forms a thick layer of biodegradation and of nitrogen redistribution across a landscape of contemporary waste cultivation and power generation. On this bigger canvas, brown is the new green.

Growth without production becomes a newfound land: economic liquidation through material recirculation. Here the world money market melts into a material market, realizing the wet dream of Turgot's unabated, unobstructed circulation of ideas, not just capital. All that is solid thus dissolves into data. Storage and accumulation—the fundamental problems of industrial urbanization—evaporate into the atmosphere to form clouds of information. The new oceans of distribution, dispersion, and diffusion pour out as the new project and space of the next urban century.

As material scarcities, both inert and living, go hand in hand with material ecologies and economies, so will alternatives proliferate and cycles increase, leading to dynamic markets of material substitutions, constantly in motion and circulation. Metabolist prophet Ivan Illich reminded us of flow's unintentional novelty:

> Circulation is as new and as fundamental an idea as gravitation, preservation of energy, evolution, or sexuality. But neither the radical newness of the idea of circulating 'stuff' nor its impact on the constitution of modern space has been studied with the same attention that was given to Kepler's laws or to the ideas of Newton, Helmholz, Darwin, or Freud.

The task of urbanists—twenty-first-century waste handlers—will therefore be to ensure the design of these material flows, pathways, and routes, through their vectors and volumes, fixed and fluid structures, logistics and landscape, extending material longevity in addition to the technological substitutions already under way. In this urban world, then, materials become part of a metabolic system, producing new materials and requiring new energies, with certain resource endpoints that are enabled by multitudes of use and limitless programmatic substitutions.   Recycling surpasses reuse and looks more like sanctioned abuse. A new dawn rises on the world market of capital commodities where steel, oil, and gas are abandoned, becoming virtually free or junk, as a result of imminent leaps in efficiency and synergy, while the free and irreducible resources of today (water, wind, soil, seed, sunlight) become a capital media, over which new wars will be fought and new territories formed.

From Marxist environmentalism to Taylorist engineering, the thawing of historic oppositions between capitalism and ecology further exposes a latent reciprocity and unintended equilibrium between the conveyance of capital and the pluralization of ecologies. As mutual agents, capitalism and ecology coexist and co-evolve from islands of exclusion toward an open sea of materials, elements, and entities through the opening of resource streams, the weaving of material sheds, the preordination of processes, the generation of ground effects, and superintendence of time.

Profiled in David Wachsmuth's Three Ecologies,   this revolution in ecological thought produces a cascading, compounding effect across the twentieth century: *Human Ecology* from the Chicago School (1.0), *Industrial Ecology* from the Danish School (2.0), and *Political Ecology* (3.0). Two subsequent expressions can be proposed: Ian McHarg's long-lasting concept of *Regional Ecology* (4.0) from the University of Pennsylvania School of Design as an intergenerational model and process technique to study and spatialize ecologics. Finally, a fifth evolution and radical requalification of ecology emerges in the twenty-first century. *Ecology 5.0* not only reverses the waterfall of all former concepts, but pluralizes them as the model of all models: Urban Ecologies.

Ecology 5.0 is a new living ground manifested through cross-dependencies, contradictions, conflicts, coercions, and complementarities associated with open and closed systems. *5.0* includes the overlapping landscape of social, material, vegetal political, logistical geographic, and temporal scales. *5.0* is a material enlightenment that recapitulates the circular and synthetic thinking of ecology—potentially the greatest overlooked concept of modernity—a path toward perpetual growth set against the great nonrenewable resource on the planet: time. As in Olafur Eliasson's Timeless Garden, the dithering concept of infinity becomes a more productive substitute for the concept of sustainability—a spatial, systemic, and material paradigm by which universality, lightness, transparency, and interconnectivity can be expressed, implied, and translated. Conservation, made possible without conservationists.

But the metabolic subject moves beyond the mere industrial connections rooted in the antiquated space of networks and network theories, or of the Euclidean points and lines. *5.0* is also based in logistical ecologies that offer the potential for understanding how economies can be saturated, irrigated, liquidated, inundated, and flooded by a range of alternative flows.

Looking beyond the residual reclamation of industrial wastes as a catalyst for growth, the profiling of emerging waste ecologies traces the contours of contemporary urban geographies. Beyond the cold accumulation of credit in cities, *5.0* delineates a landscape of flows and fluids that they influence and engender. Form therefore follows fluidity, not function.

Through this fluidic characterization of urbanization as field of flows, materials approximate fluids with different concentrations and chemistries, in different volumes and viscosities with different formations and fixities. The field entails the design of the speeds, cycles, synergies, and synchronicities of these interconnections. The vectors of ships and planes transporting cargo across the ocean and atmosphere look more like managed monsoons of materials moving across continents and clouds. Vectors cause storms that we call economies, across different tides of supply and demand, a morphology of socio-economic ebbs and flows. Infrastructures, fixed or fluid, are their landfalls and landfills.

As a recapitalized strategy, the metabolic representation of urbanization thus advances the contemporary ecologic subject, whose premise is advanced by a near infinite circulation of materials. As a market within markets, it is a system without a system engineer. Supersizing Abel Wolman's modern model of the "Metabolism of Cities," we can move beyond the linearity of sanitary engineering and set a course toward an endless loop of material resources, a landscape of responsive geographies and perpetual motions, amid intelligent orbits of exchange, overlapping arcs of empowerment, and synergistic spheres of circulation.

Notes

01. Henri Lefebvre, The Production of Space, trans. David Nicholson-Smith (Oxford: Blackwell Publishers, 1991; 1974), 46.
02. Sabine Barles & Laurence Lestel, "The Nitrogen Question Urbanization, Industrialization, and River Quality in Paris, 1830–1939", Journal of Urban History 33 (July 2007): 794–812.
03. See "Circulation and Progress: Turgot" in Rosalind Williams, "Cultural Origins and Environmental Implications of Large Technological Systems, Science in Context 6, no. 2 (1993): 385–387.
04. Ivan Illich, H2O and the Waters of Forgetfulness (London: Marion Boyars, 1986), 40.
05. Howard T. Odum, Environment, Power, and Society (New York: John Wiley and Sons, 1971).
06. David Wachsmuth, "Three Ecologies: Urban Metabolism and the Society-Nature Opposition," Sociological Quarterly 53 (2012): 506–523.
07. Abel Wolman, "The Metabolism of Cities," Scientific American 213, no. 3 (1965): 179-190.

Pierre Bélanger

Projective Views on Urban Metabolism

Conference
Postscript
by Daniel Daou and
Pablo Pérez Ramos

conference organized by:
Daniel Ibañez
Nikos Katsikis
Ali Fard
Daniel Daou
Taraneh Meshkani
Pablo Pérez Ramos

conference sponsored by:
Advanced Studies Program – Doctor
of Design (DDes) Conference
Urban Theory Lab
Energy and Environment Lab
New Geographies Lab
Department of Architecture
Department of Landscape Architecture
Urban Metabolism Student Group

Harvard University Graduate School of Design
Piper Auditorium, Gund Hall
48 Quincy Street, Cambridge, MA
Friday, February 7, 2014
10am to 6pm